Preaching Luke's Gospel

A Narrative Approach

Richard A. Jensen

CSS Publishing Company, Inc.
Lima, Ohio

Scripture quotations are from the *New Revised Standard Version of the Bible*, copyright 1989 by the Division of Christian Education of the National Council of the Churches of Christ in the USA. Used by permission.

Library of Congress Cataloging-in-Publication Data

Jensen, Richard A.
    Preaching Luke's Gospel : a narrative approach / Richard A. Jensen.
        p.   cm.
    Includes bibliographical references.
    ISBN 0-7880-1110-3 (alk. paper)
    1. Bible. N.T. Mark — Homiletical use. 2. Bible. N.T. Mark — Criticism, Narrative.
I. Title.
BS2595.5.J46   1997
251—dc21   97-11701
                                                    CIP

This book is available in the following formats, listed by ISBN:
0-7880-1110-3   Book
0-7880-1111-1   Macintosh
0-7880-1112-X IBM 3 1/2
0-7880-1113-8   Sermon Prep

For Bonnie:
Companion in
the Gospel.

Table Of Contents

Preface

Preaching Luke's Gospel: A Narrative Approach is the second in a series of works which examines narrative implications for preaching the Synoptic Gospels. The first work, *Preaching Mark's Gospel: A Narrative Approach,* contains in its preface a rationale for this approach to biblical exegesis and preaching. Some of that material needs to be repeated briefly here as orientation to this work. I refer you to the preface to *Preaching Mark's Gospel* for a fuller treatment of my own journey in thinking about biblical exegesis and about preaching in a story telling mode.

Three Eras of Human Communication

In 1993 I published a book on preaching titled *Thinking in Story: Preaching in a Post-Literate Age.* In this work I trace the human evolution in communication and the homiletical implications of that evolution. The human race has experienced three quite different eras of communication. The first era is usually called the era of Oral Communication. The ear is the human sense organ that receives the information in an Oral Culture. The story teller (rhapsode) is the primary communicator. The story teller functions by stitching stories together for his/her audience. The story teller *thinks in stories.* He/she ponders just what selection of stories to stitch together in order to create the meaning necessary for this moment. The hearers participate in these stories in their imagination and work together along with the story teller in discerning the meaning, the reality, the point of the telling.

I have speculated on what preaching might have been like in an Oral/story telling culture. It seems clear that those charged with telling forth the biblical faith would have been tellers who "thought" in stories. The Old Testament and the New Testament

Gospels bear witness to this reality. The mode of communication is story. Preachers, in turn, told these stories and other stories, too, we presume. In an Oral Culture the preacher most probably was a story teller telling stories in which the audience participated toward the creation or emergence of meaning.

The second era of human communication is Literate Culture. Experts in the field tell us that this era in communication began in Greece in the eighth century B.C. It was the creation of the phonetic alphabet that led to a whole new mode of communication and thought. The phonetic alphabet is unique because it separates sight and sound. The reader needs no sounds to interpret the meaning of this script. Learning can now take place through the eye alone! The eye replaces the ear as the fundamental human sense engaged in the learning process. The human sensorium is recalibrated. Eyes replace ears as the sense that receives and organizes knowledge.

Literate communication, of course, reached only a small percentage of the human population. Gutenberg's invention of the printing press in the 1450s A.D. democratized the literate world in the West! Print material could now find its way to the hands of the masses. This had a very important theological implication. Protestantism came to its birth on the wings of print. Could Luther and Calvin and the other reformers have possibly succeeded in their tasks without the aid of the printing press? Hardly! It is hard to imagine a Protestant apart from print. Protestantism, I might add, is having a very difficult time adjusting to today's Post-Literate culture.

In the Literate world teachers of ideas replaced tellers of stories as the primary communicators. Literate thought is usually described as conforming to the needs of the eye. It is linear, well ordered, carefully structured, analytic, and so forth. If thinking in an Oral culture was primarily a right brain activity of story telling, then thinking in a Literate culture was primarily a left brain activity of organizing ideas or concepts.

Preaching followed suit. Throughout most of the era of Literate culture preaching has been conceived of as being a matter of organizing ideas rather than of telling stories. Stories or examples are often used, but they are used to *illustrate* ideas. We all know about three point sermons. Someone once said that Protestant preaching is basically "three points and a poem." However we say it, the fact is clear. Preaching in a Literate culture moved from the telling of stories to thinking in ideas. The goal of the sermon is not so much the *participation* of the hearers in the life of the stories as the *understanding* by the hearer of the ideas that have been presented.

Preaching as the telling of stories. Preaching as the explanation of ideas. In many ways that is a basic choice we face each week as we deal with biblical texts for preaching. It is not too simplistic to suggest that this is one of the very first things a preacher must decide about the given text. How shall I communicate this text? Shall I tell stories or engage in other right brain activity that might *evoke* meaning in the life of the hearer? Or, should I explain the ideas or engage in other left brain activity that might help *explain* the meaning of the text? Evoke or explain! Preachers choose between these basic options on a weekly basis.

It is a fact that although most of the biblical material is in story form, most preaching in our time deals with ideas. Who taught us this?! Who was it that decided that our "points" about the Prodigal Son story, e.g., were more important than the story itself? Literate culture has led preaching down a very problematic path. The Bible is full of stories. We have been taught to explain the stories. In so doing we have often failed to appreciate the *power of stories.*

One of the great preachers of our time, Garrison Keillor, put the matter very well in a December 1995 interview with the magazine, *Door.* Keillor said:

> *... I think people do want to hear the Gospel in the form of a story. There's a story at the heart of every sermon. I think sermons fail when they take that story, stick it in a corner, and make it into a lecture. That won't work for people ... A story allows people to come into it. You can somehow envision yourself as a participant in a story. It engages the imagination in a way that a lecture does not ... a story has a magical power to draw people into it....*

13

Story telling is all the more important as we move into the third era in human communication. The name for the emerging communication culture might be Post-Literate or Electronic. The radical change is the change in the balance of the human sensorium. Marshall McLuhan talked about the fact that Western culture gave us an *eye for an ear.* We moved, that is, from an Oral world (ear) to a Literate world (eye). In this Post-Literate world we face a polymorphic barrage on our senses. Think of watching television. Our eyes are engaged. Our ears are engaged. Our central nervous system is engaged as we make a total response to a sensory bombardment. Electronic communciation engages our physical senses far more powerfully than does any form of communication that has preceded it.

This electronic massage of our senses that we experience in many forms of electronic communication (think of Virtual Reality!) changes us! People who experience this sensory implosion on a day to day basis come to our churches on Sunday morning with very different (even if unspoken or unformed) expectations than the people formed by Literate communication who populated our pews until recently. Simply put: A person who primarily *reads* throughout the week will come to church on Sunday and not be at all put off by a service that is primarily literate and heavy on information. A literate sermon with three points is just fine. But a person who is primarily *plugged in* during the week to television, radio, the Internet, etc., will have a great deal of difficulty relating to a service and a sermon that is primarily literate in nature.

One of the experts in human communication, Walter Ong, describes our emerging communication culture as "secondarily oral." By this he simply means that *ears have made a comeback.* You can function in a Literate culture with very little need for hearing. Our Post-Literate culture brings messages to our ears in a host of new ways. In my mind, Ong's comment is very helpful in determining the way preaching needs to move in a Post-Literate world. Ears have returned. Oral people communicated to ears. They told stories. I am fundamentally convinced, therefore, that we ought to learn a lesson from the world of the ear. What worked in an Oral culture will also work in its own way in a Post-Literate culture.

That is, we can learn again to "think in stories" and we can learn again to be *story tellers*. In taking this path we return to our roots. The Bible is a book of stories. We can tell these stories in our day, unleashing their power for reshaping our lives in their image!

One of the ways that we can respond to a new world of communication, one of the ways that we can preach in a way that speaks to the changed perceptions of Post-Literate people, is to become story tellers again. Please note that I say "one of the ways" we can respond is through story telling. Other books are coming out with different guidance for preaching in a Post-Literate culture. Story telling is one approach among many that will be proposed. When we choose to be story tellers, our sources for such stories can be our own autobiography; the stories of the lives of individuals and communities of faith; the arts and fictive stories that we create. I am more and more convinced, however, that *our most important source of stories for the telling is the Bible.*

Narrative Criticism

The Bible is getting new readings these days! Narrative critics are concerned precisely with the way that biblical stories work. I am convinced that this move to narrative readings of the Bible is a response to the change in communication culture as I have outlined it above. That is the case, I believe, whether these critics know it or not. There is simply a different communication environment at work in the world which is more open to "story" as an important means of communication.

Mark Alan Powell has written a brief book on this subject titled *What Is Narrative Criticism?* In listing the benefits of Narrative Criticism he makes the following statements with which I heartily concur:

> *Narrative criticism unleashes the power of biblical stories for personal and social transformation. There is increasing appreciation among scholars today for the ability of stories to engage us and to change the way we perceive ourselves and our world ... [A narrative*

15

hemeneutic] assumes that revelation can also be an event that happens now, in a present encounter with the text. To be sure, the Bible is a record of how God spoke to people in the past, but it is also a channel through which God speaks to people today.[1]

God speaks to us today through the stories of the Bible. That is Powell's conviction. That is my conviction as well. In my tradition we speak of the Bible as a "means of grace." The Bible, that is, is a vehicle, an instrument through which God speaks to us today. But I do not hear God speaking to me through much of the preaching that I read or experience. What I hear, rather, are *explanations* of that which God would speak. I hear *explanations* of God's love and forgiveness and justification. I am tempted to say, "So what?" My need is not to understand forgiveness. My need is to be forgiven. If I sit in your pew I want to hear you *be a voice of God* for me. I need to hear God's voice far more than I need to hear an explanation or some points about God's mercy.

For preaching this means that we need to be particularly alert for those texts in which Jesus speaks. Many times Jesus' word is a word of forgiveness or of healing. The preaching task at this point is to enable our hearers to *hear again* the words of Jesus. Be a voice for Jesus. Speak on behalf of God. This means that we must cast our living word of the text for our hearers in *first or second person, present tense* language. We say, "What Jesus is saying to us in this text is: 'The Spirit of the Lord is upon me. I have been anointed to bring good news to all who are poor. I have come to bring release to captives. I have come to give you your sight. I have come to proclaim the year of the Lord's favor for you' " (Luke 4:18-19). In those cases where Jesus does not speak in such direct language we can recast the text in such a way that we say to our hearers what it is that Jesus means to say through this text. Such preaching moves beyond mere explanation of forgiveness and healing. Such preaching makes forgiveness and healing happen!

Homiletical Directions are provided in each chapter of this book for the Lukan texts. Often concrete suggestions are given as to what first or second person, present tense proclamation we might make with a given text. These samples of proclamation are suggestive, of course. Let my words evoke your words of judgment and grace.

Another of the narrative critics who has been helpful to me in understanding the narrative character of biblical texts is Robert Alter. Alter is a Jewish literary critic who sought to bring his literary skills to a reading of the Bible. Two of his most helpful works are *The Art of Biblical Narrative* and *The World of Biblical Literature.* Two of Alter's terms have been of immense help to me in beginning to read the Bible with new eyes. Alter speaks of *narrative analogy* and *allusion.* By the term "narrative analogy" Alter means that the biblical writers often use parallel stories or acts or situations to comment on each other. Stories comment on other stories!

The concept of "narrative analogy" leads us to a new form of exegesis. The kind of exegesis that most of us have learned is a kind of "microscopic" exegesis. We put the text under a microscope and dissect it until we find bits here and there which may finally come together as a sermon. Almost all commentaries function on this microscopic level. Alter has taught me also to do a more "panoramic" form of exegesis. The question is: Which other stories in Luke's Gospel help to shed light on the text at hand? There are an increasing number of commentaries, however, which deal with this more holistic reading of the Bible.

The other Alter term referred to is the term "allusion." Alter uses this term to instruct us to put the disparate pieces of biblical narrative back together again. The biblical writers, he maintains, constantly link their texts with other texts in order to amplify their meaning. Other biblical scholars use the term "intertextuality" to mean much the same thing as Alter's "allusion."

This narrative commentary on the Gospel of Luke is written with the assumption that "narrative analogy" and "allusion" are at work in the biblical text. What I seek to point out in a brief examination of each week's text is the way that the given text is linked to other Lukan texts. I assume that you will read your normal share of "microscopic" commentaries each week. I am interested, however, in the panorama of Luke. I am interested in seeing how Lukan stories fulfill, complete, and amplify each other.

The Homiletical Directions section of each chapter will suggest ways to stitch Lukan stories (and sometimes also stories outside of Luke) together in order to create a sermon. This is preaching as biblical story telling, pure and simple. I do not suppose that one would do this every week! But preaching as biblical story telling is certainly one legitimate way of conceptualizing the homiletical task. My structural definition of such a sermon is this: *A stitching together of one to four biblical stories centered in or leading to a word of proclamation.* Proclamation is understood here to be a first or second person, present tense word of God or Jesus spoken by us out of the world that opens before us as Luke's stories interact with each other. Our word of proclamation, that is, grows out of the panoramic reality of Luke's use of "narrative analogy" and "allusion."

The Gospel of Luke

I am certainly not capable of doing this kind of panoramic exegesis of Luke's Gospel alone. I have been most helped in this task by the work of Robert Tannehill and David Tiede. Tannehill's work is titled *The Narrative Unity of Luke-Acts, Volume 1.* Tiede's work is titled *Luke: Augsburg Commentary on the New Testament.* I also recommend a book by Barbara Reid titled *Choosing The Better Part.* She has some wonderful narrative insights on the many passages in Luke that include women.

As you will see in the following pages I have leaned upon these authors extensively in my own study of Luke. I make no claims to uniqueness in my biblical work. I have borrowed from those biblical scholars who have done narrative work on Luke's Gospel. The creative task before me is to listen to these scholars, listen to narrative analogy in Luke, and propose ways of preaching based on this kind of panoramic exegesis.

Tannehill begins his work with the assumption that Luke-Acts is a *narrative unity.* On the first page of his preface Tannehill writes:

> *Despite the episodic style of large portions of Luke, it traces the unfolding of a single dominant purpose. This*

> *unifies the gospel story and unites Luke with Acts, for*
> *this purpose is not only at work in the ministry of Jesus*
> *but also in the ministries of Jesus' witnesses. Luke-Acts*
> *is unified narrative because the chief human characters*
> *... share in a mission which expresses a single controlling*
> *purpose — the purpose of God.*[2]

Tannehill notes the fact that Luke-Acts is the longest and most complex narrative in the New Testament. The rise of the discipline of narrative criticism emboldens Tannehill to seek to discover the unity of this story.

> *In this work I am not concerned with developing narrative*
> *theory ... but with using selected aspects of narrative*
> *criticism to gain new insights into Luke-Acts ... Jesus,*
> *the central character of Luke's Gospel, has a mission*
> *which he must fulfill ... the mission is received from a*
> *higher source. It entails responsibility for the realization*
> *of God's purpose in the world ... Luke-Acts has a unified*
> *plot because there is a unifying purpose of God behind*
> *the events which are narrated, and the mission of Jesus*
> *and his witnesses represents that purpose being carried*
> *out through human action.*[3]

Tannehill is convinced that Luke discloses his purpose in certain kinds of material. Angelic announcements, prophetic hymns in the birth narratives, quotations from Isaiah in Luke 3:4-6 and 4:18-19, and Jesus' own passion predictions inform the reader of the purpose and flow of the story. Working from these texts Tannehill seeks to present in his study the panoramic vista of Luke-Acts. In doing this Tannehill speaks much of "narrative analogy" and "allusion," though he doesn't use those terms. He demonstrates in a myriad of instances the way stories comment upon each other in Luke-Acts; the way Lukan stories are linked together in order to create a larger meaning than is available in any single text. My task will be to suggest how a sermon might be formed from these interlocking Lukan stories.

Tiede informs us in his Introduction that his reading of Luke's story will highlight at least three aspects of narrative:

> Luke's "Gospel" is a narrative. It is to be assessed and interpreted as a literary project. It has a beginning (Chaps. 1-2), middle (Chaps. 3-21), and end (Chaps. 22-24) as a good story does. It can be outlined into major sections, and it possesses a sense of "plot" or development. This is not the plot of a modern novel in which the central characters undergo psychological development or change, but it is the story of the interaction between God's reign and plan as deployed in Jesus and the determined will of humanity which resists, accepts, and betrays God's Messiah.[4]

Tiede notes further that his reading of Luke's narrative is based on the assumption that Luke has written a scriptural commentary. Luke tells the stories of Jesus as a comment on the stories of God's work with Israel. Jesus Christ fulfills in promise and judgment the scriptural will, plan and reign of God. Such is the panorama of this Gospel. Tiede also comments on the fact that Luke's narrative ultimately bears witness to the truth about God.

> All theological histories are finally a kind of "theodicy," justifying the ways of God in human affairs ... Luke's testimony is to Jesus the Messiah and Lord as God's way of ruling the world, God's will at work in the world.[5]

Methodology

In the preface to *Preaching Mark's Gospel* I laid out a three-fold methodology for the work. I wish to repeat that for you in this place. This work has the following purposes:

1. To call us beyond analysis of bits of information into the larger world of Luke's story.

2. To invite us to preach on Luke's Gospel at times and perhaps quite often by putting individual Lukan texts in the context of Luke's larger story.

3. To invite us to become Lukan story tellers, inviting hearers to participate in Luke's story in such a way that the story begins to lay hold of people as it seeks to change their lives in light of the storied presence of Jesus Christ.

There is much biblical illiteracy in our time. This is a tragedy. Making use of our sermon at times to tell a number of Bible stories is certainly one way of responding to this illiteracy. This is a very compelling contemporary rationale for Bible-story-telling-sermons! These stories need to be known. As we come under the inspired power of these biblical stories we will find our lives and the lives of our hearers begin to be shaped by these stories. These biblical stories do have the power to shape our lives!

In telling Lukan stories it will not be the case that each and every story we tell will have some kind of immediate impact on our hearers. We are quite like the Sower at this point. We sow the seeds of these stories in people's lives. When we do so, persons like Elizabeth and Zechariah, Mary and Gabriel, Jesus and John will come to live in people's imagination. This could be considered as a rationale for preaching. *We preach in order to put the stories of biblical people into our people's imagination.* Once the seed is sown these Bible folk will come to function for people in their lives as a kind of living guide to life! The story of Zechariah helps us get through when our faith is small. The story of Elizabeth helps us when giving birth is difficult. The story of the Good Samaritan helps us in our stewardship of life. The story of the Prodigal Son helps us as we relate to family members. The list goes on and on. When we plant these biblical stories in people's imaginations we sow seeds that will yield much fruit down through the years! It is not just our *ideas* that help to guide people in their living. Our *stories* of biblical people also help to guide people through the vicissitudes of life.

The methodology proposed here also helps to fill the gaps in the Lukan story. Many Lukan stories do not appear in the Lectionary. When we include some of these omitted stories in our preaching by linking them together ("narrative analogy") with the assigned stories, we help to give our congregation a more complete hearing of Luke's story.

Finally, let me note that the order of the chapters in this book follows the order of Luke and not the order of the Church Year. This helps us remember that Luke is a unified story. It is not just bits and pieces here and there that can be treated in any order we like. The pericope system genuinely fails us at this point. When we follow the Lectionary we are jumping around all over the place in Luke's story. Imagine reading a novel this way! The chapter placements, therefore, stand as a constant reminder that Luke gave his material an order for a purpose. Think panorama, not microscope!

Richard A. Jensen

---

1. Mark Alan Powell, *What Is Narrative Criticism?* (Minneapolis: Fortress Press, 1990), pp. 90, 98.

2. Robert C. Tannehill, *The Narrative Unity of Luke-Acts, Volume One* (Philadelphia: Fortress Press, 1986), p. xiii.

3. *Ibid.,* pp. 1-2.

4. David L. Tiede, *Luke: Augsburg Commentary on the New Testament* (Minneapolis: Augsburg, 1988), p. 25.

5. *Ibid.*, p. 27.

Luke 1:39-45 (46-55)

The narrative possibilities of today's text are almost endless. We must first of all come to terms with the fact that the first Lukan story in Cycle C begins in 1:39ff. This creates instant problems. In the first place, this means that Luke's preface (vv. 1-4) — which sets forth the purpose for the entire Gospel and for the Book of Acts which follows — is omitted from the lectionary cycle. Somewhere in the Luke year it is important that we deal with this preface. It might best be considered on Advent 1 when the Luke year begins.

The second narrative problem is that today's assigned text begins in the middle of Luke's carefully crafted story in Luke 1 that tells *parallel annunciation stories* of Zechariah and Mary. Luke intends that we catch the fullness of his meaning by hearing these stories together! What Luke has joined together no lectionary system should rend asunder! In fact, Luke 1 is so rich with images that in order to set forth the foundation for the entire Gospel we occasionally ought to use the first chapter of Luke for the entire season of Advent. There is more than enough material to accomplish this and we would then have set our preaching for the Lukan year on a very solid foundation.

The assigned text itself can be dealt with both as the climax of the parallel annunciation stories which precede it and as the introduction of the themes of Luke's Gospel which follow it. Let's deal first with the parallel annunciation stories. There is not space here to permit us to set forth the many parallelisms of these stories. The story begins with one of the powerful in Israel, a priest named Zechariah. He and his wife were righteous people but they had no child; Elizabeth was barren. The barrenness of important women is a constant biblical theme. By lot it fell to Zechariah to enter the temple and burn the incense. This was the chance of a lifetime!

Zechariah entered the temple in fear and trembling and was met by an angel who said to him, "Do not be afraid." Gabriel then announced that Elizabeth was to have a son and the son was to be named John. Gabriel proceeded to sing a song of great praise to the son to be born to Zechariah and Elizabeth. Among other things this son, John, would be filled with the Holy Spirit and prepare the people for the coming of the Lord. So far, so good.

But Zechariah wasn't buying! "How will I *know* that this is so?" he demands of the angel. Answer: "I am Gabriel. I stand in the presence of God and have been sent to speak to you and to bring you this good news" (1:19). We have a test of faith here. Zechariah has heard the word of the angel and has not believed it. He wants proof. He wants to know. Unfaith always wants to know. But the angel of God is not about *knowing*. The angel calls for faith and punishes Zechariah for his lack of faith. *"Because you did not believe my words ... you will become mute ..."* (v. 20). And it was so. Zechariah stands before us as a model of a person of unfaith.

Mary, on the other hand, stands before us as the model of faith! The contrast between Zechariah and Mary is stark. He is a priest of the highest order in Israel. Yet he does not believe. She is a common peasant woman. But she believes! She is all that Zechariah is not. The angel Gabriel comes to her six months after his visit with Zechariah. "Greetings, favored one! The Lord is with you." Thus spoke Gabriel. And Mary was afraid. "Do not be afraid," the angel said. That's exactly what Gabriel said to Zechariah. "Do not be afraid." This must be the first thing you learn to say in Angel School.

A second annunciation. Mary is to have a son. He will be the Son of the Most High. He will inherit the throne of his father, David. Luke introduces here a twofold understanding of Jesus' nature. He is the Son of God (vv. 32, 35), and he is the Son of David (vv. 32-33). These themes are played out throughout Luke's Gospel. We will deal with these themes in relation to later Lukan texts.

A third theme that is important to Luke's Gospel is touched upon here for the second time. Jesus is somehow to be born by the power of the Holy Spirit. (Note the connection of John and the Holy Spirit in 1:15.) This theme of the Holy Spirit is of vital importance to Luke.

And Mary believed the words of promise. Gabriel had scolded Zechariah because *he did not believe the words of promise.* Zechariah is the model of unfaith. Mary models faith. "Here am I," she says, "the servant of the Lord; *let it be with me according to your word"* (1:38). Faith has everything to do with hearing the promised word of God and trusting that word. That's a simple yet profound understanding of faith!

The important point to grasp here is that Luke tells us these two annunciation stories which in their fulness communicate the realities of faith and unbelief. Today's Gospel reading appoints only Mary's story for us to hear. To hear Mary's story, however, without hearing also Zechariah's story, is to miss a wonderful homiletical opportunity! These stories belong together.

We come now to the second great problem with the assignment of this Gospel text. You will have noticed that verses 45-55 are optional. The *Magnificat* is optional! Mary's song which sings the themes of Luke's Gospel is optional. This cannot be. The Magnificat simply cannot be an option. It could be said that the entire Gospel of Luke is a commentary on this song! We must somehow solve this lectionary problem. Luke 1 simply demands more attention from us than one Sunday can afford.

One of the key themes in the Magnificat is the theme of *reversal.* Luke 1:46-50 speaks of the reversal of the fortunes of Mary. Luke 1:51-53 speaks of the reversal of the fortunes of Israel. These reversals will bring all kinds of upheaval! The world will get turned upside down! This is a radical message in a radical Gospel. Luther thought that these verses ought to be the Magna Charta of every ruler. Mary sets forth what a model Christian ruler would be like.

Before we look at just a couple of lines from the Magnificat we need to note another important narrative connection with respect to Mary's song. The connection is to Hannah's prayer as we have it recorded in 1 Samuel 2:1-8. Please check out Hannah's prayer and note the similarities. Mary's song is clearly modeled on Hannah's prayer. Hannah's prayer sets the stage for the coming of

David. Mary's song sets the stage for the coming of Jesus. There is a narrative sermon possibility in weaving the Hannah and Mary stories together!

There are two lines from the Magnficat which so wonderfully summarize key Lukan themes. The first is, *"God has brought down the powerful from their thrones, and lifted up the lowly ..."* (1:52). This theme is played out in other stories in Luke's Gospel. See, for example, Luke 7:36-50; 13:22-30; 14:11-24; 16:19-31; 18:9-14 and 24. Luke 24 is, of course, the Easter story. Easter is the final demonstration of the God who lifts the lowly and puts down the powerful from their thrones!

A second theme from the Magnificat which pulses throughout Luke's Gospel is, *"... God has filled the hungry with good things, and sent the rich away empty"* (1:53). The motif of poverty and riches dominates Luke's Gospel as no other. The following stories play out this theme: Luke 6:17-31; 12:13-24; 16:19-31; 18:18-30; 19:1-10 and Acts 2:43-47; 3:1-10; 5:1-10.

These two verses from the Magnificat, 1:52 and 53, suggest a myriad of possibilities for narrative preaching. We will comment on these other passages as we come to them in the lectionary cycle. We cannot add them to this week's possibilities for narrative preaching!

Homiletical Directions

As we have seen, there are numerous possibilities for stitching Lukan stories together with Luke 1:39-45 (46-55). Mary's story definitely belongs together with the story of Zechariah. When the Magnificat is included we have the possibility of stitching together Mary's Song and Hannah's Prayer. Or we can stitch a theme or themes from the Magnificat together with stories in Luke's Gospel which pick up one of these themes.

On this Sunday prior to Christmas we might want to give consideration to Mary as the model of advent waiting. Mary had heard, as we have heard, the promise of the coming Son. Mary's "advent" is spent in quiet expectation that God will fulfill God's Son-promise. And what a Son this will be! He will be Son of God and Son of David. Is this the One we await?

What kind of Son must this mean? The Magnificat itself gives us themes of the coming Son who will put down the mighty, lift the lowly, fill the hungry with good things and send the rich away empty. Is this the One we await? This might be an unnerving picture for our polite Christmas celebrations which have become thoroughly enculturated. This Son clearly intends to turn cultural expectations on their heads. This is a dangerous Son, indeed, for all of us in our routine preparation for a nice little Christmas!

The first choice suggested here for preaching is a narrative sermon that tells the parallel annunciation stories. Story One would tell the story of Zechariah the priest from the point of view of his lack of faith. Story Two would tell the Mary story from the point of view of her faithfulness. "Let it be with me according to your word." That's the expression of Mary's faith. Mary's faith can serve as the very definition of faith for today's faithful ones.

Having told these two stories so that they properly stand in contrast with each other, we are immediately tempted to leap to judgment. "Don't be like Zechariah!" we would like to shout out. "Be like Mary." It is always tempting to preach the Law in such fashion.

But it really doesn't work that way in these stories. In the first place, we are all quite obviously more like Zechariah than we are like Mary. In the second place, we have not as yet heeded the whole story of Zechariah. Yes, he became mute. But his inability to speak was limited in scope. Once the child was born, Zechariah got it! His tongue was set loose and he blessed God (1:64). When the bystanders wondered what this child might be (1:66), old Zechariah was filled with the Holy Spirit and his tongue burst loose in wondrous song. We call his song the Benedictus (1:67-79). If you have a musical version of the Benedictus this is the day to sing it!

Zechariah, too, comes to faith in God's promise! His faith timetable is just a little slower than Mary's! Remind you of anyone? The proclamation for this sermon might go like this. God is the speaker. God says: "I am a God who makes promises. I am a God who keeps promises. I made a promise to Zechariah. Zechariah, like many of you, was slow to believe. But I kept my promise! I made a promise to Mary. She got it immediately and trusted the word of promise. I kept my promise to Mary, as well. In Jesus Christ, the Son to be born, I make a promise to you. Some of you will get it right away. Some of you might ponder the matter for some time. But never fear. I am a God who makes promises. I am a God who keeps promises. I will keep my Christ-promise to you." Amen.

Luke 2:1-20

The story of the Nativity of our Lord is narratively connected to much of the biblical story. This is hardly surprising in the sense that the birth of Jesus stands near the center of the biblical story. Luke sets this universal story within the particular context of Caesar Augustus, head of the Roman Empire. Caesar, "the august one," was deemed worthy of divine favor and human adulation. The biblical claim is that Jesus also deserves such favor and adulation. This passage speaks of two divinities. Caesar is known throughout the empire in all of his power and might. Jesus is a baby wrapped in diapers and lying in a manger. If God is truly revealed in Jesus then God is a God who is revealed in hiding! At the other end of this manger story stands a story about a cross. Truly, this God is a God who is revealed in hiding.

Joseph and Mary went to Bethlehem in order to be enrolled in the tax plan of Caesar Augustus. Bethlehem is designated here as the city of David. (Normally it is Jerusalem that is called the "City of David.") Joseph and Mary go to Bethlehem to be enrolled because they are of the lineage of David. Luke's story of Jesus, therefore, is immediately tied to the story of David. David was born in Bethlehem (1 Samuel 16:1; 17:12, 58; Micah 5:2-4).

David is very important to Luke's story of Jesus. It was to David, after all, that the messianic promise was given: 2 Samuel 7:8-16. This may be the most important passage in the Old Testament. It is the foundation of all of Israel's hope for the One who would come and usher in the messianic age.

There are also ties to the David story in the appearance of the angels to the shepherds. In each of the three stories told of David's origins in the book of 1 Samuel David is identified as a shepherd. The prophet/judge Samuel is commanded by God to go to Bethlehem to anoint the next king. Samuel went as he was commanded to the house of Jesse. How proud Jesse must have been that day. He heard Samuel's mission and immediately produced his eldest son (that's the way you did things in those days) for anointing. But God said, No! Samuel heard God say, "Do not look on his appearance or on the height of his stature, because I have rejected him; for the Lord does not see as mortals see; they look on the outward appearance, but the Lord looks on the heart" (1 Samuel 16:7). This passage could serve as a commentary on the story of Jesus' birth!

The other stories of David's origin also place him in the fields with the sheep. David is out in the fields keeping watch over his sheep when the word comes to him that the king, Saul, needs someone to play soothing music over his troubled spirit: 1 Samuel 16:14-23, *19*. The story of David's mighty slaying of Goliath also begins with David amongst his sheep: 1 Samuel 17:1-58, *15*.

Luke's shepherds come on the scene basking in the glory of the Lord as it shone around them. The angel spoke to them. (Note how often in these first chapters of Luke that an angel brings God's message!) "... I am bringing you good news of great joy for all the people: to you is born this day in the city of David a *Savior*, who is the *Messiah*, the *Lord.*" This Christologically-loaded proclamation is our clearest clue so far as to Luke's understanding of God's plan in, with, and under the birth of Jesus. (We will talk of God's plan in Luke's Gospel many times.)

Luke is the only Gospel writer to use the term *Savior* in reference to Jesus (cf. Acts 13:23). His primary Christological references to Jesus are as *Messiah* and *Lord*. This first announcement of the angels speaks of Jesus as *Messiah* and *Lord*. These same titles appear in the conclusion of the first Christian sermon preached by Peter on the day of Pentecost. Peter's sermon is recorded in Acts 2:14-36. The sermon concludes with these words: "Therefore let the entire house of Israel know with certainty that God has made him both *Lord* and *Messiah*, this Jesus whom you crucified." We might think of an arch extending from the angels' promise to Peter's sermon. This arch begins and ends with the proclamation of Jesus as *Messiah* and *Lord*. Luke's entire Gospel lives under that arch, within these bookends.

For the Nativity text we will focus our attention on Jesus as *Messiah.* In Christmas 1 we will explore the *Lord* theme a bit more. The title, *Messiah,* connects Jesus to David and messianic promise. This theme has already been spoken by the angel Gabriel to Mary. The son born to Mary is to inherit the throne of his father David and inaugurate an everlasting kingdom (1:32-33). When old Zechariah cut loose with his Benedictus he blessed God for visiting and redeeming God's people and for raising up a horn of salvation in the house of God's servant, David (1:67-69). This theme begins early in Luke!

As Luke's Gospel unfurls the *Messianic* theme occurs many times. After Jesus' early healing miracles the demons knew that he was the *Messiah* (4:40-41). In Luke 7:18-23 the messianic question of the ages is raised with respect to Jesus. Israel lived with the confident hope that God would keep the promise and send the *Messiah.* With the dawn of every new kingship, with the advent of any wonder-working agent of God, the question arose: "Are you the one who is to come, or are we to wait for another?" John the Baptist sent his disciples to ask Jesus this question. Jesus' reply gives us Luke's first real attempt to fill the concept of *Messiah* with his substance. Jesus said: "Go and tell John what you have seen and heard: the lame walk, the lepers are cleansed, the deaf hear, the dead are raised, the poor have good news brought to them. And blessed is anyone who takes no offense at me" (7:22-23).

This passage complements what may be Luke's most programmatic assertion of Jesus' mission and identity in Luke 4:18-19. We'll deal with that passage often in our narrative journey through Luke.

In Luke 9:18-24 we have another pivotal passage about the meaning of the *Messiah.* Jesus asked the disciples who people thought he was. He asked them who they thought he was. Peter got it right. He answered Jesus, "The *Messiah* of God." Jesus accepts Peter's designation and reorients the notion of *Messiah* as the one who will suffer many things, be rejected and killed, and on the third day be raised. Furthermore, Jesus indicates that if we wish to be followers of the *Messiah* we will have to deny ourselves, take up our cross, and lose our life in order to save it. This *Messiah,* diaper-wrapped and manger-born, will ultimately ask us for our life. Merry Christmas!

The last *Messianic* references in the Gospel of Luke underscore this theme of the *suffering Messiah*. On the first Easter day Cleopas and his friend were discussing the events of the day when Jesus, unrecognized, joined them on the road to Emmaus. Jesus spoke to open their eyes. "Was it not necessary that the *Messiah* should suffer these things and then enter into his glory?" Jesus said to them (24:13-35, 26).

And, finally, Jesus tells his disciples that the work of *the Messiah* was to fulfill the law, the prophets, and the psalms (24:44-49). "Thus it is written, that the *Messiah* is to suffer and to rise from the dead on the third day, and that repentance and forgiveness of sins is to be proclaimed in his name to all nations, beginning from Jerusalem" (24:46-47). Such is the work of the *Messiah*. Such is Luke's sketch for us of the plan of God for humanity. God's plan includes the suffering of the Messiah. The day will come, however, when the *reversal* of which Mary sang will come true for the *suffering Messiah*!

Homiletical Directions

Our narrative advice for the Nativity of our Lord is to tell stories of Jesus, the *Messiah*. Such storytelling can move in one of two directions. The first possibility is to tell stories of David as the background for the story of Jesus. There are stories that tie David to Bethlehem. There is the story of David's anointing as *Messiah* at the hand of Samuel. There is the promise made to David that his son will rule after him to all eternity. Next tell the birth story of Jesus emphasizing his connections to David: the birth city, the shepherds, the message that the angels bring to the shepherds, and so forth.

The closing proclamation to this grouping of stories can take the shape of God's promise to David in 2 Samuel 7. It might go something like this: The angel that spoke to the shepherds long ago speaks to us today. The angel speaks for God when he announces that the Messiah is now born among us. God says, "I made a promise to David long ago. I promised an everlasting kingdom. Today that promise is fulfilled in your hearing. I have sent my *Messiah* among you as a diaper-wrapped king. Through my son I offer you my kingdom. I offer you rest from life's trials. I offer you life in my kingdom. I offer you, this day, eternal life. It is yours. Now. It's my Christmas gift to you." Amen.

The second possibility of Messianic story telling for today is to tell what Jesus' *Messianic* rule is like based on other stories in Luke's Gospel. We might begin with the word of Gabriel to Mary, the promise of *Messiah* (1:32-33). Zechariah's song can be referred to as well (1:67ff). Substance for the *Messianic* theme begins to unfold when John sends his disciples to Jesus to ask if he is the One to come or if they should look for another. Jesus' answer to John gives substance to the *Messianic* promise. The blind receive their sight, the lame walk, lepers are cleansed, the deaf hear, the poor have good news preached to them. This is the essence of *Messianic* promise for Luke.

For Jesus to be *Messiah*, however, means he must suffer. The story in 9:18-24 sets that forth. So do the references to the *Messiah* in Luke 24:26, 46. These stories can be told leading to the announcement at the end of Luke's Gospel that sets forth the plan of God that — as a result of the suffering, dying, and rising of the *Messiah* — repentance and forgiveness of sins should be preached to all nations.

Preaching to all nations. That's what you are about today. You are bringing the *Messiah's* word of forgiveness to today's people. Your closing proclamation in this case might focus on forgiveness of sins. Forgiveness of sins is where Luke takes this *Messianic* theme. Announce this forgiveness to your congregation in the name of the hidden child in the manger.

Or focus your closing proclamation on Jesus' words in Luke 7:22-23. Your sermon could simply end in the proclamation of this word of Jesus, this word of the *Messiah* spoken for all nations to hear. "The blind receive their sight, the lame walk, the lepers are cleansed, the deaf hear, the dead are raised, the poor have good news brought to them. And blessed is anyone who takes no offense at me." Amen.

Luke 2:41-52

This is the only story that Luke tells from Jesus' childhood. As we have it here it is quite stylized and similar to the stories of Moses and Samuel. (See especially 1 Samuel 1-3. Cf. 1 Samuel 2:21, 26 with Luke 2:52.)

There are at least two strong themes that appear in this childhood story which have narrative connections to Luke's larger story. The first of these themes is that of the *temple*. When Joseph and Mary finally found the disobedient lad he was in the *temple* disputing with Israel's teachers. Amazement and astonishment were the order of the day as the boy taught the teachers a thing or two. His own parents were amazed. "Look," said his mother, "your father and I have been searching for you in great anxiety" (2:48). Even when Jesus explained why he must be in the temple his parents still didn't get it (2:50). Mary pondered these things. As we shall see below, Jesus' word that he *must* be in his Father's house hints at the suffering he is to endure. Who among us understands this suffering of the Son of God? Mary was puzzled. Joseph didn't understand. How do we grasp the irony of a Son of God who *must* suffer for us?

The theme of the *temple* is very important to Luke's Gospel. He begins his story with Zechariah in the temple (1:8ff). There Zechariah experienced the presence of God. The temple was for Israel the place of God's presence.

After the story of Jesus' birth the first thing we hear is that Joseph and Mary brought him to the temple to present him to the Lord (2:22-24). While in the temple they met a man named Simeon who was inspired by the Holy Spirit to sing praise to God that the salvation he had longed for had at last come to pass (2:25-32). There was also a woman named Anna who lived in the temple (2:36-38). When she saw this baby she gave thanks to God and became the first evangelist as she told of the child to all who were looking for the redemption of Jerusalem. The temple had much significance for Jesus even before he came to debate the elders when he was twelve.

Most students of Luke's Gospel identify chapters 9:51—19:27, material mostly unique to Luke, as the "Travel Narrative" or some such name. It begins with Jesus setting his face to go to Jerusalem (9:51). For the next ten chapters Jesus journeys in a rather zig-zag fashion through the land and on toward Jerusalem. Some scholars suggest that a traveling story was a common literary convention of Jesus' time. It was a convenient way to organize material! Traveling was the thread with which many disparate stories could be stitched together.

The "travel" chapters do bring us finally to Jerusalem but, more importantly, to the *temple in Jerusalem.* After his Palm Sunday entrance into the city and his weeping over the faithlessness of Jerusalem, Jesus goes directly to the temple (19:45). Every day that he was in Jerusalem he was teaching in the temple (19:47). (See other references to his presence in the temple: 20:1; 21:5; 21:37-38.) In the sixth hour of the day of crucifixion, the sky turned black at midday, and the *curtain of the temple was torn in two.* The presence of God would no longer be confined to the temple. With the death and resurrection of God's Son, the presence of God would find a new expression in the form of a people, a church.

Luke's Gospel ends as it began: *in the temple* (24:53). The temple was also the very first meeting place of the disciples of Jesus in the light of Pentecost (Acts 2:43-47). The first miracle performed by Peter in the name of Jesus Christ also occurred in the temple: Acts 3:1-10.

The story of Jesus in the temple, therefore, is not an isolated incident in Luke's story. The temple is an integral part of Luke's narrative. The temple was the place of God's presence for the people of Israel. The events of Pentecost, however, bring an end to the temple as the central place of God's presence among God's people. We call Pentecost the "birthday of the Christian Church." Pentecost was an event in which Jesus Christ was preached and the Spirit was poured out in order to bring the Jesus story alive in the hearts and lives of those who heard the story. In this sense *Jesus replaces the temple.* The Church replaces the temple. The Church exists wherever two or three people gather around the story of Jesus. Whenever and wherever the story of Jesus is told, there the Holy Spirit is at work. The church is the workshop of the Holy Spirit!

The theme of the *temple* is, therefore, a strong theme throughout Luke's Gospel. There is a second theme that arises in this story which is also an integral part of Luke's broader narrative. This is the theme of Jesus as *Son of God.* The Son of God theme is first raised in Luke by the angel Gabriel who tells Mary that the child born to her will be "Son of God" (1:32, 35). The angels' announcement to the shepherds also contains this message: "... to you is born this day in the city of David a Savior, who is the Messiah, *the Lord*" (2:11).

In the temple story Jesus' identity as Son of God comes forth from his own lips. "Did you not know that *I must* be in my *Father's house*?" (2:49). These are the first words Jesus speaks in Luke's Gospel. First words are always important words. The first words of Jesus tell us that he is the Son of the Father whose temple this is!

"I *must* be...." This divine *must* occurs in many passages in Luke's Gospel: 4:43; 9:22; 13:33; 17:25; 22:37; 24:7; 26:44. God has a plan and a purpose that *must* be carried out in Jesus' life and ministry. That plan and purpose, the *"divine must,"* almost always has reference to the suffering that the Son of God *must* undergo. In taking up the cup of suffering Jesus carries out God's plan for us. Life is not capricious. That would seem to be Luke's point. Life has a purpose. For all those who believe in Jesus Christ, the Son of God, life has a purpose and a destiny! This may be the central way that Luke talks about the salvific work of Jesus.

The *Son of God* theme is a very important one in Luke's Gospel. For a more extensive treatment of this theme see the material on Luke 3:15-17, 21-22 appointed for "The Baptism Of Our Lord" Sunday.

Homiletical Directions

We have looked at two themes in this week's passage that are connected to many other narratives in Luke's writings. The *Son of*

God theme is triggered by the very first words that Jesus speaks in this Gospel. His words are certainly Christological words! "Did you not know that I *must* be in my *Father's* house?" We have seen the nature of his suffering that this *divine must* sets in motion. These *must* passages certainly do set forth the nature of God's plan according to Luke.

Many scholars note that Luke does not talk about Jesus' life and death in the more traditional categories. What is clear in Luke's Gospel is that God has a plan for human life that is carried out in Jesus. Life has a meaning, a purpose, a destiny as we live in the One who *must* suffer and on the third day be raised from the dead.

One possibility for preaching on this text would be to follow these *musts* that underscore the nature of God's plan in Jesus. (See references above.) Speaking for God out of this narrative flow would lead to a proclamation something like this: "The boy Jesus stands at the beginning of my plan. This Son of mine *must* suffer. But suffering is not my last word through my Son. Resurrection is my last word. Hope is my last word. Destiny is my last word. So it shall be in your lives that are often marked by suffering. Trust my plan and realize that suffering is not to be endured in vain. Your life with me has a purpose. Your life with me has a destiny. Your life with me will one day blossom into life eternal as my plan of the ages is fulfilled." Amen.

The second dominant theme in this assigned text is the theme of the *temple.* A narrative sermon could relate the role of the temple in Luke's Gospel. The sermon would begin with Zechariah and Simeon and Anna in the temple of God. It would tell how the journey which Jesus embarks upon in 9:51 — as he sets his face to go to Jerusalem — ends really in the *temple!* (9:51—19:27 is the "Travel Narrative.") Upon arrival at Jerusalem Jesus goes to the temple day in and day out. At the hour of his death the temple curtain is ripped in two. The presence of God is set loose from the temple. It is loosed on Pentecost as the Holy Spirit begins the work of church creation. The Christian Church is the "temple of God's presence" in our time. God is present, that is, the Holy Spirit is at work, when two or three gather in the name of Jesus. The Church is people gathering around the story of Jesus.

37

You, my readers, come from many different denominations of the Christian Church. This story of Jesus in the temple which does move us finally to Pentecost affords us an opportunity to talk about the nature of the Church, the nature of God's presence for us in the world. The conclusion to the *temple* theme, therefore, might be a bit of teaching in the tradition of your denomination on the nature of the church. The Christian community replaces the *temple* in Luke's story. There is good news for us all in the new community of God's people who gather around the story of Jesus and experience the work of the Holy Spirit in our individual lives and in the life of our community.

Luke 3:1-6

Many commentators note that these verses are really the beginning of Luke's Gospel. Luke anchors the story very concretely in time: "In the fifteenth year of the reign of Emperor Tiberius...." It is this historical aspect of revelation, of course, that is unique to the biblical religions.

John the Baptist, the preacher to whom the word of God came in the fifteenth year of Tiberius, opens the drama. This is the first time we come to John the Baptist's story in the lectionary cycle. There are no texts appointed for Advent from Luke 1 until the Fourth Sunday in Advent. This means that John the Baptist pops up in our story out of nowhere. Such is not Luke's intention. Luke 1 tells a long story of a double annunciation and the birth of two sons: John and Jesus. It is vital that the beginning of the ministry of John the Baptist be set in its broader Lukan context. If you have access to the Anchor Bible commentary, *The Gospel of Luke,* by Joseph Fitzmyer, you can find a chart on the *step-parallelism* in the stories of John and Jesus on p. 313ff. (See further commentary on the annunciation stories in Chapter 1 of this work.)

John the Baptist is presented by Luke as a prophetic figure (the "word of God" came to him) who is to usher in a new age of salvation. The story of John the Baptist, therefore, has many narrative connections to the Old Testament. The song of Gabriel (1:14-17) and the song of Zechariah (1:67-79) hymn those Old Testament allusions as they prepare the way for the one who would prepare the way. John's prophetic call in these verses reminds us of the call of prophets in the Old Testament. See Isaiah 6 and Jeremiah 1:4-19 as parallel examples of prophetic calls. John the Baptist stands in this tradition! What we must finally say here is that the ministry of John the Baptist is meant to prepare humankind for the fulfillment of the whole of Old Testament promise!

John preached a baptism of repentance for the forgiveness of sins. We understand this baptism to be a Jewish ritual of cleansing and preparation. It is *not* Christian baptism. The New Testament does not teach two forms of Christian baptism, one of water, one of Spirit. Rather, there is this *pre-Christian* baptism of human action which prepares the human for the coming of the new, and Christian baptism which is baptism in water and Spirit. The agent of action in pre-Christian baptism is the self. The agent of action in Christian baptism is God present through the work of the Holy Spirit. See John 3:15-17.

The basic message of John's preaching is to call people to *repentance and forgiveness.* This forgiveness theme is already present in Zechariah's song: "And you child, will ... give knowledge of salvation to his people by the *forgiveness* of their sins" (1:76-77). We will hear an intriguing word on the repentance theme when we deal with the parable of the Prodigal Son.

There are many narrative connections in Luke's Gospel and in Acts for this repentance and forgiveness theme. When Jesus was in his hometown synagogue in Capernaum he read from Isaiah 61:1-2. Jesus identifies his ministry as the ministry of the One upon whom the Spirit of God rests. Among other things he will proclaim *release* to the captives. The word for "release" is translated by some as forgiveness. We shall see later that these Isaiah verses in the mouth of Jesus, along with the Magnificat and Jesus' answer to John the Baptist (7:22), form the base line of the message of Jesus in the Gospel of Luke. (One or all of these verses could be on banners for the Lukan year.) Part of Jesus' fundamental ministry is the ministry of forgiveness of sins.

There is a wonderful story of forgiveness told in Luke 5:17-32. This passage, which does not occur in the Lukan lectionary cycle, is a wonderful story of Jesus' power of forgiveness. The scribes and the Pharisees quite properly accuse Jesus of blasphemy, of doing the work only God can do, when they hear him announce forgiveness. The bottom line of the story, however, is that "I have come to call not the righteous but sinners to repentance" (5:32).

The "Christological drama" in Luke 7 also ends with a story about forgiveness. (Many of the Luke 7 stories occur in the lectionary in the Pentecost season.) The Christological drama arises in 7:16 where the crowd speculates that Jesus must be a prophet since he can raise the dead. In the next story John the Baptist wonders about the identity of Jesus and sends his disciples to ask Jesus Israel's question of the ages: "Are you the one who is to come or are we to wait for another?" (7:19). The end of the drama in this chapter which seems to focus on Jesus' identity is the story of a woman who was a sinner and who entered the house of one of the Pharisees. Having entered the room she began to wet Jesus' feet with her tears, and wipe them, and anoint them with oil. The Pharisees could see that Jesus was certainly no prophet, for if he were a prophet he would know what kind of woman this was who cradled and caressed his feet. She was a sinner! In the course of the story Jesus announces the word of forgiveness to this woman: "Your sins are forgiven" (7:48). Luke only mentions forgiveness in this way in this story and in the one we have discussed from Luke 5:17-32, *20*.

There are many passages in Luke-Acts which deal with the theme of repentance. See 10:13-15; 11:29-32; 13:1—5:15; 16:30-31. The combined theme of repentance and forgiveness is to be the message preached by the post-Easter church: "... that repentance and forgiveness of sins is to be proclaimed in his (Christ's) name to all nations beginning from Jerusalem. You are my witnesses to these things" (24:47-48). The conclusion of the first Christian sermon — the sermon preached on the first Pentecost — is precisely a call to repentance and forgiveness. When the crowd was cut to the heart by his sermon and asked what they could do, Peter answered: "Repent, and be baptized every one of you in the name of Jesus Christ so that your sins may be forgiven; and you will receive the gift of the Holy Spirit" (Acts 2:38).

This means that when John comes preaching a message of repentance and forgiveness of sins he comes as a *prototype* of the Christian evangelist. John is recalled by the early evangelists as they proclaimed Jesus to the Gentiles. See Acts 10:34-43, *37*; 13:17-27, *24, 25*.

A final narrative connection is an allusion to the Old Testament that we are well aware of. John the Baptist announces the purpose of his mission by quoting from the book of the prophet Isaiah. Luke continues the quotation from Isaiah a bit further than do Matthew and Mark. Luke concludes with the verse: "... all flesh shall see the salvation of God." In Luke's Gospel even John the Baptist's ministry points to the salvation of all flesh: the *Gentiles!* The theme of salvation for the Gentiles is a one of the dominant themes in Luke-Acts. For more on this theme in Luke see the comments on Luke 10:25-37.

Homiletical Directions

The possibilities for making narrative connections with this text from Luke 3:1-6 are almost endless. You can tell the birth story of John the Baptist to set his ministry in context. You can make connections with any number of Old Testament passages, for John appears as a prophet sent to prepare the way for the fulfillment of the promises of old. You can pursue the theme that the One whose way is prepared by John will bring salvation even unto the Gentiles. All of these are advent themes!

It is here recommended, however, that you work with the repentance and forgiveness theme that is the theme of John the Baptist's ministry and central to the ministry of the One for whom John prepares the way. Tell the textual story first with an accent on the repentance/forgiveness motif. Move then to the story of Jesus in his hometown synagogue of Nazareth. This story (4:14-21) will occur on the Third Sunday after the Epiphany, so the focus in this telling of this absolutely central passage in Luke's Gospel ought to be most simply on the words "release to the captives" which many interpreters see as an allusion to Jesus' ministry of forgiveness.

Next tell the story in Luke 5:17-32. The focus for this telling should be on Jesus' word of absolution to the paralytic: "Your sins are forgiven." Focus secondly on the follow-up story which finds the Pharisees and scribes upset with Jesus once again for his association with sinners. This man eats with the wrong people! Jesus replies: "I have not come to call the righteous, but sinners."

You can next move to the stories in Luke 7. These texts do appear in the Pentecost season and you may wish to omit them for consideration at this time. In using Luke 7 you might briefly set up the Christological drama that is woven through this chapter. The focus, however, needs to be on another sinner. The woman who comes to caress and cradle Jesus' feet is clearly labeled as a sinner (7:37). Jesus is still eating with the wrong people! It is often true in Luke's Gospel that meal time is a time of revelation! So it is here. What is revealed is that God loves sinners in Jesus Christ. Focus your story here, as with the story in 5:17-32, on Jesus' word of absolution. "Your sins are forgiven," says Jesus to a sinful woman.

If time allows, you can point out how Jesus' last words to the disciples commission them precisely to be about a ministry of repentance and forgiveness in his name (24:46). The climax of the first day of the life of the Christian church, Pentecost, is a sermon which finally calls people to repentance and forgiveness in the event of Christian baptism (Acts 2:38).

This theme of repentance and forgivness is, of course, an absolutely central aspect of the Christian proclamation. Don't we do this all the time? Why do it again with this John the Baptist text? Answer: because this is one of the few occasions in the Lukan year that you can naturally bring this theme to center stage.

The climax of this sermon on repentance and forgiveness needs to be a call to repentance today and the announcement of the forgiveness of sins to all who hear and repent. After having told the Lukan stories you might quickly find ways to identify yourself and your people as sinners. As sinners we are called upon to repent. We are called upon to acknowledge our sinfulness and admit that we do not have the power within us to stop our sinful ways. We need someone to help us! The Advent message today is that there *is* someone who can help us. There is One who is coming, there is One who now is, who says to you today what he said to a paralytic man and sinful woman long ago: *Your sins are forgiven.*

In whatsoever way you do it, this sermon should end with these simple words of absolution in the mouth of Jesus. Say it — and sit down! Now the work of the Holy Spirit begins. The Holy Spirit works to take the word you have proclaimed on the longest journey of all. The Holy Spirit works to take the word of absolution all the way from human ears to human hearts!

Luke 3:7-18

This week's text presents us with the preaching of John the Baptist. John is a preacher in the tradition of the Old Testament prophets, so the narrative connections with respect to the content of his preaching are primarily Old Testament connections. This sermon begins with a call to repentance (3:8) which is part of John's fundamental message as we explored in Chapter 4. John's call for repentance would brook no simple answers. The people of Israel would be tempted to say to John, "We are the children of Abraham." This would not do! A new age is dawning. Answers which draw upon God's action in the past are insufficient. Other places in this Gospel, however, Luke treats the Old Testament promises of God with more seriousness (Luke 13:10-17, *16*; 19:1-10, *9*).

There are references to Isaiah and Malachi in vv.15-17. Malachi 3:2 speaks of "the refiner's fire." Isaiah 4:4-5 mentions "purifying with water and fire," and Isaiah 41:15-16 uses the metaphor of threshing and winnowing to speak of God's judgment upon Israel's enemies. John is cast in prophetic mold! As God's prophet he points to the age which is to come. He himself, of course, will not be part of that age.

The work of the Holy Spirit is given fuller expression in the Gospel of Luke than in any of our Gospels. At one level John the Baptist casts the difference between his forerunning work and the work of the Mightier One as a difference of Spirit. John has baptized with water. The Mighty One will baptize with the Holy Spirit. Luke's Gospel paints for us a wonderful picture of what it means that Jesus is the Spirit Bearer.

In the Old Testament the work of God's spirit is most fundamentally the work of *life-giving.* In Genesis 1:2 we hear: "... a wind from God swept over the face of the waters." Footnotes in most Bibles note that the word for "wind" could also be translated as "spirit." The root word in Hebrew is *ruach*. With this word we are in the "wind family." Biblical talk about the "spirit" is "wind" talk. It is talk about the air we breathe that gives life to us and to all creation. (Cf. Psalm 33:6; Psalm 104:27-30.)

In Genesis 2:7 we hear that humans have life only when God *breathes* (Hebrew: *nephesh*) upon them. (Cf. Job 27:3; 33:4; 34:14-15; Ezekiel 37:1-10; Ecclesiastes 12:7.) Life is animated dust according to this passage. God breathes and we are alive. When God takes breath away, we die. We have our life as a gift of God's spirit/breath.

In a very important book on the subject by Michael Welker (*God the Spirit,* Fortress Press, 1994), the author notes that the earliest figures in the Old Testament to be "charismatic," filled with God's Spirit, were the judges. As we might expect, their ministry was primarily the ministry of preservation of the *life* of God's people. (Cf. Judges 3:7-11; 6:33-35; 11:6-7.) Later in Israel, as the prophets saw God's future with God's people, they spoke of a Spirit resting on the Messiah in such a way that the Messiah would usher in the dawn of universal peace, justice, mercy, and the knowledge of God. The promised Spirit Bearer would bring human *life* to its fullest flower. (Cf. Isaiah 11:1-10; 42:1-4; 61:1-4.)

From the Old Testament we learn, therefore, that talk of the work of the Holy Spirit is talk about *life-giving*. As Luke tells the story of Jesus he clearly presents Jesus as the promised Spirit Bearer in whom the *life of God is incarnate*. Jesus is first of all the *child* of the Spirit. His *birth* is wrought by the Spirit of God: Luke 1:34-35. In his baptism the Spirit of God descends upon him as a dove: 3:21-22. Clearly, Jesus is the child of the Spirit!

As Luke tells the story, Jesus understands himself as the Spirit Bearer promised by the prophets. One of the most central Lukan texts is the story of Jesus in his hometown synagogue. Jesus is asked to read from the Scripture. Jesus reads to them from Isaiah 61:1ff., one of the passages we noted above. "The Spirit of the Lord is upon me ..." Jesus reads. When he finishes reading he sits down and the eyes of all the hometown folk are fixed upon him. We can read their minds. "Isn't this Joseph's son?" they think.

"No," says Jesus. "Today this Scripture has been fulfilled in your hearing" (4:21). "I am the Spirit Bearer." That's Jesus' announcement of his identity to those closest to him. Unfortunately, those closest to such a person, then and now, usually don't get the point.

The ministry of the Spirit Bearer is to be a *life-giving* ministry. Good news to the poor. Release to captives. Sight to the blind. Liberty to the oppressed (4:18-19). That's just what one might expect from the Spirit Bearer, from the One in whom God's Spirit of life is incarnate. Luke uses a title for Jesus in Acts 3:15 that fits this description perfectly. It's a title for Jesus that never got very far. Too bad. It's of vital importance if we are to grasp the depths of Luke's story of Jesus. In this passage the writer simply refers to Jesus as the *Author of Life*. What a perfect title for the ministry of the One filled with the Spirit!

In his resurrection Jesus becomes more than Spirit Bearer. He becomes the One who *sends* life, who gives life, for the world. Jesus gives life to the world by sending the Holy Spirit. The Holy Spirit is the ongoing ministry of Jesus among us. The Holy Spirit is the active presence, the present activity of Christ. Jesus' last words to the disciples in the book of Luke are his call to his disciples to *wait in Jerusalem* to receive that which the Father promised. "And see, I am sending upon you what my Father promised; so stay here in the city until you have been clothed with power from on high" (Luke 24:49).

This promise is clearly fulfilled in the story of the day of Pentecost as told in Acts 2:1-38. Peter's sermon plays a crucial role in the strange events of that day. We would expect that Peter's sermon on the first Pentecost would be a sermon about the Holy Spirit. Wrong. Peter's sermon is about Jesus. The climax of his sermon tells us why this is so. Peter's sermon reaches its climax as he talks of the resurrection of Jesus. *The resurrected Jesus is the author of Pentecost.* That's the conclusion of Peter's sermon. "Being therefore exalted at the right hand of God, and having received from the Father the promise of the Holy Spirit, he (Jesus) *has poured out this that you both see and hear*" (Acts 2:33).

Jesus sends the Spirit. Jesus sends forth the Holy Spirit upon us so that his life-giving ministry may continue even in our time. That's the good news of the reaction to Peter's sermon. People were cut to the heart by Peter's sermon and asked, "What shall we do?" (That same question is addressed to John the Baptist three times in this week's text!) Peter said: "Repent, and be baptized every one of you in the name of Jesus Christ so that your sins may be forgiven; and *you will receive the gift of the Holy Spirit*" (Acts 2:38). Be baptized! Simple enough. We all have access to this Holy Spirit of life sent forth on the earth by Jesus. But let's broaden this beyond baptism. The crowd wants this Holy Spirit of life. Peter's answer to their question calls upon them to focus their life in Jesus Christ. It is "in the name of Jesus" that the Holy Spirit is poured out. The Holy Spirit works on earth wherever and whenever (Word and Sacraments) we tell the story of Jesus! That's our word of promise to all who yearn for the gift of the Holy Spirit in their lives. Tend the story of Jesus. Center your life in this Spirit Bearer. It is in centering your life in Jesus that you will receive again and again the Spirit of the Life of God breathed into your dusty bones.

"We believe in the Holy Spirit, the Lord, Giver of Life...." The Nicene Creed has it just right. The Holy Spirit is the giver of life to all creation and to all of us who inhabit God's created order.

Homiletical Directions

Luke's Gospel is filled with material that helps to set forth something like a "theology of the Holy Spirit." This theme of the Holy Spirit comes up in a significant way for the first time in this week's lection. John contrasts his ministry with the ministry of the Mighty One who is to come by saying that his baptism of repentance is a washing in water only. The Mighty One will baptize with the Holy Spirit and with fire.

Preachers need to pay attention and clearly set forth these Holy Spirit themes that are before us in the Lukan year. What we have given above by way of a brief biblical overview of the work of the Holy Spirit covers far too much ground for a single teaching sermon. Many of these texts will come up in the course of the lectionary year. Do make it part of your plan for this year of Luke to spend time in several sermons setting forth Luke's clear teaching on the work of the Holy Spirit.

The Third Sunday in Advent is probably not the place to undertake a complex teaching sermon on the biblical and Lukan view of the work of the Holy Spirit. We can take our cue from John the Baptist, however. John prepares the way for the ministry of the Spirit Bearer. That's a starting point. Having raised this fact about John, however, begs the question, "What or who is the Holy Spirit?" That's a question that lay people ask all the time. There is an even more important question people ask: "How do I get or receive the Holy Spirit?" That question points us precisely to Christmas! Here is a piece of the Holy Spirit mystery that does fit a teaching sermon for this week.

In this sermon we can do an abbreviated version of the biblical material we have looked at above. It is important to get to the question that the lay people asked on the first Pentecost: "What should we do?" (Acts 2:37). Peter invites the crowd to be baptized in Jesus' name in order to receive the Holy Spirit. Therein lies the answer to the commonplace question: "How do I get or receive the Holy Spirit?" You get the Holy Spirit by centering your life in Jesus Christ.

John the Baptist points us to Jesus, the One who gives the Holy Spirit. He points us to new life and new birth by pointing us to the new life and new birth of the baby wrapped in diapers. In this manger lies the One born of the Spirit. In this manger lies the One whose ministry will be a ministry of life-giving breath. Center your life in this One. Tend his story. The Holy Spirit works whenever and wherever the story of Jesus is told.

Chapter 6
Baptism Of The Lord; Epiphany 1

Luke 3:15-17, 21-22

This story of Jesus' baptism has manifold narrative connections in Luke's Gospel. We note first of all that verses 15-17 of this week's assigned text were part of the text appointed for the Third Sunday in Advent. (See Chapter 5.) The heart of the matter for this week, of course, is the baptism of Jesus. The main purpose of this baptismal scene would appear to be the heavenly identification of Jesus as Son of God. Our comments, therefore, will focus on this theme and its important narrative analogies to what follows.

Before we pick up the Son of God theme, however, we should note the *bodily* descent of the dove upon Jesus. No other Gospel writer makes the point of the descent of the Spirit upon Jesus in this striking language. Bodily descent has the character of *permanence.* The Spirit not only descended upon Jesus; the Spirit of God came in bodily form and it will *remain* upon Jesus. A biblical way of getting at the meaning here might be to remind ourselves of Israel's charismatic judges. The spirit of God certainly descended upon these *saviors* of Israel. The effect of this descent of the Spirit, however, was always *temporary.* The spirit-filled judges freed Israel from her enemies and brought forth a new time of peace and justice, but only for a fading moment. We can imagine the people of Israel crying out for a more permanent arrangement. They might have asked a question like: "Will there ever arise among us a *savior,* a *judge,* in whom the Spirit permanently resides?" The story of Jesus' baptism as told by Luke gives an affirmative answer to this longing from of old! Jesus is truly the child of the Spirit!

The identification of Jesus as Son of God is vital to the message of Luke. We have touched on this Son of God theme in Chapter 3. Earlier references to this theme in Luke are found in 1:32, 35 and 2:41-52. Here we will set forth the narrative connections with this theme in what follows Jesus' baptism. If you do not choose to follow this path in this week's preaching you can pick it up in several other places in Luke's story.

To begin with, many commentators note that the announcement of Jesus as the Son of God has narrative resonance with Psalm 2. Psalm 2 has been identified as a "royal Psalm." God speaks here to Israel's messiah: "You are my son; today I have begotten you" (v. 7). There is this heritage in Israel that the Anointed One is an "adopted" Son of God.

The story of Jesus' baptism proclaims the divine sonship of Jesus. What does it mean that Jesus is the Son of God? The story begs this question. The question, in turn, usually propels us to the church's theological thinking about "Son of God." In theory all one would need do here is consult one's own denominational theology of Jesus as Son of God, and you've got a sermon! This kind of non-narrative thinking circumvents Luke's own answer to this question. Luke's answer to the question of the meaning of "Son of God" comes in the course of the next four stories. (Of these stories Luke 4:1-13 is appointed for the First Sunday in Lent and Luke 4:14-21 is appointed for the Third Sunday after the Epiphany.)

What does it mean that Jesus is the Son of God? Luke's first answer to this question is related in the next verses in the form of a genealogy (Luke 3:23-38). The climax of this story is that Jesus is "... the son of God." No other Gospel writer used the genealogy to make such a point!

A story from Papua New Guinea gives life to this genealogy. There is a story told of a man who translated the Bible into one of the many languages of the people of Papua New Guinea. His translating procedure was to translate a passage, have his assistant read it to the people, and revise the translation accordingly. In doing this the translator skipped the genealogy for the same reason we pay so little attention to it: boring! At the end of the task, however, he did translate the genealogical list and he was present when it was read to the people. As the names of the ancestors were rattled off the translator noticed that a hush fell over the room. So quiet did it get with the crowd pressing in on him that he thought he must have violated some tribal taboo in his translating. But no! When the reading was finished the people stood in amazement. "Why didn't you tell us this before?" they asked. "No one bothers to write down the ancestors of spirit being but only of real persons. The Bible must mean to say here that Jesus is a *real person*! Jesus was a real man on our real earth and not just a part of some spirit world; not just some of the white man's magic!"

The people hearing this genealogy had been Christians. But they had never understood that the Son of God was a real person. Only this genealogy, similar to their own genealogical thinking, convinced them of Jesus' true nature. Perhaps the world of Luke was much like this world of Papua New Guinea. Luke knew, therefore, that the most important way he could answer the question of what it means that Jesus is the Son of God was by giving his genealogy. For Luke and his audience this "boring" genealogy was very exciting stuff!

The baptismal story announces that Jesus is the Son of God. Jesus' genealogy is given to help clarify what Son of God means. Then the devil enters the picture: Luke 4:1-13. The thrust of his temptation is to help Jesus get a "better" understanding of what it means to be Son of God. *"If you are the Son of God*, command this stone to become a loaf of bread" (v. 3). *"If you are the Son of God* , throw yourself down from here ..." (v. 9). At a very important level this story is a *commentary on Jesus' baptism* and the nature of divine sonship. The devil has its own understanding of what it means to be Son of God: it means to have power on earth and to have it now! "I will give you glory now!" the devil shouts (v. 6). "If you are the Son of God, for God's sake, act like one! Do something. Show us. Let us see your glory!" The devil appears to have a "theology of glory."

Jesus spoke to the disciples on the road to Emmaus. He said to them: "Was it not necessary that the Messiah should suffer these things and *then enter his glory*?" (Luke 24:46). The time for glory would come. The devil was reading from the wrong time chart! At any rate, the devil left Jesus after being unable to convince this Son of God that being the divine Son was about the Son's glory! The devil would be back at a more opportune time! (4:13).

The next story takes place in Nazareth. It is the fourth consecutive story that meditates on the Son of God theme. What does
it mean that Jesus is Son of God? Jesus reads to the hometown
folks from Isaiah 61:

> *The Spirit of the Lord is upon me,*
> *because he has anointed me*
> *to bring good news to the poor.*
> *He has sent me to proclaim release to the captives*
> *and recovery of sight to the blind,*
> *to let the oppressed go free,*
> *to proclaim the year of the Lord's favor.*
>
> (Luke 4:18-19)

And Jesus said: "Today this scripture is fulfilled in your
hearing" (Luke 4:21). This passage serves many functions in
Luke's Gospel. It may be the most pivotal verse in the entire
Gospel. Seen in the context of the Lukan stories that immediately
precede it, this reading from Isaiah is Jesus' way of saying what it
means that he is Son of God. Being Son of God is not about the
glory of the Son! Being Son of God is about being a servant to all
in need. The Nazareth assembly, of course, didn't get it. They
didn't perceive whose son he was. As far as they knew, he was
Joseph's son (v. 22).

The Son of God theme is also touched upon in Luke 4:40-41.
The demons recognize Jesus as Son of God! This is true also of
the story told of the Gerasene demoniac in Luke 8:26-33, *28*.

The heavenly identification of Jesus as the Son of God is
repeated in the Transfiguration story: Luke 9:28-36. This text is
appointed for the last Sunday after the Epiphany.

The fate of the Son of God is told in the parable Jesus tells in
Luke 20:9-18. The owner of the vineyard sends his "beloved son,"
and the son is killed by those wicked inhabitants of the vineyard.
Jesus confirms with this parable that the destiny of the Son of God
is a destiny of suffering. This parable of Jesus is not appointed for
the lectionary year.

At Jesus' trial the themes of Son of God and Messiah merge a
bit (Luke 22:66-67). The chief priests put the question to Jesus

baldly: "Are you the the Son of God?" Jesus answered: "You say that I am." And they replied: "What further testimony do we need? We have heard it ourselves from his own lips!" To claim to be God was a blasphemous claim. Such a man should be killed. So they took him to Pilate. The Son of God must suffer. Luke presents Jesus as the One who must suffer far more strongly than do the other Gospels.

Homiletical Directions

The preaching possibilities on the few verses assigned for this week are many. One might focus on the baptismal theme. Such a sermon might tell first the story of this week's text focusing on God's announcement: "You are my Son, the Beloved; with you I am well pleased." We could talk about Christian baptism as containing this same promise for us today. This word might strike with particular power in the lives of those who feel lonely, alone, alienated, orphaned. To such people it is indeed good news to hear: "You are my child. You are my son. You are my daughter. I am pleased with you."

A second preaching possibility would be to follow up the Son of God theme in Luke's Gospel. The most obvious way to do this would be to link the four Lukan stories together as a meditation on what it means to be Son of God. We refer to the stories in 3:21-22; 3:23-38; 4:1-13; 4:16-21. The climax of these stories is Jesus' reading from the book of Isaiah. Jesus defines the meaning of Son of God through this Isaiah passage as the life of a servant. The Son of God/servant cares for the poor, the captives, and all who are oppressed. In our baptism we are called "sons" and "daughters" of God. It follows that our *baptismal vocation* is precisely to live the life of servants. We, too, are called upon to care for the poor, the captives, and the oppressed. Such a sermon is obviously a call to the children of God to take up the yoke of Christian discipleship and live lives that are focused not on self, as the devil would have it, but on the needs of others.

This same Son of God theme can be developed out of four consecutive Lukan stories (the other texts we have touched upon might also be used) toward a strong word of proclamation. These four stories from Luke need to be told in sequence somewhere in the church year. The stitching together of these stories means telling each story toward the end so that the meaning of "Son of God" becomes clear. Such a sermon might well end with Jesus' reading of Isaiah. We can turn the meaning of "Son of God" into proclamation of this passage. We can say: What Jesus is saying to us today about the meaning of "Son of God" is something like this. "I am the Son of God. I have come to preach good news to the poor. I have come to proclaim release to the captives. I have come to bring sight to the blind. I have come to set at liberty those who are oppressed. I have come to announce to you that the acceptable year of the Lord is at hand." Amen!

Luke 4:1-13

In the early years of the Christian Church a dominant theme of the Lenten season was the conflict between demonic powers and Christian life. The text appointed for this First Sunday in Lent, the story of Jesus' temptation, picks up this ancient theme. There were obstacles on the way as Jesus sought to live out his vocation as Son of God. There are obstacles on our way as well as we seek to live out our vocation as children of God.

We have looked at this passage briefly in Chapter 6. It appears to be part of a series of stories (3:21-22; 3:23-38; 4:1-13; 4:16-21) that develop the Son of God theme in Luke's telling of the Jesus story. Jesus was declared to be Son of God in his baptism and through the instrument of a genealogical list. In this week's story the devil tries its hand at interpreting the meaning of Son of God. The devil operates from a "theology of glory." "If you are the Son of God," the devil says, "command this stone to become a loaf of bread." In this and its other temptations the devil seeks to persuade Jesus to "count equality with God a thing to be grasped" (Philippians 2:6). "Show us your God stuff," the devil hisses. "Let's see the glory now!" But Jesus would not. He remained an obedient Son of his God. He would walk the road of suffering to the cross. Glory would have to wait for another day. (See Luke 24:26.)

Jesus does not succumb to temptation. In so doing he establishes his identity as the obedient Son of God. The writer of the book of Hebrews picks up this theme in a pastoral way. "For we do not have a high priest who is unable to sympathize with our weaknesses, but we have one who in every respect has been tested as we are, yet without sin" (Hebrews 4:15). We see in Jesus, therefore, the One who overcomes temptation on behalf of all humankind! He becomes, in turn, a model for Christian discipleship.

Jesus turns away the temptations of the devil by quoting from the Old Testament, specifically from the book of Deuteronomy. Jesus quotes from Deuteronomy 8:3; 6:18 and 6:16 in turning back the devil's lying promises of glory. The context in the book of Deuteronomy is that of the people of Israel in exodus to a new land. According to most biblical accounts Israel's time in the wilderness was a time of *temptation and failure!* In the wilderness Israel was tempted and failed. In his wilderness Jesus was tempted and did not fail.

The early Christian theologian Irenaeus made use of this wilderness analogy and several other Old Testament analogies in his doctrine of *recapitulation.* Irenaeus spoke of Adam and Eve in Paradise as moral and spiritual children. Humans were intended to grow into full humanity, into ever closer resemblance with God the Maker of all. The devil's temptation (Genesis 3:1-7) was too much for those in the childhood of the race. They were tempted to "be like God." How can any human refuse such an offer? So Adam and Eve ate of the tree. They acted in *disobedience.* Through this act the whole of the human race became enslaved to the devil (Romans 5:12-21).

According to Irenaeus, the whole human race fell under the power of sin, death, and the devil through the disobedience of one man. If the human race fell into bondage through the *disobedience* of one man, it can be put back together again by the *obedience* of one man: "... just as by the one man's disobedience the many were made sinners, so by the one man's obedience the many will be made righteous" (Romans 5:19). As Irenaeus put it: "God in Christ became what we are, in order to enable us to become what He is." This is *recapitulation.* The word itself comes from the fact that mathematical addition in the ancient world put the sum at the top of the column. The solution is the "summing up" process. So, according to Irenaeus, all things are "summed up" in Christ; all things are "recapitulated" in Christ.

The temptation story, therefore, recapitulates the story of the fall. Adam was disobedient. (This is Irenaeus' way of putting the matter. Today we seek to include Eve in the story, too.) Jesus was obedient. Adam (and Eve) did count equality with God a "thing to

57

be grasped." Jesus did not count equality with God "a thing to be grasped." Indeed, Christ became what we are in order that we might become what God is! Because of Christ's act of obedience we are free from the powers that held us in bondage.

The major significance of Irenaeus' theology was its polemic against Gnosticism. Harold Bloom, an author who defines himself as a Gnostic Jew, has written a recent book called *The American Religion: The Emergence of the Post-Christian Nation.* His fundamental thesis is that the religion that is native to American soil is Gnosticism. He defines Gnosticism as follows:

> *... the Gnostics, in a narrow sense, were a proto-Christian sect of the second century of the Common Era, whose broad beliefs centered in two absolute convictions: the Creation, of the world and of mankind in its present form, was the same event as the Fall of the world and of man, but humankind has in it a spark or breath of the uncreated, of God, and that spark can find its way back to the uncreated, unfallen world, in a solitary act of knowledge.*[1]

Gnosticism, that is, believes that humans have fallen from a spiritual world that existed before the creation. We are now captives of a material world. But there is hope. God is within us! The uncreated is within us. The unfallen world is within us. Therefore, by a "solitary act of knowledge" (*gnosis* means knowledge) we can leave this material world and return to our rightful place among the gods.

The aim of Bloom's book is to show how the new American religions of the nineteenth and twentieth centuries are at heart gnostic. The major nineteenth century new religions in America were Mormon, Christian Science, Seventh-Day Adventism, Jehovah's Witness, and Pentecostalism. All are gnostic, proclaims Bloom. The cults that have sprung up among us in recent years are gnostic as well. Most of what passes for "spirituality" in the media today is also gnostic. Bloom's analysis of the gnostic tendencies of so much of what passes for "spirituality" today is essentially on target!

The single passage of Scripture that could be used as a theme for a book on these religions and cults is Genesis 3:5: "... for God knows that when you eat of it your eyes will be opened, and *you will be like God,* knowing good and evil." Gnostics of every time and every place *count equality with God a thing to be grasped.* God is within them, and all they need to do is to *know* this, and act upon this knowledge, and they will be reunited with the gods.

Against such did Irenaeus rail. So must we. Today's text is a very important bulwark against manifold forms of false spirituality! Jesus Christ did *not count equality with God a thing to be grasped.* Counting equality with God a thing to be grasped is perhaps the fundamental human sin. We were not created to be gods. We were created to be human beings. We were created to live in obedience to God. Jesus demonstrates that obedience for us in the temptation story. As Risen Lord he takes our fallen humanity and *restores* it to full humanity. As Risen Lord he grants to our humanity eternal life.

Homiletical Directions

In its narrative setting in Luke's Gospel the story of the temptation is part of a series of stories in Luke 3 and 4 which gradually reveal for us the meaning of Son of God. If you did not deal with this narrative sequence on the Sunday of the Baptism of the Lord you may wish to deal with it here. See Chapter 5 for the exposition of the Son of God theme in Luke and possible directions for this week's sermon. We have put the story of Jesus' temptation in much broader narrative perspective in what we have said above. It is quite natural to place the story of Jesus' temptation alongside the first story of human temptation in the Genesis garden. Story One of our sermon, therefore, would be the Genesis 3 story of temptation. The final focus of the telling of this story should be on the fundamental human temptation to play God. "Eat it," the devil said, "and you will be like God."

Before turning to today's story it might be wise to play out this "be like God" motif in the human story. A story or two of how we humans seek to play God might be told. Or you might enter the gnostic world which we introduced through Irenaeus' theology of recapitulation. This week's text affords us an excellent opportunity to deal with the nature of much of the spirituality that runs rampant in our culture today. People claim to be more "spiritual" than ever even though formal religion or going to church has nothing to do with it. Much of the spirituality that surrounds us is gnostic. The assumption is that God is by nature within us and that what we need for a fulfilling life is to make contact with the God within. Spirituality that does this lives out the fundamental human sin. Such spirituality makes equality with God a thing to be grasped!

If you deal with the gnostic theme it would be wise if you can tell a story from the cult world or the world of contemporary "spirituality" that makes the point. You might also wish to say a few words about Irenaeus to indicate that Jesus was obedient where humans were disobedient. Jesus did not count equality with God a thing to be grasped! The usage of Philippians 2:6 is very important in a sermon that focuses on the center of human temptation — the temptation to want to be like God.

Finally, tell the story of the temptation. Tell it with a focus on Jesus' obedience, on the fact that he did not grasp equality with God. In doing so Jesus Christ won the victory over the tempter and the temptation. In his victory we have new human possibilities for our life of discipleship. Irenaeus was right. Jesus became like us in order that we might be like him!

A concluding proclamation would enable Jesus to speak to us of his empowering victory. Jesus says to us today: "The human race succumbed to temptation. Humans wanted to be God. So I have come from God as a human. I have overcome the temptation. I have overcome the tempter. I have come to set you free from temptation. I have come to live within you in order that you may be as I am. Walk with me as a human being empowered by my presence. Walk with me and I will empower you to no longer count equality with God a thing to be grasped. Walk with me and I will enable you to live for others and not for yourself." Amen.

---

1. Harold Bloom, *The American Religion: The Emergence of the Post-Christian Nation* (New York: Simon and Schuster, 1992), p. 2.

Luke 4:14-21

With this week's text we come to the absolute center of Luke's concerns. David Tiede understands Jesus' reading of Isaiah as the inaugural address of Jesus' ministry: "... this portion of Isaiah announces the program of Luke's Messiah Jesus in the most specific terms possible."[1] Tiede points out that Peter's sermon on the first Pentecost is the inaugural address of the Book of Acts (2:14-41).

Several themes of Luke's Gospel are present in this week's appointed verses. We spoke of this passage in relation to the Lukan theme of the Holy Spirit in Chapter 5. In these verses Jesus identifies himself as the One upon whom the Spirit of the Lord is present! In Chapter 6 we related how this passage is the conclusion of four consecutive Lukan passages that deal with the Son of God theme. The verses from Isaiah which Jesus read to the people set forth Jesus' understanding of the vocation of the Son of God as a ministry of service to those in need.

These verses must also be examined from the point of view that they set forth the program that Jesus will pursue in the succeeding chapters of Luke. Robert Tannehill speaks of the importance of this story in understanding Luke's Gospel:

> *I previously stated that important clues to what is central in the narrative, giving it continuity, can be found in four types of material: major Old Testament quotations, statements of the commission which an important character has received from God, previews and reviews of the course of the narrative, and disclosures of God's purpose by characters presented as reliable. The quotation from Isaiah which Jesus reads in the Nazareth synagogue fits all four of these categories. As Scripture, it is viewed as testimony to God's purpose. As a statement*

by Jesus, it comes from the human character of highest
authority within the narrative. It is a statement of what
the Lord has sent Jesus to do, i.e., a statement of Jesus'
commission, which should lead us to expect that it is also
a preview of what Jesus will in fact be doing in the fol-
lowing narrative ... The quotation from Isaiah is a public
disclosure of Jesus' commission from God which
functions as a guide to the reader in understanding the
following story of Jesus' ministry.[2]

We have spoken earlier of the two other theme passages for
Luke's Gospel. One is the Magnificat, 1:46-56. The second is
Jesus' answer to the question of John the Baptist when John sent
his disciples to ask Jesus if he was the One who was to come,
7:18-23. In some way we need to lift up these three passages for
meditation and consideration during the Lukan year. Use your
imagination on this!

The Isaiah passage from which Jesus reads (Isaiah 61:1-2)
begins with the words, "The Spirit of the Lord is upon me...." We
have spoken earlier about the sense in which Jesus identifies himself
here as the "Spirit's child," the "Spirit's man," the "bearer of the
Spirit." There is also a prophetic overtone to this quotation. Luke
will develop the theme that Jesus is a "prophet like Moses." (See
Acts 3:17-26.) We will track this theme in later chapters.

Jesus understands himself to be anointed for a ministry to the
poor. Luke deals with the theme of poverty far more than the
other Gospel writers. This, too, is a theme that will be touched
upon in later chapters.

Jesus further understands his ministry to be a ministry shaped
by the Jubilee Year tradition of Israel. This is how many interpreters
understand the reference to the "acceptable year of the Lord." See
Leviticus 25 for a description of the Jubilee Year. In this fiftieth
year Israel was not to farm the land. Any who had lost their land
were to return to it. Israel was to remember in this way that the
land belonged to the Lord and they were always strangers and
sojourners in God's land. The proclamation of the acceptable year
of the Lord was to be part of Jesus' ministry. "Today this scripture
is fulfilled in your hearing," Jesus said (4:21).

This word (4:21) of Jesus about *today* as the fulfillment of scripture is important to Luke in many ways. Luke has a broad historical perspective on the ministry of Jesus. With the coming of Jesus a new era of salvation has arrived. The Time of Israel is over. Scripture has been fulfilled. The Time of the Church is yet to come. *Now* is the time of Jesus' work of bringing God's plan to fruition.

As we have said above, the themes from the Isaiah passage which Jesus came to fulfill are played out over and over again in the stories which follow the story of Jesus in his hometown synagogue. The poor are lifted up, captives are released (forgiveness is one manifestation of this), the blind receive their sight and so on. We will give just a few examples:

* 4:31-37: Jesus speaks a powerful word and sets free one who is oppressed by a demon.
* 4:38-39: Peter's mother-in-law is healed.
* 4:40-41: Healing the sick who had various diseases.
* 4:42-43: Preaching the good news of the kingdom.
* 5:12-16: Lepers are cleansed.
* 6:6-11: Healing a man with a withered hand.
* 6:20-26: Good news to the poor.
* 7:1-10: Healing by the power of the word! Faith is that which trusts the word it has heard!

And so it continues to be in Luke's Gospel. Jesus identified himself as the One of whom Isaiah spoke. From that day forward Jesus went forth to do what the prophet had foretold.

You will note in looking at these stories that Jesus most often healed by the power of a spoken word. (7:1-10 might be the best example of this.) Jesus' word was like God's word. God had only to speak and what was spoken came into being. God said, "Let there be light," and there was light. Jesus comes among us as *God's word incarnate.* He, too, spoke and it came to pass. This is the reality in passage after passage in Luke's telling of the story. Jesus came to announce new realities. Faith arises at the intersection where Jesus' word is heard and believed.

It is from this reality of the power of the word of proclamation that this author is moved to emphasize *proclamation in Jesus' name* as the heart of preaching! We speak for God, we speak for Jesus and the Holy Spirit makes it so! God's spoken word creates new realities! Preaching has awesome power. We pray that we might be good stewards of the power of the proclaimed word.

Homiletical Directions

We made reference to Chapter 5 which deals with the Holy Spirit theme and Chapter 6 which deals with the Son of God theme. If you have not as yet dealt with these themes in a sustained way you can certainly do so this week. Sermon suggestions on those themes are contained in the respective chapters.

This matter of the Jubilee Year is intriguing! Think of the economic realties of such a year. Debts were forgiven. Land was returned. Everyone went back to square one. Whether Israel ever actually lived this Jubilee out in practice is not the point. The point is in the vision of how God's people are to live as strangers in the land that belongs to God. This economic vision is about as far removed from American capitalism as it can get. The year of Luke is a very tough year for our American sensibilities. Passage after passage excoriates the rich. Passage after passage extols the poor. That starts already in the Magnificat.

We'll have much more to say about poverty and wealth in Luke's Gospel as we walk through this year. For today let's just think about the possibility of holding up this Jubilee Year as a kind of new vision of a way a society might be economically organized. Luke's Gospel does call forth from us some new forms of obedience in respect to poverty and wealth. Paul Ricoeur once said that *obedience follows the imagination.* One preaching possibility is that we set forth the vision of the Jubilee Year as a way of stretching people's imaginations about economic justice. We don't need to advocate a return to the Jubilee Year. That's not the point. The point is simply to enlarge the imagination of people; help them think in some new ways. Obedience follows the imagination! Let the vision do its own bending of minds. It might prepare us for passages to come!

We have pointed out a number of passages in Luke 4-7 that carry out the themes of Jesus' quotation from Isaiah. An obvious sermon this week would be, first, to isolate a theme from the Isaiah quotation. Second, tell those stories from the following chapters that carry out the theme. Close each section by putting the proclamation in the mouth of Jesus. The first theme, for example, is "good news to the poor." We can tell the story from Luke 6:20-26 where Jesus blesses the poor. (Jesus also has words of woe for the rich!) Conclude this section by speaking for Jesus: "I have been anointed to preach good news to the poor."

This procedure can be followed for each of the themes in the Isaiah quotation. The Isaiah themes coupled with the stories that follow would lead us to several proclamations: "I have come to bring release to the captives," "I have come to bring sight to the blind," "I have come to set at liberty those who are oppressed," "I have come to bring the year of Jubilee."

You can leave the sermon at that. Your congregation has heard Jesus read from Isaiah and carry out his ministry in fulfillment of these themes. At the conclusion of each theme they have heard Jesus' proclamatory word. They can be left to make applications of these words to their own lives. The other option is that after completing the above proclamation we put our hearers in the place of those to whom Jesus ministers today and speak his word of proclamation to them as a word of present tense address.

----

1. David Tiede, *Luke: Augsburg Commentary on the New Testament* (Minneapolis: Augsburg, 1988), p. 106.

2. Robert Tannehill, *The Narrative Unity of Luke-Acts, Volume One* (Philadelphia: Fortress Press, 1986), pp. 61-62.

Luke 4:21-30

The text assigned for the Fourth Sunday after the Epiphany overlaps the text appointed for the Third Sunday after the Epiphany. The text for the Third Sunday *ended* with, and the text for the Fourth Sunday *begins* with, v. 21: "Then he (Jesus) began to say to them, 'Today this scripture has been fulfilled in your hearing.' " We have commented above on the importance of this verse in terms of Jesus' self-identification. Jesus understood himself as the Spirit Bearer promised of old. Jesus understood himself as Spirit Bearer, as Son of God whose life was to be given for the poor, the captives, the blind, and the oppressed.

So far, so good. But now the mood changes in the story told by Luke. The One who had come to proclaim the acceptable year of the Lord is not acceptable to his own people! "Isn't this Joseph's son?" they queried. In his commentary on Luke, David Tiede writes that this question on the lips of the people is the dramatic hinge of the narrative. Up until this story in Luke's telling people had come to faith in the workings of God toward the birth of a Son. Zechariah believed, though his faith was slow in coming. Mary asked simply that God's word of promise be done to her. Elizabeth and Simeon and Anna believed. Jesus' hometown folk, however, did not believe! Their question could sound neutral enough. "Isn't this Joseph's son?" Jesus' reply to their question, however, makes it clear that their question was a question of unbelief.

In his book, *Prophecy and History in Luke-Acts,* David Tiede makes much of this passage of rejection.[1] At the time that Luke wrote his Gospel, he maintains, there were many questions in the air about God's promises to Israel. Things did not appear to have worked out the way Israel's hopes would have preferred. There was *rejection* on every hand! But why? Why must a prophet be rejected in his own country (4:24)? (See also the immediate rejection of the prophet [Jesus] by the Samaritans: 9:51-56.) The fact of the matter is, however, that people did not accept Jesus' identification of his own mission. That's why this prophet is not acceptable in his own country. This rejection of Jesus and his mission continues as a theme in Luke-Acts until its very last pages: Acts 28:23-31. Luke concludes his entire story with the word that the telling of the story, preaching and teaching the kingdom of God, will be carried on. The end of Luke's two-volume work, that is, leaves the final question of belief and unbelief up to us. The preaching is still going on. Will we have faith?

In answer to the question about his parental origin Jesus identifies himself as a prophet. (The Lukan theme of Jesus as prophet is discussed in Luke 7:11-17.) Jesus states it as a fact that prophets have never been accepted in their own country. To prove his point he tells stories of two such prophets. Notice how Jesus answered the questions of the people. He told stories. Jesus thought in stories! In his first story Jesus pointed out that Elijah could only miraculously produce food for a woman in the land of Sidon at a time of great drought (1 Kings 17:8-16). Elisha could only perform healing powers on a Syrian named Naaman (2 Kings 5:1-19). Unbelief, that is, is nothing new! It's been around for a long time. Prophets, those bearing the word of God, are not acceptable in their own home countries!

Unbelief grows apace in the Lukan narrative. The Pharisees appear as leading spokespersons for those who doubt. They raise questions about Jesus' every move: 5:17-26, *21*; 5:29-39, *30, 33*; 6:1-11, *2, 7, 11*. The first reaction to Jesus among the Samaritans is the same as the first reaction of his own townspeople. Neither would they receive him (9:51-56)! The end result of this whole process of unbelief, of course, is that the Son of Man *must suffer.* Unbelief finally got Jesus killed.

Satan had a hand in this, too. We remember that after tempting Jesus the devil left him and waited for a more opportune time. In Luke 22:3 we read that the devil entered Judas Iscariot. A more opportune time indeed! Judas betrayed Jesus. Jesus was handed over to the authorities. There was a trial, a conviction, and a crucifixion. Truly, a prophet has no honor in his own country!

Homiletical Directions

This week's text from Luke 4 is an ideal time to preach on faith and unbelief. Story One would be the story from today's text. The focus of the telling would be on the unbelief of Jesus' friends and neighbors. You might imaginatively expand the story in your telling by describing certain kinds of people who had known Jesus all their lives. Now they sit in the synagogue and hear him say that he is the fulfillment of the word of the prophets; he is the fulfillment of scriptural promise. They hear, but they cannot believe. "Isn't this Joseph's son?" Jesus' friends and neighbors do not believe. *They do not believe the words Jesus speaks!* They do not believe that the Spirit of the Lord is upon this son of a carpenter. They do not believe that this day Holy Scripture is fulfilled in their hearing.

Story Two might recall the story of Zechariah and Mary in Luke 1. (See Chapter 1 for our earlier comments on Zechariah and Mary.) In this week's text unbelief raises its ugly head in a very serious way for the first time in Luke's story. Before this we heard of faithful responses to *God's words of promise.* Zechariah did not believe the words of promise right away. Zechariah is kind of the patron saint of all who come slowly to faith. Zechariah's unbelief is described precisely. "You did not believe my words," Gabriel says to Zechariah when Zechariah wanted to know *how* God was going to fulfill God's promise (Luke 1:20). This is precisely the problem with the people in Nazareth. They did not believe the words they had heard from Jesus' mouth. Zechariah's unbelief was temporary. Once the child was born his tongue was set loose and he burst forth in song (1:67-79).

Unlike Zechariah, Mary believed right away. Her faith is also defined in precise language. "Let it be with me according to your word," Mary said upon hearing the word of promise from the lips of the angel Gabriel (1:38). Faith believes the word that it hears. Unbelief does not believe the word that it hears. So it was in the synagogue in Nazareth when Jesus read from the prophet Isaiah.

Story One and Two of our sermon are complete. We may need to pause here to catch the big picture. Luke's story begins as a story of the faithful, as a story of those who believe what they hear. In Nazareth unbelief appears for the first time in the story. We referred above to the Pharisees as those who follow up the Nazareth unbelief with unbelieving questions of their own. They didn't believe the words Jesus said either. Nor did the Samaritans (9:51-56). Nor did those whose unbelief led to Jesus' betrayal, trial, and crucifixion.

Story Three might be the story that follows today's text: 4:31-37. It is a story that demonstrates the power of the word that Jesus incarnates. There was a man in the synagogue with an unclean demon. The man with the demon shouted at Jesus. "Be silent and come out of him," Jesus said. And the demon came out. When Jesus speaks, demons listen. "What kind of utterance is this?" the people said. "For with authority and power he commands the unclean spirits and out they come" (4:31-37)! Jesus' word has power because he is God's Word incarnate! As God's Word incarnate Jesus is the author of our faith.

A theological summary of where we have been would go like this: Faith is created by the words that come forth from the mouth of God. Faith is created by the words that come forth from the mouth of God's Son. *Faith is created by the word of God incarnate in Jesus Christ.*

Story Four could focus on Acts 28:23-31. This is the end of the story as Luke tells it. Unbelief is still a problem, especially for the Jews who hear but never understand, who see but never perceive. So the message of God's Word incarnate must be taken to the Gentiles. Luke's two-volume work ends in preaching, ends in the telling of the story to the Gentiles, ends in the telling of the story to us. The final question of Luke's story, therefore, is the question of belief or unbelief addressed to us.

Today Jesus speaks to us. He says to us what he said to the people in Nazareth long ago: "The Spirit of the Lord is upon me. I am God's word of promise to you. I fulfill the promises of Scripture for you. I have come to set you free from all that oppresses you. I have come to set you free from the powers of sin. I have come to set you free from the powers of death. I have come to set you free from the powers of the devil."

"What kind of utterance is this? For with authority ..." he speaks! (4:36).

Such a sermon might end with a prayer to the Holy Spirit to enable us to believe the words that we have heard.

---

1. David Tiede, *Prophecy and History in Luke-Acts* (Philadelphia: Fortress Press, 1980), Chapter 2.

Luke 5:1-11

The first four chapters of Luke prepare the way for all that is to come. Very importantly we have heard Jesus identify himself with the vision of the prophet Isaiah (Luke 4:18-19). Jesus shall preach good news to the poor, proclaim release to the captives, and so forth. These themes dominate the portrayal of the earthly ministry of Jesus. The lectionary skips over Luke 4:31-44. In these verses Jesus carries out his prophetic commission by teaching with authority, casting out demons, and healing the sick. At the close of these verses Jesus reiterates his calling: "I must proclaim the good news of the kingdom of God to the other cities also ..." (4:43).

As we enter Chapter 5 Jesus is preaching the good news and the crowds have gathered around him to hear "the word of God." Preaching the word of God is central to God's mission as portrayed in Luke-Acts. We have already learned from Luke that the word of God has the power to do what it says. The word of God is a creative word that calls into existence things that are not (Romans 4:17). Peter responds to the power of the word in Jesus' mouth through his obedience in putting out into the deep even though he and the others have fished these waters before. "At your word I will let down the nets," Peter says.

By a word Jesus calls Peter to discipleship. Peter let out the nets and caught a back-breaking abundance of fish. Peter realized that he was in the presence of someone great. He repents! "Go away from me, Lord, for I am a sinful man!" This is the first word we hear from Peter in Luke's Gospel. The last word we hear from Peter in Luke is his words of denial of his Lord: 22:54-62. The story of Peter's denial ends with the words: "And he went out and wept bitterly" (22:62). Repentance at the beginning. Denial at the end. We understand this first of the disciples pretty well. He is a lot like most of us!

71

This, of course, is not the end of the matter with Peter. He will be called forth again by the forgiving and empowering word of God in order to take his place as bold proclaimer of the gospel. The Book of Acts completes Peter's story. Peter is there at the moment of Jesus' ascension (Acts 1:6-14). More importantly he is there on the day of Pentecost to preach the vital sermon which is to explain to all who have gathered that it is Jesus, whom you have crucified, who has sent forth this that you have seen and heard (Acts 2:14-36, *33)*. The Acts story continues to announce to us the boldness of Peter as he leads the young church into mission.

> *The Peter who turns away from following Jesus to trial before the Sanhedrin in Luke speaks boldly in Jesus' name before the Sanhedrin in Acts 4-5. His willingness to go to prison and his boldness in witnessing to Jesus before threatening authorities contrast sharply with his previous denials.*[1]

We have heard Peter's opening and closing lines in the Gospel of Luke. We have been reminded that the Book of Acts makes it clear that Peter had been filled with new power to preach boldly the name of Jesus Christ. God in Jesus Christ had to lift Peter from his knees of repentance more than once in order that Peter might be empowered for mission. Throughout Luke's Gospel we watch Peter struggle to grow into the fullness of God's call. When Jesus asks his disciples who he is, for example, it is Peter who comes closest to a right answer. Peter's answer to Jesus' question is: "The Messiah of God" (9:18-22, *20)*.

When Peter went with Jesus and James and John to the mountain of Transfiguration a few days after Peter's confession, however, Peter's lack of understanding is underscored (9:28-36). Peter thought they ought to build booths and stay on the mountain. Luke tells us that Peter didn't know what he was saying. When the incident was over the disciples and Peter kept quiet about the matter. The following stories (9:37-43a; 43b-48) demonstrate the lack of understanding of the disciples and Peter. These stories lay the foundation for the Travel Narrative which comes next in Luke

(9:51—19:27). One of the key ingredients of the Travel Narrative is that of Jesus teaching his followers the meaning of discipleship. Peter is also in need of such learning.

The repentance and forgiveness theme which is evident throughout Luke's story has been discussed in Chapter 4. The story of Peter's call is also a story of repentance and forgiveness. We hear Peter's word of repentance: "Go away from me, Lord, for I am a sinful man!" Jesus' word of forgiveness is the word that the angel Gabriel spoke to Zechariah (1:13) and Mary (1:30): Do not be afraid! Do not be afraid, Peter, there is a mission to accomplish. God's word has the power to do what it says. God's word made a saint out of a sinner. God's word made a disciple out of Peter!

Today's story ends with a very important note. We are told that the disciples *left everything* and followed Jesus (5:11). This will be a very important item to remember as we move through Luke's Gospel with its deep concern with possessions. Luke sees possessions and wealth as inimical to discipleship. True disciples *leave everything*. This theme will come up many times. We will need to remember that the disciples have already left their possessions behind. In this practice they are models of discipleship in the Lukan story.

Homiletical Directions

This week's text is about the divine call to mission centered in the story of Peter. This is truly a call we wish all in our congregation to hear and experience. The first story to tell is the story of Peter as told in this text from Luke 5:1-11. It's a story that can be told with great drama. The focus of the story might well center on the fact that Jesus calls a sinner to mission. Later in Luke 5 there is the story of a tax collector named Levi who is called to mission (5:27-32). Tax collectors and sinners are the categories of the despised in Luke's Gospel, but these are the people Jesus calls! "I have come to call not the righteous but sinners to repentance" (5:32). This story of Levi is not part of the lectionary for Cycle C so it might be helpful to include it with the story of Peter to underscore the reality that Jesus does, indeed, call sinners to mission. In the case of Peter it appears to be the power of Jesus' word, "Do not be afraid," which offers forgiveness for Peter's sins and empowerment for the exciting task of catching people for God.

Structurally speaking, it would be possible to end each of today's stories we choose to tell in our sermon with the word of Jesus: Do not be afraid. As people hear the story of Peter and Levi and hear that they, like the disciples of old, are sinners called into mission, it might be good for them to hear Jesus' word of comfort: Do not be afraid. Jesus' word addresses us yet today. Jesus' word is God's word. It does what it says!

Our suggestion is that the stories we tell in preaching today be stories that follow the life of Peter. Story Two might, therefore, be the story of Peter's confession in 9:18-22. This story is not used in this lectionary year. The point of the story is that sometimes Peter got it right. This story is followed immediately, of course, with the Transfiguration story (9:28-36; Last Sunday after the Epiphany). Here Peter and the others get it wrong. They don't understand the matter of Transfiguration. They want to camp out in glory just after Jesus has called them to a life of the cross. The stories in 9:37-43a and 9:43b-48 tell further stories of the disciples and Peter getting it wrong. Such is the way of discipleship. Sometimes we get it right; sometimes wrong. Always we live under the call of Jesus: Do not be afraid.

A third story of Peter to tell is the story of Peter's denial as told in 22:54-62. This story only occurs in the lectionary as part of the long reading for the Sunday of the Passion. This is as good a time as any to tell this story of Peter's denial. The story has no happy ending. Peter is reduced to bitter tears. All who are called to mission know these moments! It is clear, however, that Jesus did not give up on Peter even in this time of denial. As Luke tells the story, Peter is alive and well preaching on the Day of Pentecost (Acts 2:14ff) and speaks without fear to the Jewish leaders. The word of Jesus has sustained him. "Do not be afraid!" Easter has transformed him. Such is the hope of disciples in every age!

As suggested above it might be well to apply each of these stories of Peter to your own hearers as you go. The structure would be: story of Peter, word to today's disciples. Second story of Peter, word to today's disciples. Third story of Peter, word to today's disciples. It has already been suggested that Jesus' word to Peter, "Do not be afraid," might serve as the word of God which continues to empower sinners to catch people for the Kingdom of God.

1. Robert C. Tannehill, *The Narrative Unity of Luke-Acts, Volume One* (Philadelphia: Fortress Press, 1986), p. 265.

Luke 6:17-26

A considerable portion of Luke's narrative is omitted as we move from the Fifth Sunday after the Epiphany to the Sixth Sunday after the Epiphany. The material in Luke 5:12—6:16 is not appointed for any Sunday in Cycle C. The first segment omitted is 5:12-16 which is the story of Jesus' healing of a leper. "I do choose," Jesus says in this narrative. "Be made clean." Jesus is seen in this pericope to be carrying out his mission (Luke 4:18-19). He carries out his mission in this instance through the instrumentality of his powerful word!

The next section omitted is a block of material from 5:17—6:11 which contains a number of controversy stories. We see in these stories reactions to Jesus on the part of the scribes and Pharisees. Tannehill suggests that Luke presents Jesus' relation to the scribes and Pharisees through four recurrent "type-scenes": (1) Jesus eats with tax collectors and sinners; (2) Jesus heals on the Sabbath; (3) Jesus eats in the house of a Pharisee; (4) a Jewish leader asks Jesus a question about eternal life.[1]

In this material Jesus enters a time of testing of his mission. Objections are raised to what he says and does. The questions come fast and furious: "Who can forgive sins but God alone?" (5:21). "Why do you eat and drink with tax collectors and sinners?" (5:30). "Why don't your disciples fast like our disciples and the disciples of John?" (5:33). "Why are you doing what is not lawful on the Sabbath?" (6:2). As Luke presents the material Jesus answers the questions satisfactorily. Jesus' theme answer may be his word that new wine cannot be poured into old wineskins (5:37). His questioners are not impressed: "... they were filled with fury and discussed with one another what they might do to Jesus" (6:11). This One may be the Messiah upon whom the Spirit of the Lord rests, but his ministry will be met with much rejection! Luke apprises us of this reality early on.

The material in 6:12-16 has to do with Jesus' appointment of the Twelve whom he called apostles. We have dealt with the call of Peter and mentioned the call of Levi (Luke 5:27-32). According to 6:13 many disciples have been called. The Sermon on the Plain (6:20-49) begins Jesus' instruction of his disciples. David Tiede calls the Sermon on the Plain, "... a major policy statement of the kingdom."[2] As Jesus and his disciples come down to the plain a great multitude of people gathers around them. Jesus preaches and heals. The power of his touch healed them all! The mission announced in 4:18-19 is engaged. This is what Jesus has announced that he will do as he brings God's kingdom.

Jesus then looks upon his disciples and blessed them. "Blessed are you who are poor," Jesus begins. This is a departure from Matthew's version of this beatitude. In Matthew, Jesus blesses those who are *poor in spirit* (Matthew 5:3). In Luke, Jesus blesses real poverty, the poverty of his disciples. The disciples, we remember, left everything to follow Jesus (5:11, 28; 18:28). They are the poor! In their missionary work they must count on the hospitality of others (9:4-5; 10:8-11).

Jesus' announced mission was that he was to bring good news to the poor. This theme of favor upon the poor was present already in Mary's Magnificat. "He has brought down the powerful from their thrones, and lifted up the lowly; he has filled the hungry with good things, and sent the rich away empty" (1:52-53). Mary's song for her Son is a vision of radical social reversal. Jesus' word to his disciples in the Sermon on the Plain is a precise echo of this reversal. The poor are blessed and the hungry filled. On the other hand, the rich will receive woe and find themselves hungry.

> *Indeed, the woes in 6:24-25 use some of the same vocabulary as 1:53 in announcing the same reversal ... The disciples are the vanguard of a larger group who will experience the upheaval announced in 1:51-53. They are the poor who know about the good news because Jesus has proclaimed it to them, and they have responded with initial acceptance.*[3]

Homiletical Directions

It is difficult to escape the theme of the blessing of the poor and the word of woe to the rich in this week's text. This might be one of the weeks in the Lukan year to tackle this challenging theme. Jesus' Sermon on the Plain with its words of blessing and woe to the disciples needs to be set in its Lukan context. An introduction might refer both to the Magnificat (1:53) and Jesus' adoption of Isaiah's words for his mission (4:18-19, "preach good news to the poor") as background to this address to his disciples. We need also to remind our hearers that the disciples are poor! They have left everything to follow Jesus.

This theme of the rich and the poor occurs several times in Luke. When we discussed 1:53 from the Magnificat we noted the following Lukan passages which also deal with the theme of rich and poor: 12:13-14 (Proper 13); 16:19-31 (Proper 21); 18:18-30, and 19:1-10 (Proper 26). It is suggested that you tell two or more of these stories along with the story of the text for this week's sermon.

Story One in a sermon on this rich/poor theme would begin with setting the context followed by a simple proclamation of Jesus' word to his disciples. Memorize the blessings and the woes. Announce them! Our suggestion is that you avoid explanation in dealing with these blessings and woes and with the stories you weave together with them. Announce the blessings. Announce the woes.

Proceed to Story Two. Use any of the stories listed in the above paragraph. Just tell them as they are. Some of them do occur in the lectionary cycle, but your use of them at this point would simply be in the telling. Tell the story of the rich man who built ever bigger barns, for example. Now he could eat, drink, and be merry. But, no! He is a fool. He is not rich toward God. Follow the telling of this story by a repetition of the blessings and the woes from 6:20-26. Again, don't explain the story. Just tell it. Follow it with the blessings and woes.

Story Three can repeat this same process with another of the Lukan stories that deal with this theme as listed above. Just tell the story. No explanation. Follow it with a repetition of the blessings and woes.

Tell as many of the Lukan stories as you have time for. Follow them with the blessings and woes. After your final Lukan story and your final word of blessing and woe, say Amen. Your sermon is over. You have let Jesus say a hard word about riches and poverty. It is better that Jesus say these thorny words than that you say them. Let the stories do their own work on the imagination of your hearers. A closing prayer and/or a hymn following your story telling and blessing/woe pronouncing would provide time for your congregation to meditate on what these words and stories of Jesus mean for their life of discipleship in America today.

----

1. Robert C. Tannehill, *The Narrative Unity of Luke-Acts, Volume 1* (Philadelphia: Fortress Press, 1986), pp. 169-176, has a general discussion of the material in 5:17—6:11.

2. David Tiede, *Luke: Augsburg Commentary on the New Testament* (Minneapolis: Augsburg, 1988), p. 13.

3. Tannehill, *op. cit.*, p. 208.

Luke 6:27-38

This week's text is a continuation of the Sermon on the Plain. Jesus begins to set forth here a kind of ethics for the kingdom of God. David Tiede comments on this section of Luke as follows:

> *This section is an ethical exposition of the Beatitudes, and the church's situation ... As ethics, this counsel is in the realm of law. The brilliant usage of these commands by Tolstoy, Ghandi, and Martin Luther King in developing the philosophy of nonviolence have demonstrated the power of the address as a strategy for social change. It offers an alternative vision, especially in Luke where the particularities of poverty, reprisal, extortion, and loan policy are so prominent.*[1]

"Love your enemies," Jesus begins. This is precisely the realm of *radical reversal* that we have met in the blessings and woes that begin the Sermon on the Plain. Jesus calls for behavior to match Mary's song wherein reversal is the theme of the kingdom. The proud are scattered. The mighty are put down from their thrones. Those who are lowly are exalted. The hungry are filled with good things. The rich are sent away empty (Luke 1:52-53). The poor are blessed. The rich hear a word of woe. Enemies are loved. Good is done to the hated. An alternative vision of life, indeed! The reversal theme of Jesus' ethics as presented here stands in close relationship with the very nature of the kingdom he brings.

Another Lukan theme that appears in Jesus' ethics is the theme of *renunciation of possessions*. We tracked this theme in Chapter 11. If someone takes your jacket give him your overcoat as well. Give to all who beg. Share your possessions with the needy. There seems to be an echo here of some of the preaching of John the Baptist (3:10-11).

In his comment on verses 32-33 Tiede notes that the Greek word translated here as *credit* can also be translated as *grace* (Greek: *charis*). " 'What kind of grace is that for you?' indicates that the issue is not merely *how much* one has done, but the *kind* of 'grace' which is at work. The grace of the kingdom is qualitatively different."[2]

God's graciousness to sinners makes all the difference in the world when it comes to living a life of radical reversal. Graced people are empowered people. They do not live out of an alternative vision in order to gain favor with God. They live such a life because they have received the favor of God in unlimited abundance.

"Be merciful, just as your Father is merciful" (6:36). This theme of mercy picks up the theme of credit/grace. Mary sang of this mercy (1:50, 54). Zechariah sang of this mercy (1:72, 78). The kingdom of the Coming One is a kingdom nourished by mercy. In light of the incredible mercy of God we can be called to live lives of mercy as well!

Homiletical Directions

We have identified themes from the verses appointed for this week that live in harmony with wider themes from Luke's Gospel. Our sermon for this week could track one or more of these themes as we seek to understand our calling to live lives of radical reversal.

In this instance, however, it might be more important to tell stories of people who have lived upside down kind of lives in our contemporary world. Tiede has given us some macro examples: Tolstoy, Ghandi, Martin Luther King. If one were to tell just one of these stories of people who lived their lives out of an alternative vision of reality, the story of Martin Luther King is to be commended. In the first place, we are not far from the celebration of Martin Luther King, Jr. Day (January 15). In the second place, King's story gives us an opportunity to tackle the issue of racial injustice in our land.

If we choose to tell stories of contemporary people who live out this ethic of Jesus, we need to tell some micro stories along with the macro story of a person like King. We need, that is, to tell stories of ordinary people who have lived lives of reversal. The more local these people are, the more ordinary, the better.

Such a sermon would begin by identifying "radical reversal" or some other theme from the text as an introduction. Stories of people who have lived out such lives would follow. We don't need to say much in terms of application of these stories. The stories work on people's imagination. They make the point!

It is important that such a sermon end on a note of mercy and grace. No one in your congregation has the power in and of themselves to live a life out of an alternative vision. We all need to be empowered for such living. Our empowerment comes from the mercy of God. Mary and Zechariah could be called forth as witnesses at this point! Life in the kingdom is life in the grasp of a God who has mercy on all who fear God and "in remembrance of mercy" saved Israel. Life in the kingdom is life in the grasp of a God who has had mercy upon us in the past and in whose tender mercy we receive the forgiveness of our sins.

A closing word of proclamation to such a sermon might go like this: Jesus' word for us today is: "I call you to live your lives out of an alternative vision of reality. I call you to live your lives as lives that reverse the values of this culture. I call you to love your enemy; turn the other cheek; give your possessions to those in need and judge not the lives of others. Be merciful even as I am merciful. I have come to nourish your entire life with my mercy. I have come empower you with mercy in order that you may, indeed, live a new kind of life in this world." Amen.

---

1. David Tiede, *Luke: Augsburg Commentary on the New Testament* (Minneapolis: Augsburg, 1988), pp. 142-143.

2. *Ibid.,* p. 144.

Chapter 13
Epiphany 8
Proper 3: Sunday between May 24 and May 28

Luke 6:39-49

We note first of all that this week's text is doubly appointed for the Lukan year. When there is an Eighth Sunday after the Epiphany in the Church's Year, Proper 3 will be omitted. In the Revised Common Lectionary the first several Sundays after Pentecost may or may not be used depending upon the date of Pentecost. Older lectionaries typically omitted selections from the last Sundays of the Church Year.

This week's text is the third text appointed from the Sermon on the Plain in which Jesus teaches a kind of ethic of the kingdom of God. Verses 43-49 do form many narrative connections with what follows in Luke. These verses are concerned with the *heart of the matter* in relation to ethical living. Jesus distinguishes between roots and fruits. Ethics for Jesus is a matter of roots, a matter of the heart. The good person does outwardly good deeds (fruits) because the heart (root) is pure. The evil person, likewise, is evil because of his heart (root). Christian ethics is a root matter, not a fruit matter!

This root/fruit analogy speaks to the issue of "good works." Good works are the fruits our life produces. Good works flow forth from a pure heart. The heart is the key to the matter of good works. Our good works cannot make our heart good. But our heart can make our works good. And what is it that makes our heart good? Making our hearts good is beyond human capacity. The One who created human hearts is the only One who can re-create human hearts. It is God's Word that makes hearts pure!

The analogy shifts to foundations: verses 46-49. This section of the material parallels that in verses 43-45. The good person who produces good from the heart (v. 45) is like the person who hears God's word and does it (v. 47). *Hearing God's word is the foundation of good life.* The one who hears and does has built the house of life on a firm foundation. The evil person, on the other hand, is one who produces evil from the heart (v. 45). This one builds without a firm foundation. The evil one hears but *does not do* the word of God that is heard (v. 49). We note again that the firm foundation of our life in the world comes from God's word. Ethical living begins in our ears. Ethical living begins in listening to words that transform our hearts and set our lives on a firm foundation.

The creative power of God's word is a theme in Luke's Gospel. We saw it in Jesus' first deed of ministry in 4:31-37. "For with authority and power he commands the unclean spirits, and out they come!" (4:36). We saw it again in the synagogue when Jesus healed a withered hand with the power of his word. "Stretch out your hand," Jesus said and the man was healed (6:6-11, *10*). The very next story in Luke (7:1-10) is the story of the centurion who understood very clearly the power of the word. He had people under his command. When he spoke, they obeyed. The centurion clearly believed that Jesus' word had the same kind of power. Jesus commended the centurion. "I tell you, not even in Israel have I found such faith" (7:9). Faith believes what it hears! Jesus calls upon us to be *doers of the word*. Jesus calls upon us to hear the word of God and keep it. His word creates new hearts. His word is the sure foundation of ethical living.

The theme of God's creative word is touched upon in 7:18-23. John the Baptist has sent his disciples to ask Jesus if he was the One who was to come or whether they should wait for another. Are you the Christ? That's what John wanted to know. Jesus answered: "Go and tell John what you *have seen and heard*" (v. 22). Jesus' word has been heard and as a result of such hearing the blind can see, the lame can walk, lepers are cleansed, the dead are raised, and the poor have heard the good news. *God's word does something!*

The story of the Sower in Luke 8:4-15 also picks up the theme of hearing and doing God's word. (This text is not appointed for the Lukan year.) Jesus tells the story of a sower who sows prodigally. In his prodigality some seed falls on the path, some on the rocks, some among the thorns and some on good soil. "Let anyone who has ears listen!" (8: 8). That's Jesus' conclusion. Ears and listening. That's how humans receive God's word from the Sower named Jesus.

But, of course, not everyone hears and does! Verses 11-14 tell us that the seed the Sower sows is the *word of God* (8:11). But not everyone does what he hears! Often the devil, or a time of testing, or the cares, riches, and pleasures of life rip up that which has been sown. Luke is probably most concerned here with the disciples who wilted in time of testing and who were always tempted by the abundance of life's possessions.

Finally, in Luke 8:19-20, Jesus defines the family of God. "My mother and my brothers are those who *hear the word of God and do it.*"

Homiletical Directions

The topic of this week's sermon should probably have something to do with the lifestyle of the members of God's kingdom. We can begin with the text, especially verses 43-49. Draw out the parallels between the good person, the treasure of the heart, and the one who *does the word* thus building life on a firm foundation. The other parallel is between the evil person, the evil treasure of the heart, and the ones who do not do what they have heard, thus building life on a shaky foundation. The key reality here is that the power of the kingdom in our lives comes through God's word. We become God's kind of people through listening and receptivity. Only God through the power of God's word can transform our human hearts so that we become doers of the word.

We have listed a number of stories that can be told that demonstrate the power of God's word: 4:31-37; 6:6-11; 7:1-10. The first two of these stories do not occur in this lectionary year, so they may be the best stories to tell at this point. The centurion's story in 7:1-10 should probably not be totally neglected because of its wonderfully clear description of the power of the word and its definition of faith. On the nature of faith remember also Mary's classic response to God's word of promise: "... let it be with me according to your word" (Luke 1:38). The faith of the centurion and the faith of Mary are described in very similar ways. Each of them comes to faith as a result of a word that is spoken to them. God's word creates the very possibility of human faith.

Not everyone believes what has been heard. Not all are doers of the word. The Parable of the Sower who sows "the word of God" can be told to bring this reality to life (Luke 8:4-15). The Parable of the Sower is about receptivity. "Let anyone with ears listen." It is about God's incredible prodigality in sowing the word on every kind of soil. But not everyone hears and does! There are challenges to our hearing. There are challenges to becoming doers of the word. Perhaps a prayer to the Holy Spirit is in order inviting the Spirit to open our ears to the hearing of the word in order that it may take deep root in our hearts.

Proclamation at the end of these stories might go something like this. Jesus' word for us today through these stories is: "I call on you to hear my word. I have sown God's word on the soil of every person's heart. Listen. Receive. Believe. My word has the power to transform your heart. My word has the power to make you doers of the word and not hearers only. Remember, life in my kingdom always begins in your ears. You keep on listening to my word. I'll keep on transforming your heart that you might be doers of my word and not hearers only." Amen.

Chapter 14
Proper 4: Sunday between May 29 and June 4

Luke 7:1-10

Luke 7:1 marks a transition in the flow of material in this Gospel. We move from the sayings of Jesus to the deeds of Jesus.

> ... *Luke has pulled together the following stories into a "Christological drama" in which the authority of Jesus' messiahship will be revealed, while still hidden in the mystery of the necessity of his rejection and death. "Who Jesus is" will be made evident in a variety of displays, but "why he must die" becomes the motive power of the plot of the narrative ... Luke's "Christology" is ... a persistent demonstration that Jesus is truly the anointed one of God, the fulfillment of God's promises and the faithful revelation of God's will and rule. This "Christological drama" is, therefore ... a dynamic demonstration of God's will and greatness, driving finally to the mystery of the necessity of the death of the Messiah.*[1]

Tiede also points out that the material in Luke 7 has to do with Jesus as the *prophet* of God. We will take up this prophet theme in Chapter 15.

In this particular story we hear about a Gentile, a centurion in the Roman army, who comes to Jesus on behalf of his sick slave. We have discussed the faith of the centurion in Chapter 9. His faith is so much like the faith of Mary. "Only speak the word, and let my servant be healed," says the centurion (7:7). "Let it be with me according to your word," says Mary. (1:38). Faith is created by the power of God's authoritative word. Faith is response to the power of this word!

Another common Lukan theme touched upon in this story is the theme of the power and authority of God's word. We have heard of Jesus' powerful word in many of the earlier Lukan stories. This story puts it so very well as the centurion, who knows the power of his word, also grasps the power of Jesus' word.

Still another common Lukan theme is part of the life of this centurion's story. The centurion is a *Gentile*!

> *The barrier which excludes Gentiles is only gradually broken down in Luke-Acts. Jesus is willing to heal the centurion's servant and even willing to come to his house. But the centurion assumes that this is too much to ask and prevents him. In Acts 10 another Gentile centurion appears. Peter does associate with him and stays in his house, behavior which he must defend when he returns to Jerusalem.*[2]

The theme of the "light for the revelation to the Gentiles" (Luke 2:30-32, *32*) appears early and often in Luke's Gospel. It is one of the dominant themes of the Lukan material and deserves at least one Sunday of full attention. Simeon's song in Luke 2 makes reference to Isaiah 49:6: "It is too light a thing that you should be my servant to raise up the tribes of Jacob and restore the survivors of Israel; I will give you as a light to the nations, that my salvation may reach to the end of the earth." In his commentary David Tiede says that this Isaiah passage might very well be the thematic statement of Luke's entire narrative!

This theme is next touched upon in Luke 3:4-6 where Luke identifies John the Baptist with the quotation from Isaiah 40. This is not new. Both Matthew and Mark also quote Isaiah 40 with reference to John's ministry. Only Luke, however, continues the Isaiah quotation through Isaiah 40:5: "Then the glory of the Lord shall be revealed, and *all people* shall see it together, for the mouth of the Lord has spoken." (Emphasis mine.) Luke places the theme of mission to the Gentiles on the lips of John the Baptist. This is of vital importance for Luke.

The next reference to the Gentile theme is the genealogy of Jesus as given by Luke in 3:23-38. Matthew's genealogy (Matthew 1:1-17) traces Jesus' lineage to Abraham, the ancestor of the

Israelite people. Luke's genealogy goes back to Adam, the ancestor of all people!

Luke 7:1-10, the text appointed for this week, presents us with our first Gentile person! He is a good person, a model of faithful response to the powerful word of the Savior.

Luke 21:20-24 speaks of the times of fulfillment for the Gentiles.

Luke 24:44-51 contains Jesus' last words to his disciples in Luke's way of telling the story. This is a very important passage because in this passage Luke presents us with a summary of Jesus' mission. Jesus has fulfilled all that is written in the law and the prophets. The Messiah had to suffer in order that repentance and forgiveness *should be preached in his name to all nations.* The disciples are given this charge to mission and then asked to wait. They are to wait in Jerusalem for the promise of the Father. It will be through the power of the Holy Spirit that the message of Jesus Christ will be preached to all nations.

Luke opens the book of Acts where he has left off. Again we hear Jesus charging the disciples to wait in Jerusalem for the promise of the Father, to wait for the empowerment of the Holy Spirit: "... you will receive power when the Holy Spirit has come upon you; and you will be my witnesses in Jerusalem, in all Judea and Samaria, and *to the ends of the earth*" (Acts 1:8). Pentecost is coming, and Pentecost is about a mission to all peoples.

Acts 2:1-47 tells of the Pentecost that happened in Jerusalem. That's where Jesus said things would begin. Acts 8:4-24 tells of the "Samaritan Pentecost." The Holy Spirit is at work breaking down the barriers between people. The Holy Spirit is at work fashioning a new kind of "inclusive" community. Acts 10:1—11:18 tells of a "Gentile Pentecost." Here is another Roman centurion who plays a key role in the movement of the Spirit which gathers Gentiles into God's coming kingdom.

The book of Acts ends with a note of mission to the Gentiles (Acts 28:23-31). This closing story is dominated by the ongoing unbelief of the Jewish people. They hear but they do not understand. They see but they do not perceive. So Paul announces: "Let it be known to you then that this salvation of God has been sent to the Gentiles; they will listen" (Acts 28:28). Luke closes his two-volume work with the word that Paul did what he said: he preached the kingdom of God in Rome. He preached openly. He was not hindered.

The book of Acts ends, that is, with the reality of preaching to the Gentiles. Will they listen? Will we? Do we? At this point Luke's writing really ends in our human heart. We are the Gentiles. Do we listen? And, if we have listened, do we join in our own way to keep this preaching going to all the peoples of the earth? Like much of Holy Scripture, Luke-Acts has an open-ended conclusion. It concludes with an existential question for each human heart!

Homiletical Directions

The directions for preaching on this text are manifold. The reality of the centurion's faith could be highlighted along with other stories of faith in Luke. Chapter 9 can give guidance on this possibility.

Another possibility is to deal with the theme of the authority and power of God's word. Earlier chapters have also dealt with this theme.

Chapter 7 of Luke is a kind of Christological drama. It raises the question of the identity of Jesus. The centurion understands Jesus to be a man with a powerful word. The people of Nain see Jesus as a prophet: Luke 7:11-17, *16*. (This text is Proper 4 in the Lukan lectionary cycle.) Luke 7:18-35 (none of this material appears in the lectionary year) deals with Jesus' identity in relation to John the Baptist. John asks who Jesus is and Jesus, in turn, speaks of the relationship between the ministry of John and his own ministry.

In Luke 7:36-50 (Proper 6) the question arises again about whether or not Jesus might be a prophet. If so, he reveals himself to be a prophet who associates with sinners and who has the power on earth to forgive sins.

Certainly these stories in Luke 7 could be put together sermonically as a way of addressing the question of Jesus' identity. This sermon could end in a wonderful first person proclamation wherein Jesus announces to us, "My word is powerful; I give life to the dead; I associate with sinners; I announce the forgiveness of sins." Jesus' answer to John's question, "Are you the one who is to come...?" (7:20-22) could also be used in this series of closing proclamations.

Still another very important sermon possibility with this text is the Gentile theme that is raised by the appearance of the faithful centurion. This is a dominant theme in Luke and should really be touched upon on more than one occasion during the Lukan year. We have cited a number of passages that touch the mission to the Gentiles theme in Luke. Put together the stories that best suit the way you wish to narrate this theme.

The direction of the Gentile theme itself can move in a variety of directions. It can certainly be used to lift up the theme of mission. A missionary challenge can be issued to our congregations. A theme of such a sermon might be, "Have you left Jerusalem yet?" See Acts 1:8.

A second possibility with these Gentile stories is to touch the theme of the inclusive character of the gospel message. This theme is of vital importance to Luke! We hear the challenge to be an "inclusive church" quite often these days. It's probably too bad we have to borrow "politically correct language" to talk about the all-embracing intention of the gospel. It might be better if we challenged each other to be "pentecostal churches." The pentecostal stories in Acts (in Jerusalem, Samaria, and the ends of the earth) are wonderful stories which tell of incredible boundaries being broken down between peoples as the Spirit-empowered message of Jesus Christ enfolds peoples of all nations within its household.

---

1. David L. Tiede, *Luke: Augsburg Commentary on the New Testament* (Minneapolis: Augsburg, 1988), pp. 147-148.

2. Robert C. Tannehill, *The Narrative Unity of Luke-Acts, Volume One* (Philadelphia: Fortress, 1986), p. 115.

Chapter 15
Proper 5: Sunday between June 5 and 11

Luke 7:11-17

In Chapter 14 we referred to David Tiede's understanding that Luke 7 is a kind of "Christological drama." The question of the identity of Jesus comes into full view here. In Luke 7 it is clearly Jesus' identity as a *prophet* that is most seriously explored.

Robert Tannehill comments on the theme of Jesus as Prophet as follows:

> *Jesus is "a prophet mighty in work and word" (24:19) and yet is rejected and suffers a violent fate. The rejection, as well as the mighty work and word, belongs to a pattern of prophetic experience which is important for understanding the Lukan view of Jesus. This prophetic pattern enables the narrator to hold together as a meaningful unity Jesus' message, acts of power, and violent death. We distort the Lukan view of Jesus' mighty acts when we isolate them from the prophetic context which unifies these three facets of Jesus' story.*[1]

What kind of prophet is Jesus? According to the story in this week's appointed text he is a prophet "like Elijah." (The Elijah stories are told in 1 Kings 17-19; 2 Kings 1-2.) 1 Kings 17:8-24 tells the story of Elijah's healing of a widow's only son. The story of Jesus healing a widow's only son and Elijah's healing have much in common. It is not surprising that the crowd in Nain concluded from Jesus' healing activity that "A great prophet has risen among us!" (7:16).

Some commentators suggest that Jesus' healing of the centurion's slave in 7:1-10 has affinities with the story of Elisha's healing of Naaman, a commander in the Syrian army. See 2 Kings 5. (The Elisha stories are found in 2 Kings 2-9, 13.)

Jesus is a prophet like Elijah and Elisha. This combination in relation to Jesus appears first in the scene in the synagogue at Nazareth. Jesus had read to the people from the prophet Isaiah. "This Scripture is fulfilled in your hearing," he had told them. Jesus thus announced that he would do *wonder-working deeds.* He would preach good news to the poor, bring release to captives, sight to the blind and liberty to the oppressed! When the hometown folk rejected such notions Jesus quoted to them an old saying: "Truly I tell you, no prophet is accepted in the prophet's hometown" (Luke 4:24). Jesus then proceeded to tell stories of Elijah and Elisha in order make his point (4:25-27).

Of a prophet like Elijah and Elisha one expects wonder-working deeds! On the road to Emmaus on Easter's first evening the confused disciples try to explain to the yet unrecognized Jesus that Jesus of Nazareth was a prophet mighty in word and deed (24:19-21; see also Acts 2:22). Other discussions of Jesus as a prophet occur in Luke 7:24-30; 9:7-9, 18-23; 9:51-56.

Another prophetic theme in Luke-Acts portrays Jesus as a "prophet like Moses." In Acts 3 Peter preaches a rather lengthy sermon in the portico called Solomon's in order to explain the fact that he had just performed a wonder work himself. Peter had called a lame man to walk. In his sermon Peter lays out God's plan of salvation. He accuses the people of killing the Author of Life (Acts 3:15. This is a uniquely Lukan title for Jesus that needs to be revived as a useful metaphor for speaking of the salvation that Jesus brings to humankind!). This, says Peter, is part of the plan of God as foretold by the prophets. "Repent therefore," Peter continues, "and turn to God so that your sins may be wiped out, so that times of refreshing may come from the presence of the Lord, and that he may send the Messiah appointed for you, that is, Jesus, who must remain in heaven until the time of universal restoration that God announced long ago through his holy prophets. Moses said, 'The Lord your God will raise up for you from your own people a prophet like me. You must listen to whatever he tells you' " (Acts 3:19-22).

In Luke's telling of the story Jesus is portrayed as a "prophet like Moses." This means that Jesus is a *suffering prophet* who completes for us the plan of God. The reference to the "prophet like Moses" is from Deuteronomy 18:15-18, *18*. What we learn from the book of Deuteronomy is that Moses was a *suffering prophet.* Please read Deuteronomy 1:37; 3:23-28; 4:21-27; 5:22-27; 9:25-29. What we hear in these passages is that Moses was not allowed to enter the promised land "because the Lord was angry with me on your account." Moses, that is, must *suffer for the sins of the people.* Over and over again the theme is repeated that the anger of God for the people's sins is directed against Moses. Moses' life is always on the line. He must put his life between the people and the God they dare not face lest they die. Moses, that is, risks death to intercede for this people. Hear these words from the psalmist: "Therefore God said God would destroy them (the chosen people) — had not Moses *stood in the breach* before him, to turn away his wrath from destroying them" (Psalm 106:23).

These pictures of the "prophet" Moses are very clear models of Jesus' ministry. Jesus is, indeed, a "prophet like Moses." He must put his life in the breach. He must intercede for us with God. He must bear the wrath of God for our sins. Jesus is a prophet who suffers for the sins of the people. Jesus thus fulfills the plan of God! That's how Luke tells the story. That's what we heard from the passage in Acts.

It is no surprise, therefore, that when we come to Luke 9 — a passage of revelation of Jesus — we hear that "The Son of Man must undergo great suffering, and be rejected by the elders, chief priests, and scribes, and be killed, and on the third day be raised" (9:22). This is what one might expect of a "prophet like Moses."

In the Transfiguration story in 9:28-36 Jesus is seen in the company of the prophets: Moses and Elijah. They talked together with Jesus about his departure for Jerusalem. The Greek word for departure is literally "exodus." Jesus is a "prophet like Moses." He, too, will make an exodus. He, too, will die at the end of the journey. (Jesus' exodus begins in Luke 9:51.)

In Luke 11:45-52 there is another reference to the killing of the prophets. Luke's view is that God's prophets die! This theme is picked up again in 13:31-35, a text appointed for the Second

Sunday in Lent. Jesus *must* (divine necessity) go to Jerusalem, a city that kills prophets.

Homiletical Directions

Our sermon could move in many narrative directions based on the material we have discussed. There is no way we can work with all the references to prophetic themes we have discussed. It might be best to confine our vision to the two major themes we have surfaced: 1) Jesus is a wonder-working, life-giving prophet like Elijah and Elisha; 2) Jesus is a suffering "prophet like Moses."

For the wonder-working theme we can begin by telling the story of this week's text with a focus on the response of the people that "A great prophet has risen among us." We can then tell the story from 1 Kings 17:8-24 where Elijah performed a very similar miracle. If there is time, the story from last week could be referred to along with a brief telling of the story of Elisha healing the Syrian commander (2 Kings 5). These stories establish the theme that prophets like Elijah, Elisha, and Jesus are wonder-workers. Reference can be made to the Emmaus road story (particularly 24:19) and Peter's sermon in Acts 2 (note verse 22) to give additional credence to this "wonder-working" theme. Other references were cited above on this theme which you may or may not choose to incorporate in this week's stories.

Once our stories have established that Jesus is a wonder-working prophet like Elijah and Elisha it might be good to pay a return visit to Luke 4:16-21. This thematically central passage in Luke's Gospel tells of Jesus in his hometown synagogue reading from the book of the prophet Isaiah. The Isaiah passage certainly suggests that the Spirit Bearer ("The Spirit of the Lord is upon me") will do great deeds of life for God's people. In connection with this passage we might also make reference to Acts 3:15 which refers to Jesus as the Author of Life. This is a very good title for Jesus, the prophet like Elijah and Elisha.

Jesus, Author of Life, would make an excellent focus for this sermon. Our proclamation might go something like this: "I am the Author of Life. I am a prophet like Elijah and Elisha. I have come to bring life to the dead. I have come to bring life to your mortal bodies. Believe in my life-giving word. Believe that I will speak the same word over your dead body that I spoke to the widow's son. 'I say to you, arise!' You can believe it, you know. I am the Author of Life."

A second possibility with this text is to shape stories around the theme that Jesus is a "prophet like Moses." Here, too, we need to tell the text's story with a focus on the response of the crowd that "a great prophet has risen among us." We can note that this is a common Lukan theme. Move next to Peter's sermon in Acts 3 which speaks of Jesus as a "prophet like Moses."

Tell Moses' stories! Tell what you can of the Moses stories from the book of Deuteronomy. Moses is the *suffering prophet.* He suffers for the people's sins. He must die so that they may proceed to the land of promise. He must stand in the breach between sinful people and righteous God.

Luke identifies Jesus with Moses in Acts 3. Throughout his Gospel he speaks of the fact that prophets get killed and that Jerusalem is the city which kills the prophets. From the Transfiguration story where Moses appears with Jesus we learn that Jesus, too, must go on an *exodus.* Jesus will make an exodus to Jerusalem. Jesus will suffer. Jesus will die. Jesus will bear our sins. Jesus will suffer in our place. In this way the plan of God is carried out among us. "Repent therefore, and turn to God so that your sins may be wiped out, so that times of refreshing may come from the presence of the Lord ..." (Acts 3:19-20).

"I am a prophet like Moses," Jesus says to us today! You can develop a closing proclamation beginning with these powerful words.

---

1. Robert C. Tannehill, *The Narrative Unity of Luke-Acts, Volume One* (Philadelphia: Fortress Press, 1986), p. 96.

Chapter 16
Proper 6: Sunday between June 12 and 18

Luke 7:36—8:3

The lectionary at this point omits the material in Luke 7:18-35. Luke 7:18-22 is the very important material in which Jesus answers the question about his identity for John the Baptist. We have spoken a number of times about the fact that these verses along with Mary's Magnificat (1:46-55) and Jesus' quotation of the prophet Isaiah (4:18-19) set forth the central pulsating themes of Luke's Gospel.

In 7:23-30 Jesus gives a lesson about the ministry of John the Baptist. In this chapter which identifies Jesus as a prophet, John the Baptist is acclaimed as "greater than a prophet" (7:26-28). Still, the least in the kingdom of God is greater than John!

In 7:31-35 Jesus speaks of the rejection of John the Baptist and himself. Jesus is condemned by many because he is a friend of tax collectors and sinners (v. 34). This leads us naturally to the text appointed for this week which puts Jesus in the company of a woman who is very clearly defined as a sinner. This story of the sinful woman rings with a host of connections to other Lukan material. In the first place, this story resonates with the contention in the flow of Luke 7 that Jesus is a prophet. As far as the hosting Pharisee is concerned Jesus is no prophet (v. 39)! How can Jesus be a prophet when he cannot even recognize a sinner when he sees one? Luke clearly sees Jesus as a prophet (see Chapter 15) who breaks the mold. Jesus is a new kind of prophet who gathers sinners in his embrace.

Secondly, in Chapter 1 we identified this story as one of many Lukan stories that play out one of the themes of Mary's Magnificat. Mary sang that her God "has brought down the powerful from their thrones, and lifted up the lowly" (Luke 1:52). Other stories that relate to this theme of *reversal* are identified in Chapter 1. If you have not as yet stitched these stories together you can certainly do so this week.

A third way that this story is connected to other parts of the Lukan story is identified by Robert Tannehill. He sees this story as one of the many *quest stories* that occur in the Lukan narrative.[1] In a "quest story" someone approaches Jesus in quest of something very important to human well-being. In a quest story we always have an ending to the quest. Tannehill cites Luke 5:17-26; 7:2-10 and 7:36-50 as early quest stories. Quest stories also appear in the final chapters of the Travel Narrative: Luke 17:12-19; 18:18-23 and 19:1-10. Tannehill is convinced, furthermore, that the thief on the cross belongs to these quest stories: 23:39-43. "The criminal is the last person who turns to Jesus for help during Jesus' ministry, he is also the one person who understands and accepts the path which Jesus must follow to fulfill God's purpose: through death to enthronement at God's right hand."[2] Quest stories show us that Jesus is One who intercedes for those who are oppressed or excluded. As such these quest stories are also part of the reversal theme of Mary's Magnificat. (For further discussion of quest stories see Chapter 37.)

Still another way, a fourth way, that this material connects to the larger Lukan material is with its reference to a *meal* in the house of the Pharisee. Luke is fond of picturing Jesus in mealtime situations. See also 10:38-42; 11:37-54; 13:22-30; 14:1-24; 15:1-32. *Eucharistic* type meals are reported in 9:12-22; 22:7-23; 24:28-35. This mealtime emphasis reminds us of another of the strong themes of Mary's Magnificat: "God has filled the hungry with good things ..." (1:53). Scholars have noted that mealtimes are often times of revelation in Jesus' ministry. This is particularly true of the eucharistic meals. Neither the meal in Luke 9:12-27 nor that in 22:7-23 (Lord's Supper) are included in the Lukan lectionary year. The meal at Emmaus (24:28-35) is dealt with only partially in the text appointed for Easter Evening. There is a great loss of key Lukan material here! Hopefully you can find occasion during this year to yoke the eucharistic type meals into one sermon. Emphasis would be placed on the revelation of Jesus that occurs through the meals. The church is a eucharistic people. We gather at table on a regular basis. In, with, and under our gathering the Lord is present to reveal himself to us. In such a meal setting Jesus is as close to us as he was to the disciples. The disciples on the road to Emmaus, after all, did not recognize Jesus until the "breaking of the bread." As today's disciples we share in this bread-breaking. Disciples of every age are fed by our Lord and in the feeding we come to ever greater recognition of who Jesus is for our life and ministry.

A fifth narrative connection for this wonderful story is to connect it with the narrative in 5:17-26. This Luke 5 story, which is not appointed for the Lukan year, is also a story of *forgiveness of sins*. Many commentators have observed that Luke often tells stories in doublets, with one story on a topic about a man and one about a woman. Luke 5:17-26 is the story of forgiveness and healing of a paralyzed man. Luke 7:36-50 is the story of forgiveness of a woman who is a sinner. (Luke 8:1-3 underscores the theme of the presence of women in the company of the One who preaches the good news of the kingdom of God.) A key phrase in both stories is Jesus' proclamation: "Your sins are forgiven." (See 5:20 and 7:48.) We remember as well that "release of sins" was one of the images of ministry Jesus claimed for himself in his reading from the prophet Isaiah in 4:18-19.

In this week's text the woman is clearly defined as a sinner. This accentuates her *vulnerability*. She is vulnerable as a sinner. She is vulnerable by entering the house of a Pharisee. She is vulnerable because she does not behave properly in a male world. Simon for one was much offended by her anointing of Jesus.

A vulnerable woman comes to Jesus in her time of need and lavishes him with ointment. Her need is fulfilled. Jesus speaks a word of forgiveness over her life. Jesus clearly understands that this woman has *believed his word of forgiveness*. Thus he can say to her: "Your faith has saved you; go in peace" (7:50). There are three other Lukan stories which end in a pronouncement concerning saving faith. These stories are the story of the woman with a twelve-year flow of blood in 8:40-48, the story of the cleansing of the Samaritan leper in 17:11-19, and the story of a blind beggar on the road to Jericho in 18:35-43. In each case vulnerable people, people in deepest need, come to Jesus for help. Jesus speaks a word of power over the lives of these people. In the case of the woman with a twelve-year flow of blood, power went out from Jesus for her healing. Four vulnerable people are recipients of Jesus' word or deed of power. They believe in his power and they are healed. Their faith saved them. Faith is clearly portrayed here as trust in Jesus in the midst of extreme vulnerability. There is, therefore, a wonderful sermon on the substance of faith in these four stories.

A final comment on the forgiveness of the sinful woman. The loving power of Jesus' word and the loving deeds of the sinful woman stand in very tight relationship in verses 47-50. These verses dare not be read in such a way that the woman's loving deeds became the ground of her forgiveness. No! It's always the other way around. Jesus' word of forgiveness becomes the ground of this woman's loving deeds. Loved people love people. Forgiven people forgive people. That's what Jesus' story to Simon is all about. There is a kind of organic relationship between Jesus' love for us and our love for Jesus. We love because we are loved. We return to Jesus' love as often as possible in order that our love might be renewed.

Homiletical Directions

Each of the five narrative connections we have examined is open to story-stitching possibilities. Which of the five you choose to develop will depend upon the particular needs of your own congregation at this juncture of their life.

The first theme we touched upon suggested that this story fits into the larger context of the "Christological Drama" of Luke 7 which underlines Jesus' identity as a prophet. "Who is this man?" (7:49).

The second story-stitching possibility is to take up the theme of the stories that have their genesis in the reversal theme of Mary's Magnificat. At some point in the church year this group of stories ought to be told together. God can reverse our fortunes as well!

The "quest stories" offer a marvelous opportunity to tell stories of the One whose ministry includes the oppressed and the excluded. It would be important to include the thief on the cross in this battery of stories.

If it is time in your congregation to talk a bit about the nature of the eucharist in Christian life, the meal stories can be stitched together. The meal story before us is certainly a time of teaching and revelation. That is also true of the more "eucharistic-type" meal in 9:12-27. The eucharistic overtones in this story occur in 9:16 with language reminiscent of the Last Supper. In the context of this meal Jesus asks his disciples about his identity and reveals to them that he is to be a suffering Messiah. The revelatory character of the Last Supper (22:7-23) and the supper at Emmaus (24:28-35) is clearly evident.

Themes of forgiveness and faith also dominate this week's text. In Luke's telling of the Jesus story, it is only in this story and in 5:17-26 that Jesus announces the forgiveness of sins. Forgiveness of sins is such a central reality of the Christian message that this theme has much to commend it. The goal of telling these two stories would be to enable our people to hear Jesus' word addressed to them: "Your sins are forgiven!"

---

1. Robert C. Tannehill, *The Narrative Unity of Luke-Acts, Volume One* (Philadelphia: Fortress Press, 1986), pp. 111-127.

2. *Ibid.,* pp. 126-127.

Luke 8:26-39

This week's text concerning the exorcism which set a captive Gerasene demoniac free is the only text appointed from Luke 8 in this year's lectionary readings. David Tiede points out that the material in Luke 8:3—9:50 sets forth the substance of Jesus' ministry in Galilee as Luke tells the story. There is a theme to the stories in Luke 8, and it is the theme of the *power of God's word.* We touched upon some of this material in Chapter 13 when we discussed the general theme of *hearing and doing* God's word.

Luke 8 begins with the Parable of the Sower. This parable is common to the Synoptic Gospels but it is only appointed as a Sunday text in the year of Matthew. We noted in Chapter 13 that this parable can certainly be read as a parable concerning the word of God. In fact, Luke is the only Gospel writer who explicitly states that the "seed is the word of God" (8:11). Jesus invites people to a careful hearing of the word of God (8:8). His explanation of the parable is about different kinds of hearing!

Beyond the Parable of the Sower the theme of God's word and human hearing is picked up throughout Luke 8. In 8:18 people are invited to take heed how they hear. Disciples are defined as those who hear the word of God and do it (8:21). Jesus' word is a powerful word. It has the power to calm the storm (8:24). It has the power to set the captive demoniac free. The demoniac himself is pictured as a person who has heard the word of God and does it (8:39). Jesus' word also has the power to raise the dead (8:49-56).

Robert Tannehill believes that Luke sees the Parable of the Sower as a call to discipleship. Disciples are those who hear the word of God and do it. He particularly believes that the second and third kind of hearers, the rocky ground and the thorny ground hearers, speak to the matter of discipleship.

The second and third cases could apply to the disciples, who have heard Jesus' word and accepted it but now are being warned that this beginning does not guarantee the harvest. So two types of danger are being emphasized in order to prepare the disciples for them. There is the danger that faith will be temporary and will disappear "in a time of temptation." There is a danger that faith will be choked out "by cares and riches and pleasures of life." ... Possessions and persecution will be major continuing concerns in Jesus' later instruction of the disciples.[1]

This week's pericope text from Luke 8 is the story of the exorcism of the Gerasene demoniac. This story appears in each of the Synoptic Gospels but is appointed in the lectionary only in the Matthew version. It is a rich story and well worth telling in all of its intricacies. Luke tells other stories of the casting out of demons. In 4:33-37 Jesus cast an unclean demon out of a man in the synagogue. This story glories in the authority of Jesus' word. "What kind of utterance is this? For with authority and power he commands the unclean spirits, and out they come!" (Luke 4:37).

In 9:37-43 Jesus cast an unclean spirit out of a young lad who was violently possessed. In this story, too, the crowds are astounded at the greatness of God! This story is optionally appointed for The Transfiguration of Our Lord Sunday.

Luke 11:14-26 is a rather lengthy story and discussion of demonic possession. Jesus' word is heard in this story and it is not believed. Those gathered accused Jesus of casting out demons by the power of demons. Jesus insisted that he cast out demons by the authority of God. "But if it is by the finger of God that I cast out the demons, then the kingdom of God has come to you" (Luke 11:20). Casting out demons is a sign of the coming of the kingdom of God. We are reminded of Jesus' quotation from Isaiah in his hometown of Nazareth: "God has sent me to proclaim release to the captives ..." (Luke 4:19).

Homiletical Directions

There are a number of ways in which the stories we have discussed could be stitched together for this week's sermon. A sermon on the authority of God's word is certainly one possibility. We could also pick up the theme of hearing and doing God's Word.

Our main recommendation for preaching, however, is that we stitch together the Lukan stories in which Jesus casts out demons. The theme of Luke's Gospel which is present in the exorcism stories is the theme of *release to the captives.* Luke clearly understands Jesus' power over demons to be a sign of the coming of God's kingdom to earth.

We have cited three additional stories of demonic exorcism from Luke in addition to the text appointed for this week. They are Luke 4:33-37; 9:37-43; 11:14-26. It is very important to note that only 9:37-43 is appointed in the Lukan lectionary year and that is an optional appointment. This week is the only week we have the possibility of dealing with a theme that is vital to Luke's understanding of Jesus' power and the nature of the coming of the kingdom of God.

The structure for this sermon is quite simple. Tell the story appointed for this week. Add two or three of the other exorcism stories as time allows. Tell the stories around the theme of release to the captives or the theme of exorcism stories as a sign of the coming of God's kingdom.

In our world today evil is a horrible reality. We usually don't talk about demonic possession or unclean spirits. But we know from experience the power of evil. We in the twentieth century have witnessed the raw power of evil. We have seen genocide rampant in China, Russia, Hitler's Germany, Central Africa, and in the former region of Yugoslavia. Evil exists. Evil reigns! Peoples are oppressed. Individuals are captive to the power of evil. What hope is there for humankind?

There are other more personal signs of possession among us. Incredible numbers of people among us are possessed by drugs, alcohol, gambling, sex, and so forth. Who shall set the captives free?

Today's stories from Luke hymn our hope! God in Jesus Christ speaks the word that is the beginning of freedom for captives. Jesus' word to us through stories such as these is: "I have come to set you free from captivity to evil. Come out, evil power, come out! Rush down the river banks and be drowned. In the name of God you are released. If I by the finger of God cast out demons then know that the kingdom of God has come upon you. Such is the power of my word. Hear my word. Believe my word. Do my word." Amen.

Luther's great hymn "A Mighty Fortress Is Our God" would be an appropriate sermon hymn. Note particularly verse 4:

> *Though hordes of devils fill the land*
> *All threatening to devour us,*
> *We tremble not, unmoved we stand;*
> *They cannot overpower us.*
> *This world's prince may rage,*
> *In fierce war engage.*
> *He is doomed to fail;*
> *God's judgment must prevail!*
> One little word *subdues him.*

How we celebrate that little word!

---

1. Robert C. Tannehill, *The Narrative Unity of Luke-Acts, Volume One* (Philadelphia: Fortress, 1986), pp. 210-211.

Chapter 18
Transfiguration (Last Sunday After The Epiphany)

Luke 9:28-36 (37-43)

The assigned Gospel text for this week is one of only two texts (see Proper 8; Luke 9:51-62) in the Lukan year taken from Luke 9. This is unfortunate because Luke 9 contains some very important material in the overall structure of Luke's story. This chapter contains important material, for instance, in Jesus' equipping of his disciples for their mission. The chapter begins with the commissioning of the twelve (9:1-6). Jesus asks the twelve about his identity (9:18-22). "Peter's confession of Jesus as *'the Christ of God'* is as central to Luke's account as Peter's differing words are to Matthew ... The term *the Christ of God* is ... as crucial to Luke's testimony as can be imagined."[1] Jesus is the One anointed to bring in God's reign.

In the light of the revelation of his identity as the Messiah of God Jesus reveals to the disciples that he "... must undergo great suffering, and be rejected by the elders, chief priests, and scribes, and be killed, and on the third day be raised" (9:22). This is a surprise to the disciples. This is new information for them. This verse stands as a kind of central word of prophecy of Jesus regarding the suffering he *must* undergo. The remainder of Luke's Gospel is a movement towards Jerusalem where the Messiah will suffer.

The necessity of Messianic suffering occurs again and again in Luke: 9:44; 12:50; 13:33; 17:25; 18:31-34; 24:7, 25-26, 44-46. The disciples have great difficulty grasping the divine necessity of Jesus' road to suffering. Still Peter's identification of Jesus as the Messiah is an evidence of growth on the part of the disciples. Jesus will be busy teaching them throughout Luke's story. Chapter 9 both reveals Jesus' identity to the disciples and demonstrates how much they have to learn. This is evident in the Transfiguration text (v. 33) and in the story that follows wherein the disciples cannot drive an unclean spirit out of a child (9:37-43). When Jesus reveals to them a second time that he must suffer, the disciples do not understand, "... its meaning was concealed from them so that they could not perceive it. And they were afraid to ask him about this saying" (9:45). In the next story, after having heard that Jesus must suffer and that those who follow him will have to take up the cross (9:23-27), the disciples want to know who among them is the greatest! (9:46-48). The picture of the disciples in Luke 9 prepares us for the Travel Narrative (9:51—19:27) in which Jesus gives much instruction to the disciples — disciples of every age.

In Chapter 16 we talked a bit about the function of meals in Luke's story. Mealtime is often revelation time when Jesus is at table. So it is in 9:12-22. Jesus has come, after all, to fill the "hungry with good things" (1:53), to bless "those who are hungry now" (6:21).

We come then to the story of Transfiguration. This passage is also bound up with the identity of Jesus. Herod has raised the question of Jesus' identity in Luke 9:9. Jesus asks the disciples about his identity in 9:18, 20. Peter has given an answer to the question of Jesus' identity. Now it is God's turn to answer! God's answer is, "This is my Son, my Chosen; listen to him!" (9:35). This word from God may be intended to serve as a corrective to the partial understanding of Jesus' identity in Peter's confession.

We have heard this word from God identifying Jesus as God's Son in the story of Jesus' baptism (3:21-22). At that point in time God's word came to Jesus as Jesus was being prepared for his ministry. In Luke 9 God's word comes to Jesus as he prepares to make his *exodus* to Jerusalem. The Greek word for departure (9:31) is literally the word *exodus*. This prophet like Moses is being prepared like Moses to make an exodus. Jesus' exodus is to the city that kills prophets! The Travel Narrative is the story of that exodus. Jesus "set his face to go to Jerusalem" (9:51).

One aspect of Luke's story of the Transfiguration that does not occur in Matthew or Mark is the statement that the disciples saw *Jesus' glory* (9:32). Jesus speaks of his glory only once in Luke's Gospel, and that is in the story of the road to Emmaus. Jesus seeks to explain the meaning of what has taken place to the two disciples on that road. He says to them, "Was it not necessary that the Messiah should suffer these things and then enter his *glory*?" (Luke 24:26). Glory would appear to be connected with Jesus' resurrection. The disciples have seen a preview of resurrection glory on the mountain of Transfiguration.

In the Transfiguration story, the climax of the first part of Luke's Gospel, there are a host of biblical references. Most good commentaries will highlight these references. The many biblical references that can be made from these verses underscore for us the crucial importance of this story. These references also suggest possibilities for narrative preaching. We can tell some of these biblical stories as the background out of which the meaning of the story of the Transfiguration will emerge.

Homiletical Directions

A first narrative possibility with the Transfiguration text is to set it in the narrative context of Luke 9. Story One of our sermon would set up Herod's question, "... who is this about whom I hear such things?" (9:9). This question sets off a series of passages which deal with Jesus' identity.

Story Two would focus on the story of the feeding of the 5,000. We have discussed the fact that meals are a time of revelation in Luke. Immediately following the story of the feeding Jesus raises the question about his own identity. "Who do the crowds say that I am?" (9:18). A variety of answers is given to this question. Some say John the Baptist, some say Elijah, and others say you are one of the old prophets risen from the grave. (We looked at the theme of Jesus as a prophet in our discussion of Luke 7.) It would be a simple matter in the telling of this part of the story to add the answers that people of today give to this question! Finally, Peter speaks. "You are the Messiah of God" (9:20). Jesus' response to Peter indicates that something is not quite right about this answer. Jesus orders them to tell no one. He proceeds to tell them about the necessity of his own suffering which surely jarred their glorious messianic expectations. Peter says Messiah and the disciples think *glory*. Jesus orders them to be silent and points them to his *cross*.

Story Three would be the story of Transfiguration itself. Here is God's revelation of Jesus' identity. "This is my Son, my Chosen; listen to him" (9:35). Tell this story with its manifold biblical references! Here is the conclusion to the question of identity in Luke 9. God gives the final answer! The fact that Jesus is God's Son, of course, is no surprise to our congregations. The accent may need to fall rather on the word, "Listen to him." This word is a challenge to disciples of every age. (There is further discussion of the "Son of God" theme in Chapter 3.)

A second narrative possibility for this sermon would be to connect the story of Jesus' baptism (Luke 3:21-22) with this story of the Transfiguration. These are the texts for the first and last Sundays in Epiphany! In these alpha and omega texts we hear the voice of God announcing the identity of God's Son. Epiphany is about manifestation, revelation. It is a season surrounded by stories of the reality that Jesus is God's Son. Such is God's Word to us in this Epiphany season. And God's word speaks with authority. What God speaks comes to pass. Jesus is the Son of God.

Our sermon, therefore, would tell both the baptismal and the Transfiguration stories. The focus will be on God's epiphany word: "This is my Son." Epiphany begins with this revelation in the context of baptism. We have been baptized as well. We have been baptized in Jesus' baptism. There Epiphany happened to us. God in Jesus Christ announces in baptism: "You are my son. You are my daughter. You are my child." What God speaks comes to pass. We are the children of God.

Epiphany ends with the admonition: "Listen to him." God speaks through Jesus to Jesus' disciples. We, too, are disciples of Jesus. The original disciples didn't grasp all the aspects of this revelation of God. We are slow to grasp it as well. So we are called to join Jesus in an *exodus* to Jerusalem. In the Travel Narrative that is coming Jesus will continue to speak to the twelve and to us as he instructs us in the life of discipleship.

Two realities are posited on the basis of the baptismal and Transfiguration stories. Reality number one is that God calls us sons and daughters. Make this a clear gospel word of proclamation.

Say it in such a way that it is today's Epiphany word to people: "You are my sons. You are my daughters. You are my disciples."

Reality number two is the fact that disciples have a lot yet to learn. "Listen to him." Join him on the exodus to Jerusalem. Take up your cross and follow! Every day can be an epiphany with the Son of God as leader of our exodus through life. There will be suffering along the way, to be sure, but at the last we shall see Christ's glory which shall become our glory as well.

---

1. David L. Tiede, *Luke, Augsburg Commentary on the New Testament* (Minneapolis: Augsburg, 1988), p. 184.

Chapter 19
Proper 8: Sunday between June 26 and July 2

Luke 9:51-62

Scholars have recognized for a long time that the material in Luke 9:51—19:27 is unique in the Synoptic Gospels. It is a peculiarly Lukan section containing such well-known stories as the Prodigal Son, the Good Samaritan, and the parable of the Rich Man and Lazarus, to cite just a few.

The material takes the form of a *journey*! Jesus sets his face to make an *exodus* (Luke 9:31) to Jerusalem. In the last story in this segment of Luke's Gospel Jesus is "near" Jerusalem (19:11). The journey ends in 19:28 where we hear that Jesus was "going up to Jerusalem." Because of the journey character of this material this section of Luke has been given a variety of "journey" titles. We will simply refer to this corpus as the Travel Narrative.

Joseph Fitzmyer describes this material thus: "The travel account [is] ... a collection of teachings for the young missionary church, in which instruction of disciples alternates with debates with opponents."[1] Scholars note that oral story tellers often organized disparate material by incorporating it into a journey. The story of the journey, that is, gives cohesion to a variety of material.

We noted in Chapter 18 that the disciples appear to have a lot to learn, from the shape of the narrative in Luke 9. On his exodus to Jerusalem Jesus will teach them many things about the nature of true discipleship.

The opening verse of the Travel Narrative indicates that the time had come for Jesus "to be taken up." We have been prepared for this event by Jesus' key prophetic word in 9:22: "The Son of Man must undergo great suffering, and be rejected by the elders, chief priests, and scribes, and be killed, and on the third day be raised." Jerusalem is to be the place of Jesus' suffering. The city of Jerusalem plays a key role in Luke's story of the Christ. (Chapter

3 discusses the central role played by the *temple in Jerusalem.*)
Luke's story opens in the temple in Jerusalem (Luke 1). In Luke
2:22ff. the parents of Jesus bring him to the temple in Jerusalem in
order to present him to the Lord. The entire central section of
Luke, the Travel Narrative, is the story of the exodus to Jerusalem.
The journey is ominous because of Jesus' word in 9:22 and because
Jerusalem is the city that kills the prophets (13:33-34). And so it
came to pass that the "prophet" Jesus would die in Jerusalem.
Jerusalem then becomes the city in which the disciples must *wait*
to begin the mission that Jesus commanded them to undertake
(24:44-49). In the book of Acts the disciples are waiting in
Jerusalem for the promise of the Spirit (Acts 1:1-5). Jesus tells the
disciples that the Spirit of God will be poured out upon them and
they will be his disciples in *Jerusalem* and in all Judea and Samaria
and to the end of the earth (Acts 1:8). Jerusalem becomes the base
camp for mission to the ends of the earth. The Pentecost story
takes place in Jerusalem as the empowering of the disciples and
the founding of the Christian community (Acts 2).

The reality of Jerusalem for Luke continues in the book of Acts.
We can see a kind of parallelism that is developed between Jesus
and Saint Paul. Jesus' journey of ministry began in Galilee, moved
through Samaria, and ended in Jerusalem. The last half of the book
of Acts tells of Paul's journeys to fulfill the mission of the church
as it moves out from Jerusalem to Samaria and on to Rome, on to
the ends of the earth.

Jesus sent his disciples ahead of him to prepare his way to enter
Samaria (9:51). In the early days of his mission it was John the
Baptist who prepared the way. The preparation did not work. The
Samaritans would not receive him. This is reminiscent of Jesus'
first appearance in his hometown of Nazareth. The hometown folk
did not receive him either (Luke 4:22-29). Now he is off to
Jerusalem. Neither will Jerusalem receive him. Jesus is a despised
and rejected man.

In the face of Samaritan rejection the disciples ask if they should
call fire down from heaven to consume those of obstinate hearts.
That's what Elijah had done (2 Kings 1:9-16). Jesus says, No!
There are many ways in which Luke's telling of the story portrays

Jesus as a prophet. But Jesus is not a duplicate of the prophets of old. With Jesus something new has entered human life. As for Samaria, its inhabitants will be visited again by Philip and the apostles from Jerusalem (Acts 8:9-25). A very important aspect of Luke's telling of the Messiah is the reality that Samaritans in particular and Gentiles in general shall be included in the renewed kingdom of God. This story is told with particular power in Acts 8 and Acts 10-11, the story of Cornelius.

In verses 57-62 the emphasis turns from journeying to following. Jesus makes a journey. People are called to follow. Jesus has set the stage for this call to follow in 9:23-27. Jesus has invited people to follow him by self-denial; by taking up the cross; by losing life to find life. Tannehill summarizes that which a disciple must give up to follow Jesus as life (9:23-25), home and family (9:57-62), and possessions.[2] Luke 14:25-33 includes precisely these three realities in its call to discipleship. With respect to possessions we remember that the rich are sent away empty (Luke 1:53). A number of the stories in the Travel Narrative touch upon the matter of possessions. The story of the wealthy ruler who wanted to gain eternal life (18:18-30) and its complementary story of Zacchaeus (19:1-10) are of particular importance here. Following Jesus is, indeed, a matter of losing our life in order to find God's life.

Homiletical Directions

The material above suggests a number of directions for a narrative sermon on this text. In some way it is important for our hearers to understand that with this material we enter into a lengthy section of Luke's Gospel which is described as a journey to Jerusalem. We will be preaching on these texts for many months now! Today can lay the foundation. It is in this week's text that Jesus' exodus journey to Jerusalem begins!

The first narrative possibility that suggests itself, therefore, is stories that lift up the importance of Jerusalem in Luke's telling of the Messianic story. We have already touched upon these texts. The Gospel of Luke begins in Jerusalem. Jesus is brought to Jerusalem to be presented to God according to the law. Our stories hold forth first of all, that Jerusalem is the beginning of the story.

113

Some comment on the importance of Jerusalem for the people of Israel might also be worth sharing at the outset.

Our storytelling can move next to the key prophecy in Luke's Gospel in 9:22. This crucial link in Luke's story is not included anywhere else in the Lukan lectionary year. The Son of Man must go to Jerusalem (this is implied) in order to undergo much suffering. Luke 9:31 indicates that Jesus will undertake an exodus to Jerusalem. The Travel Narrative in Luke 9:51—19:27 is the story of this exodus.

In the very first leg of Jesus' journey to Jerusalem he is not received by the Samaritans. This reminds us of his rejection in his hometown and his rejection in Jerusalem. Luke 22:47 through Luke 23 tells of Jesus' reception and death in Jerusalem.

Jerusalem next becomes the place where Jesus commands his disciples to remain in order to be empowered in mission (24:44-49). Acts 1 and 2 tell us how this mission got off the ground! It is a mission that is to begin in Jerusalem (Acts 1:8) and move out to the ends of the earth.

From Jerusalem to our town, to our lives. That is the flow of this story. It is a story that intends to reach beyond itself and include the whole world. It is a story that intends to reach us! Wherever we live becomes our Jerusalem. We are in turn called to be empowered in Jerusalem and to take the message of the Messiah to the ends of the earth.

Moving beyond Luke it might be appropriate to note that the flow of God's story finally ends in Jerusalem. "And I saw the holy city, the new Jerusalem, coming down out of heaven from God ..." (Revelation 21:2).

Another obvious possibility for this week's narrative sermon would focus on the second half of the text. Jesus is on a journey. We are called to follow. Story One might begin with Jesus' words about discipleship in light of his prophecy (9:22) that we are to live a life of self-denial, cross-bearing and *life-losing* in order to find the true meaning of our humanity (9:23-27).

Luke 9:57-62 could serve as a second story. The story can be told pretty much as is with your own embellishments. People are called to follow, and they come up with home and family excuses.

114

They have family values, it seems! Jesus has other values. He calls them to *leave family behind* and follow on the exodus to Jerusalem.

If we wish to add *possessions* to the triad of things to leave behind we could include the story of the rich ruler from Luke 18:18-30 in today's story telling. This story is not used in the Lukan year.

Losing life, leaving family, and giving up possessions occur together in 14:25-33. This text is appointed in the Lukan lectionary cycle as Proper 18.

Jesus' call to discipleship is a hard and challenging call. We are invited to "listen to him" when he calls (9:35). We are invited to follow, follow the One who took up his cross and gave his life for us. It is the power of his amazing love that attracts us and empowers our following!

---

1. Joseph Fitzmyer, *The Gospel According to Luke, I-IX* (New York: Doubleday, 1981), p. 826.

2. Robert C. Tannehill, *The Narrative Unity of Luke-Acts, Volume One* (Philadelphia: Fortress Press, 1986), p. 231.

Chapter 20
Proper 9: Sunday between July 3 and 9

Luke 10:1-11, 16-20

Chapters 9 and 10 of Luke are much occupied with the disciples. In 9:1-6 Jesus sent out the twelve with power and authority over demons and diseases. The disciples were sent out to preach the kingdom of God and to heal. In 9:51 Jesus set his *face* to go to Jerusalem and sent his messengers ahead of him to prepare his way. In today's text the mission is expanded. The Lord appointed 70 (or 72) and sent them ahead of his *face* to every town and place where he was about to come. He sent them, that is, to prepare his way as John had done at the beginning (Luke 1:14-17, *17*; 3:4; 7:27). More people must be sent out to prepare for the Lord because the harvest is plentiful and the laborers are few. The agricultural imagery here reminds us of the story of the Parable of the Sower in Luke 8:4-8. The harvest may be a reference to Joel 3:1-13 and/or Isaiah 27:11-12.

There is a textual problem with the number of those sent. Commentators are not of one mind on the solution to this issue. Robert Tannehill prefers the number 72:

> *Seventy-two agrees with the number of the nations of the world according to the LXX of Genesis 10, the number of the elders who prepared the LXX ... and the number of the princes and languages in the world according to 3 Enoch 17:8, 18:2f, and 30:2. If seventy-two is the original reading, it seems likely that a hint of the future universal mission is intended. The technique used here would resemble Acts 2:9-11, where a long list of nations foreshadows the universal mission within the context of the mission to Jews in Jerusalem.*[1]

However we determine the proper number of those sent out it is clear that we are dealing here with a context of mission. The role of preparing the way of the Lord shifts from John the Baptist to those whom Jesus sends before his *face.* Tannehill argues that aspects of Luke 10:1-24 provide a model for the mission of the church in Acts.[2] A fundamental aspect of John the Baptist's mission was to proclaim a message of repentance and forgiveness (3:3). As we have seen in Chapter 4 the mission of repentance and forgiveness is the message that Jesus also commissioned his disciples to proclaim (24:44-49, *47*). This is also the heart of the message of the preaching of Peter on the day of Pentecost (Acts 2:14-40, *38*). The missionary message stays remarkably the same throughout Luke's telling of the story of mission.

The mission of the 72 was to prepare the way for people to *receive* or *not to receive* Jesus' coming. Jesus' own townsfolk did not receive him (4:22-30). The Samaritans did not receive him (9:53). The list of those who do receive Jesus includes Martha (10:38) and Zacchaeus (19:6). This language of reception also occurs in the Book of Acts (8:14; 11:1; 17:11). The book of Acts also lifts up those who receive the early missionaries with hospitality.

David Tiede calls the verses before us this week a "handbook on evangelism." The word of the missionary-evangelist is "Peace to this house!" (10:5). We remember the word of the angels in Luke's Gospel: "Glory to God in the highest heaven, and on earth *peace* among those whom he favors!" (Luke 2:14. See also 7:50; 8:48.) We are to understand this message as carrying out the performative character of the word that we have discussed earlier. With this announcement peace comes to the house. The Word of God does what it says. Missionary work is the work of *proclamation.* Mission begins with the good news announcement of peace. When the missionary speaks of peace, he or she speaks in the name of God. "Whoever listens to you listens to me, and whoever rejects you rejects me, and whoever rejects me rejects the one who sent me" (10:16).

Missionaries go to houses (v. 5) and towns (v. 8). Missionary work is a public work, a public proclamation of peace. That's the kind of religion that Christianity is. Its message is public. It is meant for all. It is the first thing we say to people. This is in stark contrast to the many cults in our world today whose basic message is private and intended only for the ears of the initiates. Cults have one message for the public and quite another for the private meetings with their adherents. The message of Christianity, the message carried by our missionaries, is the same message in public and in private: "Peace to this house!"

The mission described in today's text met with great success. The 72 were overjoyed: "Lord, in your name, even the demons submit to us!" (10:17). The fall of Satan from his throne would appear to be an eschatological sign of the coming of God's reign in the world. This initial mission success will not be sustained, for it is, after all, a mission on the way to Jerusalem; a mission on the way to the cross!

Homiletical Directions

The church is mission and this week we are afforded a wonderful opportunity to undergird the mission challenge. There are many items from these texts which suggest themselves as we discuss the missionary imperative. It may be that you will wish to gather the "points" this week regarding gospel outreach and teach the nature of mission to your congregation.

One narrative approach suggests itself. That approach would seek to depict in narrative form just how deeply imbedded mission is in the Christian story. The story of Christ starts with a missionary by the name of John the Baptist who is to prepare the way of the Lord. The verses that relate to John's mission are cited above.

We might next take up the call of Simon Peter and James and John in Luke 5:1-11. We have commented on this story in Chapter 10. Jesus' call of these men to follow him in order to "catch people" comes immediately upon the inauguration of Jesus' ministry as told in Luke 4. Jesus came to preach the good news of the kingdom of God to many cities (4:43). In order to fulfill this mission Jesus calls followers to go with him on the way.

The story of the call of the twelve in 9:1-6 can also be told in this sequence of stories of mission. This story is not in the Lukan lectionary cycle so it might be well to include it with its companion story that is this week's text.

The stories we have mentioned so far can be told quite simply. The focus should be upon the fact that mission is integral to the nature of Jesus' message. We come next to today's text. Again, tell it with a focus on mission.

In the last chapter of Luke the final words that Jesus speaks to the disciples are mission words. See 24:44-49. Jesus raises a word of caution about mission. No one should undertake a mission task unless that one has been empowered by the Spirit. "Wait in Jerusalem!" Jesus tells his freshly commissioned disciples. They do wait, and on the day of Pentecost the Spirit empowers them to be disciples of Jesus in Jerusalem and in Judea and Samaria and to the ends of the earth. (See Acts 1:4-8; 2:1-40.) Mission is empowered by Pentecost. Mission is empowered by the Holy Spirit. The book of Acts tells the story of Pentecost in Jerusalem (Acts 2) and of "mini-pentecosts" in Samaria (Acts 8:4-17), and on toward the ends of the earth (Acts 10—11:18; 19:1-7).

Spirit-empowered mission is part of the basic nature of Christian discipleship. That's the message of a whole series of stories in Luke's narrative. A narrative sermon which lifts up this reality might well end in a commissioning word with a prayer for the coming of the Spirit. In prayer we call upon the Holy Spirit to empower our public mission which announces "peace" to all whom we encounter!

---

1. Robert C. Tannehill, *The Narrative Unity of Luke-Acts, Volume One* (Philadelphia: Fortress Press, 1986), p. 233.

2. *Ibid.*, pp. 233-237.

Luke 10:25-37

We come this week to one of the great Lukan stories that have found their way into the consciousness of people far and wide. A poll was taken some years ago asking people in the United States why they gave to charity. The number one answer was a reference to the story of the "good" (Luke's story does not call him good) Samaritan! "You can't just pass by on the other side" was an answer given by many in relationship to their motive for giving.

David Tiede sets this week's text into its immediate context in Luke's Gospel:

> *This cluster of stories presents Jesus teaching "on the way." The encounter with the* lawyer *(vv. 25-28) sets the context with a discussion of observing the Law and inheriting eternal life. The parable of the "good Samaritan" (vv. 29-37) provides an object lesson in loving and serving the neighbor; the exchanges with Mary and Martha (vv. 38-42) deal with the priorities of serving and hearing the word of God, and Jesus' instruction on prayer (11:1-13) depicts the confidence with which all people may love and serve God.*[1]

A lawyer rises to test Jesus. "What must I do to inherit eternal life?" That's the question. This is a question asked and answered by myriads of lawyers in the rabbinic tradition. No matter how Jesus answered this question the lawyer would be able to quote to Jesus other answers by other teachers. Jesus turns the tables on the lawyer and asks him what the law says. The lawyer says rightly! He knows that the greatest law is that which calls for love of God and love of neighbor. See Leviticus 19:18 and Deuteronomy 6:5. In Matthew 22:34-40 and Mark 12:28-31 Jesus answers a question about the "greatest commandment in the law" by giving the same answer this lawyer gives. Love God. Love your neighbor.

Love of God and neighbor is *the* biblical word on the divinely intended shape for human life. God created the first human and called upon this one to refrain from eating from the tree of the knowledge of good and evil in the *center* of the garden (Genesis 2:16-17). This *boundary at the center* was to serve as a reminder that God is the center of human life. God is to be loved above all else.

God saw that the first human was alone and that loneliness was not good (Genesis 2:18-25). God, therefore, created a woman for the man. The two were to live together in human community. They were to love each other! Human life is life lived in community with other persons. We are to love these persons.

The Ten Commandments speak in their two tables of love of God and love of neighbor. The commandments which concern the neighbor put *a boundary at the edges* of our lives. This boundary tells us what we *cannot* do in relation to our neighbor. We are to love the neighbor. The commandments do not tell us what that means. We will have to figure that out for ourselves. We do know that there are *boundaries* on our behavior with others.

The lawyer is not satisfied by Jesus' answer. He wants *to justify himself.* In order to justify himself he needs to know exactly who his neighbor is. Then he can love that neighbor and live! Then he can justify himself. We note the main concern of the lawyer. His main concern is himself. He is not really interested in his neighbor except as a means to his own justification.

This motive of self-justification occurs in other Lukan stories (16:14-15; 18:9). Jesus makes it clear in all of these stories that justification and eternal life are not rewards for the justifiable behavior of humans. Justification is a gift of God. This is particularly clear in the story of the Pharisee and the tax collector in 18:9-14. (This text is appointed for Proper 25.) In this story it is the sinner who cries, "Lord, be merciful to me," who goes home justified.

We have referred a number of times to the theme of *reversal* in Luke's Gospel. This theme is first sung by Mary: "God has brought down the powerful from their thrones, and lifted the lowly ..." (Luke 1:52). We mentioned this theme in Chapter 1. We cited Luke 7:36-50; 13:22-30; 14:11-24 and Chapter 24 as stories of reversal. This reversal is also present in today's story as the lawyer (the powerful) is brought down and the lowly (Samaritan) is lifted up. It is probably in character for this Gospel to suggest that justification is about lifting the lowly!

It has been noted by many commentators that Jesus' story of the Samaritan does not directly answer the question of the lawyer. The lawyer wanted to know who his neighbor was. Jesus' story is of a man, a very unlikely man, who was a neighbor. In order to catch the sharp edge of this story we need to remind ourselves of the status of Samaritans in relationship to Jews. John's Gospel puts it succinctly: "Jews do not share things in common with Samaritans" (John 4:9). The Samaritans were the remnant of the old Northern Kingdom in Israel who defined themselves over and against the people of Judah (the south) in the post-exilic period. It is hard for us to imagine the genuine shock value of this story in its context. A good Samaritan? Impossible!

We have talked about Luke's mission theme. The salvation that comes in Jesus Christ is for all people. See Luke 2:32; 3:6. This mission to the whole world, of course, is carried out in the Book of Acts as the disciples are empowered by the Holy Spirit to be witnesses of Christ in Jerusalem and Judea and *Samaria* and to the ends of the earth (Acts 1:8). The first appearance of Samaritans in Luke's Gospel is in the story in 9:51-56 where they would not receive Jesus as he set his face towards Jerusalem. That's what we expect from Samaritans! But in this week's text we have a *good* Samaritan. In Luke 17:11-19 it is the Samaritan leper *alone* who returns to give thanks to Jesus. (This text is appointed for Proper 23.) The grand climax of the Samaritan theme is the story of the "Samaritan Pentecost" in Acts 8:4-17. Apostles from Jerusalem went down to Samaria to pray for these newborn Christians with the laying on of hands. Samaritans become part of Christian community. Incredible!

Homiletical Directions

The narrative possibilities for preaching on this week's text are many. First, we could deal with the theme of love of God and love of neighbor. Tell only the first part of this week's story (10:25-28). This very good answer of the lawyer points to the reality of how God created us in the first place. From the Genesis material above tell the story of the creation of the first person, the tree in the garden, and the need for human community. This story says that we are created to love God at the center of our life and our neighbor as well. To live such a life is to live in the *image of God.*

Next tell the shape of the Ten Commandments. The first table of the law points to our relationship to God; the second table of the law points to the boundaries we must not cross in our relationship with our neighbor. We can add to this the fact that Jesus gives this same answer of love of God and neighbor when he is asked what the great commandment of the law is (Matthew 22:34-40; Mark 12:28-31).

Such a sermon, of course, cannot end with a command to people to love God and neighbor. That's precisely what we can't do! In Colossians 1:15 and Romans 8:29 we read references to Jesus as the *image of God.* The Romans passage tells us that it is God's intention to *conform* us to the image of God's son. There is our hope. There is our proclamation. Jesus' word is: "I am the image of God. I have come to conform you to my image. Put your trust in me and I will conform your life to be a life of love of God and love of neighbor."

A second sermon possibility would be to deal with the theme of self-justification versus justification by God. First tell the lawyer's story down to the fact that he asked in order to justify himself. See the text above for additional comments on the meaning of self-justification. Second, note the self-justification motive in 16:14-15; 18:9-*14.* It would be very helpful to tell the story of the Pharisee and the tax collector this week even though it will occur later in the lectionary cycle. It is a story that clearly explicates the justification theme. Who is justified? Confessing sinners go home justified. Play off the realities of self-justification and Christ's justification. Such a sermon can end in proclamation: "I justify sinners. I justify those who cry for mercy. I justify you when you, along with the tax collector, cry 'God, be merciful to me, a sinner.' "

A third narrative possibility would be to go with the Samaritan theme. As Old Testament background you can tell stories from Nehemiah 2:1-*20*; 4; 6:1-9. When Nehemiah came back from exile he was confronted by the political power of the Samaritans in the persons of Sanballat and Tobiah. Note the closing line of the story told in Nehemiah 2. The Samaritans have no portion or right or memorial in Jerusalem! The same was true in the earlier return of exiles to Jerusalem. See Ezra 4:1-*3*.

In Luke's story begin with the *bad Samaritans* in 9:51-56. Then comes this week's story of a *good Samaritan*. Tell his story! Reference can be made as well to the *good Samaritan* in 17:11-19. The Samaritan story ends in the book of Acts 8:4-17. The apostles from Jerusalem go down to Samaria to lay hands upon the Christians there. The Holy Spirit is poured out also on the Samaritans! Samaritans are no longer excluded from Jerusalem! This is in contrast to Ezra 4:3 and Nehemiah 2:20.

The conclusion of this series of stories might have Jesus say: "I love the outcast. I love even the Samaritans. Bad Samaritans were turned to good Samaritans in my presence. I still love outcasts today. I still love Samaritans who by some persons' definition must stand outside of my love. If I love the Samaritans of yesterday and today, then know that I love you as well."

---

1. David L. Tiede, *Luke: Augsburg Commentary on the New Testament* (Minneapolis: Augsburg, 1988), p. 207.

Luke 10:38-42

The few verses in this week's Gospel text have been the subject of much interpretation. The immediate context of these verses is the lawyer's question: "What must I do to inherit eternal life?" (Luke 10:25). Jesus invited the lawyer to answer his own question and he answered it well: "You shall love the Lord your God with all your heart, and with all your soul, and with all your strength, and with all your mind; and your neighbor as yourself" (10:27).

Love God; love neighbor. Jesus approved this answer. When the lawyer, seeking to justify himself, asked for precise directions on loving neighbor Jesus told his neighbor-love story of the Good Samaritan (10:29-37). Immediately following this story about the horizontal dimension of loving God and neighbor comes the Mary and Martha story appointed for this week. One dimension of the Mary and Martha story is that it is a story about the vertical dimension of the love God, love neighbor command. Mary sat at the Lord's feet and listened! She chose the better part!

The story of Mary and Martha has been the cause of consternation for many women down through the years. Women in the church have usually been confined to the role of *diakonia*. They have been heirs of Martha in the roles assigned to them by both church and society. (Fortunately the times are a'changing.) Yet Mary gets the praise! This has been a difficult double message to live with!

Fundamental to our understanding of this story is the question of the valuation put on women in the Gospel of Luke. Usually Luke comes off quite well in such studies. Women play a greater role in his Gospel than in any other. Most commentaries give the listing of stories about women. It is impressive. Luke has often received great praise for the exalted status of women in his pages.

This line of thinking leads to a very positive interpretation of the role of Mary in this story. She was able to choose a better way. She sat at Jesus' feet and listened. And Jesus taught her! That was unheard of in the first century. Mary is, therefore, a symbol of feminine emancipation. Mary chose, and therefore women may choose, to sit at Jesus' feet and be a disciple.

Contemporary female biblical scholars are not sold, however, on the idea that Luke's picture of women is positive. *The Women's Bible Commentary*, for example, argues that Luke keeps women in very passive and subservient roles.[1] The authors argue, for example, that women were treated as well by Judaism in the first century as they were by Jesus. The fact that Mary could sit at the feet of a rabbi and learn the scripture does not pit Christianity versus Judaism. They acknowledge that Luke has more material about women (42 passages) than the other Gospels. They do not believe, however, that Luke's treatment of women in these many passages is as positive as it has often been considered. They note, for example, that Mary is *silent* in her encounter with Jesus. She is receptive, passive. And this is typical in Luke's story. Women are quiet. They do not speak up. They do not challenge Jesus. What a contrast there is, for example, between Luke's picture of Martha and the picture of Martha given by John. In John 11:27 Martha gives the great confession. We usually credit the great confession to Peter, but in John's Gospel it is a woman who gives this confession.

The Women's Bible Commentary says this about Mary in this story:

> *The disciples and apostles in Luke learn often in dialogues ... but Mary is silent. Her attitude is that of a disciple, but she is not a disciple. She is only an audience. What she has heard and learned at the Lord's feet is private; it does not instruct and shape the whole community.*[2]

The Women's Bible Commentary gives us a helpful word of caution on what we want to say about women in the Gospel of Luke and in this week's text. Still there is much good to be said of the role of women in Luke, women who *hear the word of God and keep it.* We commented in Chapter 13 on the theme of "hearing and doing the word of God" in Luke. This theme is first triggered in Jesus' story of building our house on sand or rock (Luke 6:46-49). The story of Mary and Martha fits this theme as well. Mary is pictured as one who hears the word.

It is difficult to hear this story of Mary's listening and not to think of that other Mary who is such a faith-model in Luke's story. Jesus' mother Mary heard the word from the angel Gabriel. Her response was profound: "Here am I, the servant of the Lord; *let it be with me according to your word*" (Luke 1:38). Mary heard the word. She received the word and the word changed her life!

There is a passage in Luke 11:27-28 that fits this theme very well. A woman shouts out in a crowd in praise of Jesus' mother. "Blessed is the womb that bore you and the breasts that nursed you!" This woman defined Mary by her biology! Jesus rejected this limited definition of his mother. He knew his mother as a woman of faith. His answer to the woman makes this clear: "Blessed rather are those who hear the word of God and obey it!" Mother Mary is not to be praised, women are not to be praised, for their biology. Women are to be praised, men are to be praised, for hearing the word of God and obeying it.

In this week's text Mary serves as a model of one who hears the word of God. This is of vital importance to Luke! This Mary, like Mother Mary, is a model for us all. She is the model of one who let it be done to her according to God's word.

Homiletical Directions

Our suggestion is that this week's sermon in narrative form be shaped around the theme of hearing and doing God's word. Story One could well be the story of Mary's encounter with the angel Gabriel as told in Luke 1:26-38. This text from Luke is not assigned for the Lukan year and this might be an opportunity to use this wonderful story. The focus of the story will be on Mary as the one who hears God's word and does it. "Let it be with me according to your word." This was Mary's testimony of faith!

Mary's story in Luke could be amplified with the use of the story in Luke 11:27-28. Jesus affirms for us that his mother should be remembered among us as the one who is blessed for hearing and doing God's word.

Story Two might pick up the theme of hearing and doing God's word that begins with Jesus' story of building on rock and sand. A solid foundation for life is built by all who hear God's word and do it (Luke 6:46-49). This text was treated in Chapter 13. If you did not deal with the hearing/doing theme at that time then this story would fit well into today's story mix.

Story Three might then be the story of the Parable of the Sower as told in Luke 8:4-15. Neither is this text appointed for the Lukan year. The themes of the story are strong. Jesus is the Sower of the Seed. *The seed is the word of God* (8:11)! When we are called to be hearers of God's word it is to Jesus that we are called. Jesus is the gracious sower who sows the seed with prodigality on all kinds of soil. No one stands outside the possibility of hearing this word. Jesus' word is for all.

The second strong theme of the Parable of the Sower is the theme of *hearing*. "Let anyone with ears to hear listen!" (8:8). The seed of God's word is sown by the Sower named Jesus. All are invited to hear this word and be fructified.

Story Four is the text for this week. In light of these other Lukan stories the theme that stands out in the Mary/Martha story is that Mary is one of those people who has ears and does listen. She is not distracted from the word of the Sower by many tasks. She has seen the one thing needful. She has chosen the better part, and this will not be taken away from her.

A closing proclamation might go something like this: Jesus' word to us today is:"I am the Sower. I have come into this world to sow the seed of God's word on the soil of human hearts. I have come to sow the seed of God's word on your heart no matter what condition its soil is in. Listen to my word. Lend your ear. Don't be distracted by many things. (You will know some of the distractions in your local situation. They may be specified here.) Don't run after other words and other gods. Like Mary, hear my word and keep it. 'Let anyone with ears to hear listen!' My word shall never be taken away from you!"

A very brief closing prayer might call our hearers to respond to God's word as Mother Mary responded: "Let it be with me according to your word."

---

1. Carol A. Newsom and Sharon H. Ringe, editors, *The Women's Bible Commentary* (Louisville: Westminster/John Knox Press, 1992), p. 279.

2. *Ibid.,* p. 289.

Luke 11:1-13

One of the basic agendas "on the way to Jerusalem" is instruction of the disciples. In the Gospel text appointed for this week prayer is the topic of instruction. The text begins with Jesus at prayer. Luke presents Jesus at prayer at many decisive moments of his earthly ministry (3:21; 5:16; 6:12; 9:18, 28).

In response to the disciples' request Jesus teaches them to pray first and foremost by teaching them the Lord's Prayer. Standard commentaries will have much information on the various petitions of this prayer. Prayer is a vital aspect of the Christian life. It may well be that this Sunday's sermon should be a teaching sermon on prayer. The prayer Jesus teaches begins with an address to "Father."

> *The address of God as* Father *has troubled some people as too specifically male and authoritarian. Of course this prayer comes from a patriarchal culture, and the whole Gospel of Luke is a testimony to the authority and power of God's reign at work in Jesus. But Jesus' use of the word* Father *was probably shocking to first-century ears because it was not as authoritarian or regal as they expected.* [1]

We are reminded of Jeremias' emphasis on the uniqueness of Jesus' "Abba" prayers, though Luke uses the Greek word *patros*, not *abba*.

Jesus' instruction on prayer here not only begins with "Father," it ends with "Father" (v. 13). In Luke 10:21-22 we hear that God through Jesus has been revealed as "Father" to the disciples (babes). Prayer, therefore, is directed to the Father. But Luke gets more specific than this. Prayer to the Father elicits from the Father the gift of the Holy Spirit. *The Holy Spirit is the promise of the Father which is to sustain the life of the disciple!*

The Holy Spirit as the promise of the Father is a strong theme in Luke-Acts. This theme is enunciated by Jesus in his farewell address to his disciples (Luke 24:44-49). In these verses Jesus summarizes his mission on earth. He then commands the disciples to be witnesses preaching repentance and forgiveness beginning in Jerusalem. "And see, I am sending upon you what my *father promised*; so stay here in the city until you have been clothed with power from on high" (24:49). This theme is repeated in Acts 1:4: "... he (Jesus) ordered them not to leave Jerusalem, but to wait there for the *promise of the Father.*" The "promise of the Father" is the gift of the Holy Spirit on the occasion of Pentecost. At the conclusion of Peter's explanatory sermon on the gift of the Spirit at the first Pentecost (a sermon which is about Jesus!) he says: "[Jesus] being therefore exalted at the right hand of God, and having received *from the Father the promise of the Holy Spirit*, he has poured out this that you both see and hear" (Acts 2:33).

Prayer in Jesus' name is made to the Father in order that disciples might receive the promise of the Father, the Holy Spirit, to answer our prayers! Acts 4:23-31 is a particularly clear passage that speaks of prayer as the prelude to the coming of the gift of the Holy Spirit. When we pray to God, God sends Godself in answer to our prayers! This is an incredible assertion. Prayer does not just get the attention of a far-off God who decides what to do with our petitions. Prayer to a God as near as a Father results in God joining Godself to the one who prays. God doesn't just answer prayers. *God is the answer to our prayers.* God allies Godself with us in the form of the gift of the Holy Spirit.

A central part of the Lord's prayer is prayer that God will deliver us from trials and temptations. In Luke 12:8-12 we hear that God will send the Holy Spirit to teach the disciples what to say in the hour of trial and temptation. "Lead us not into temptation," we are taught to pray. "I will be with you in the time of trial and temptation," is the answer to our prayers. "I will send myself in the form of the Holy Spirit to stand with you in times of trial." This is part of Jesus' answer to the request to be taught how to pray. Words such as those suggested here might form a proclamatory component to a teaching sermon on prayer for this week.

131

These verses in Luke 12 refer as well to the sin against the Holy Spirit. This text is not used in the Lukan year. Luke does tell stories (he *thinks* in stories) that give narrative shape to the truth of the sin against the Holy Spirit. Peter sins against Jesus by his denials in the courtyard. These sins against Jesus are forgiven! Ananias and Sapphira, on the other hand, sin against the Holy Spirit (Acts 5:1-11). Note especially verses 3 and 9. Their sin is not forgiven! Simon the magician also sinned against the Holy Spirit by trying to get the power of the Spirit under his own control (Acts 8:9-24). Forgiveness for Simon is problematic. One must not presume to control or misuse the gift of the Spirit. Grave consequences may result.

Homiletical Directions

As suggested above, this week's text provides a wonderful opportunity to teach modern disciples something of the nature and meaning of prayer. Some of the narrative material which we have discussed could possibly be woven into your teaching.

---

1. David L. Tiede, *Luke: Augsburg Commentary on the New Testament* (Minneapolis: Augsburg, 1988), p. 212.

Chapter 24
Proper 13: Sunday between July 31 and August 6

Luke 12:13-21

"God has filled the hungry with good things, and sent the rich away empty" (Luke 1:53). This theme verse of Luke from Mary's magnificent Magnificat is presented to us in narrative form in this week's Gospel text. This text tells of a rich man sent away empty. The verses that follow, verses 22-31, tell of the hungry being filled with good things (12:22-31) but they are not appointed in the Lukan year, so they might well be considered together with 12:13-21.

We mentioned this week's Gospel in Chapter 1 when we first looked at the Magnificat. It is also included in the discussion of Luke 6:17-26 in Chapter 11.

Some scholars see these verses in 12:13-21 as part of a single discourse of Jesus which is presented in Luke 12:1—13:9. In these passages:

> *Jesus is interacting with three principal groups: the disciples, the Pharisees and scribes, and the crowd or representatives of it ... Jesus' instruction in this discourse is unusually comprehensive, embracing four topics (persecution, loss of possessions, the judgment of the returning Lord, conflict with family) which are related subjects of disciple instruction in Luke ... The narrator prefers returning to major topics of teaching repeatedly, rather than grouping related teaching in a single discourse, thus reinforcing through recurrence and suggesting that Jesus was repeatedly engaged in this type of teaching.*[1]

A major theme of the discourses in 12:1—13:9 is fear and anxiety. This week's story deals with the theme of fear for our eternal security. One of the multitude makes a request. "Bid my brother divide the inheritance with me," he asks Jesus. Getting involved in legal disputes over estates is difficult business. Jesus passes the question by and tells a story about the problematic nature of possessions. "Life does not consist in the abundance of possessions." That's the point of Jesus' story.

This theme of possessions is of constant concern to Luke. Mary's song first sings of the rich being sent away just as the man in this story is sent away because he was not rich toward God. Jesus has come for the poor. This was announced in Jesus' inaugural address in Nazareth. "The Spirit of the Lord is upon me, because he has anointed me to bring good news to the poor" (Luke 4:18). Since Jesus has come for the poor there is no need to be anxious over one's life. That's the message of the verses that follow this week's text. "Strive for his kingdom, and these things will be given to you as well" (12:31).

In the Travel Narrative there are several other passages which deal with this theme of possessions: 16:1-31; 18:18-30; and 19:1-10. As we have seen, this theme carries over also into the book of Acts as the story of Ananias and Sapphira clearly illustrates. It should not be surprising to us that the early church had a very different evaluation of poverty and wealth than we do today.

> *Most of the great "fathers" of the church held economic views which would be considered quite radical in our day. Ambrose of Milan, for instance, says that "the earth has been created in common for all, rich and poor. Why do you (the rich) claim for yourselves the right to own the land?" ... Basil the Great says to the rich: "The bread that you hoard belongs to the hungry. The cloak that you keep in your chests belongs to the naked. The shoes that rot in your house belong to the unshod."*[2]

Homiletical Directions

In Chapter 11 there are homiletical directions which include this week's text. You may wish to review the comments there. If you have not as yet grouped these passages about the rich being sent away and the hungry being filled with good things into sermonic form, this week affords another opportunity to do so.

We come face to face here again with some very difficult words from Luke's Jesus on wealth and poverty. These stories are not easy to tell in a North American context of affluence. Ours is a culture which celebrates the wealthy and sees wealth as a socially sanctioned goal for life. This week's text and the verses that follow it are downright un-American! What to do? We can avoid the hard word, the counter-cultural word. Doing so, however, is an outright betrayal of Luke's portrait of Jesus. We can preach the topic head-on, make it our own, give it all the gusto we have. In this approach we risk alienating people not only from Jesus but from us! A better approach might be to tell the stories as they are. Put the hard words where they belong — on the lips of Mary and Jesus. The words do not need our explanation. They are crystal clear. Let the Bible speak for itself. Acknowledge that these are words you struggle with as well. Pray that the Holy Spirit apply this word to the manifold needs of human hearts.

One theme for this week's sermon would simply be: God has filled the hungry with good things and sent the rich away empty. Tell first the story of Mary and her song. Let this verse stand out in the telling as the theme for the day. This theme can be buttressed by reference to the story of Jesus in his hometown synagogue announcing that he has come to bring good news to the poor (Luke 4:16-21). You may also refer to the story of John the Baptist sending his disciples to Jesus to ask if Jesus is the One who is to come. Part of Jesus' reply to John is the sign that the poor have good news preached to them (Luke 7:18-23).

With these stories as background simply tell the story assigned for this week. Close by saying: God sends the rich man away empty. Then tell the story which follows in Luke 12:22-31. Close by saying: God fills the hungry with good things.

This sermon might continue with reference to other stories from the Travel Narrative that make this same point: 16:1-31; 18:18-30; 19:1-10. Chapter 39 deals with 19:1-10 (the story of Zacchaeus) as a response to the story of the rich young ruler told in 18:18-30. You may wish to include some of that material here as well. Repeat the theme after each story: God fills the hungry with good things and sends the rich away empty.

135

Some of these same stories may be told under other themes suggested by the material in Luke 12:13-31. "Do not be anxious about your life." "Seek first the kingdom of God." In any case, these texts deal with the priorities of life.

Close with an appropriate prayer or hymn that invites the Holy Spirit to guide each heart in understanding what it means to be rich toward God.

1. Robert C. Tannehill, *The Narrative Unity of Luke-Acts, Volume One* (Philadelphia: Fortress Press, 1986), pp. 242-243.

2. Justo L. and Catherine G. Gonzalez, *The Liberating Pulpit* (Nashville: Abingdon Press, 1994), p. 54.

Luke 12:32-40

This week's text begins with a clear statement of the Gospel message. "Do not be afraid ... for it is your Father's good pleasure to give you the kingdom." There need be no cause of anxiety for disciples of Jesus when they trust that the kingdom has been given them. It has come freely. It is a gift. Life has a new and secure foundation. David Tiede refers to this verse as the theme of the entire section from 12:1—13:21.

The theme of possessions which was present in last week's assigned text (12:13-21) is picked up again. Possessions are to be sold. The kingdom given to us, the kingdom we are to desire with our heart above all things (12:31), is to be our priceless treasure. And then, suddenly, Luke plunges us into eschatological imagery.

> *At 12:35 Jesus moves into eschatological exhortation without indication of a break. This is understandable in light of indications elsewhere that detachment from possessions and from cares of daily life is an important part of readiness for the coming of the Son of Man which Jesus wishes to see in his disciples ... The eschatological instruction in 12:35-48 is ... concerned solely with the meaning of the Lord's return for his servants who are charged with responsibilities.*[1]

The story told in 12:35-40 is a story told to convey the need of a state of watchfulness for the return of the master. Those who are awake at his coming will share in the eschatological feast. At this feast the master (Jesus) will serve them! This is a gracious kingdom, indeed. Images of the eschatological banquet are present elsewhere in the Travel Narrative: 13:20-30; 14:15-24 (which are not part of the Lukan pericopes); 15:22-32.

A parallel story to 12:35-40 may be found at the very end of the Travel Narrative: 19:12-27. Both stories deal with that which should occupy the servants while they wait for the master's return. That which should occupy them is nothing unworldly and spiritual. They are to be busy with their daily tasks. They are to keep watch. They are to invest wisely. They are to be about the business of faithful living on earth.

Luke 19:12-27, a text not appointed in the Lukan year, is important not only for its parallel message to this week's text. These verses are very important as well because they are the closing words of the Travel Narrative. Jesus has drawn nigh to his destination throughout the Travel Narrative, Jerusalem (19:11). The disciples are excited! Now the king will ascend his throne. Now the promised Messiah will begin his rule. Now the glory will break forth upon them. Jesus' story pulls the rug out from under such expectations.

> ... *Jesus' parable supplies a complex corrective to such expectations by indicating that (a) harsh opposition still lies ahead in the coming of the kingdom, (b) the judgment which will come with the kingdom could be fearsome, and (c) those who are faithful servants and disciples have important responsibilities in the meantime.*[2]

In other words, this story also demystifies the coming of the kingdom. The kingdom has come. It is the Father's good pleasure to give us this gift. The kingdom is coming. Those gifted with the kingdom have responsibilities here on earth as they await the fulfillment of what has been promised.

Tannehill points out that there are three major eschatological teaching sections in Luke's Gospel: 12:35-48; 17:22-30 (not appointed in the Lukan year) and 21:34-36 which is part of the text appointed for the First Sunday in Advent. Each story underscores the reality that we humans do not know the day or the hour of the final coming of the kingdom. See 12:40; 17:22-24; 21:34. The message of this variety of eschatological stories is consistent. We do not know the day or the hour, but we do know that we are to be about our earthly tasks as we await the final day.

Homiletical Directions

We have a lot of stories to tell this week concerning the coming of the kingdom. Let's start out, however, with the best news about the kingdom. Let's start out with a word of proclamation. "God's word to you today, my friends, is gracious. 'It is my good pleasure to give you the kingdom,' God says to us in today's text. 'I gave you the kingdom in your baptism. I renew my kingdom promise each time you come to my table. It is my good pleasure to give you the kingdom.' "

Verses 35-40 (we can also use verses 41-48) tell a story about the final coming of the kingdom. Even as we revel in God's gift of the kingdom we wonder about how the promise will come out. When will God's kingdom come for good? When will God's will be done on earth as it is in heaven? And what are we to be doing on earth as we await the fulfillment of God's kingdom promise? These are the questions which the stories we have looked at address.

Having made the proclamation and asked the question, our sermon can turn to story telling. Luke tells a number of stories that deal with these very practical questions of kingdom faith. The story in today's assigned text can be told along with the story in verses 41-48. You may also tell the story in 17:22-30 and 19:12-27. None of these stories is appointed for the Lukan year.

Our sermon structure so far is simple. Make the proclamation from 12:32. Raise the questions about the final coming of the kingdom and the nature of our kingdom life on earth. Tell one to four of the stories we have suggested as a way of answering the questions. Two dominant realities emerge from this story telling. One reality is that *we don't know the day or the hour of the final coming of the kingdom.* The stories make this clear. The unknown kingdom hour secures the fact that the kingdom is ours as gift. If we knew the day and the hour we would surely get prepared. We could spend our last year, or month, or week before the kingdom dawns by getting our life in perfect order. When the king comes we would be ready! We would be prepared. And none of us would be saved! If we knew the day and the hour we would make the mistake of thinking that we could make ourselves kingdom-ready. We would rely, that is, on our good works. And no one would be saved. The

139

kingdom comes by grace. "It is my good pleasure to give you the kingdom." That's the gospel promise. The unknown character of the kingdom hour forces us to rely on God's kingdom gift alone as our means of preparation!

The second reality that emerges from this story telling is that *we know what to do until the kingdom comes.* We are to gird up our loins and keep our lamps burning for the return of the master. We are to stay awake (12:35-40). We are to be faithful stewards of what God has given us. See 12:41-48; 19:12-27. This comes very close to Martin Luther's doctrine of vocation. God has put us in many stations in life. We are parents, children, aunts, uncles, workers, citizens, inhabitants of God's earth. These are the places where we live out our kingdom lives. We stay awake. We remain faithful. We use our God-given gifts in service of neighbor, nation, and world. That's what kingdom people do until God's final kingdom comes.

We know what kingdom people are to do. But let's not end on that note. Let's end the sermon on the grace note with which we began. "Do not be afraid ... for it is your Father's good pleasure to give you the kingdom." You are kingdom people! Be kingdom people!

---

1. Robert C. Tannehill, *The Narrative Unity of Luke-Acts, Volume One* (Philadelphia: Fortress Press, 1986), pp. 248-249.

2. David L. Tiede, *Luke: Augsburg Commentary on the New Testament* (Minneapolis: Augsburg, 1988), p. 322.

Luke 12:49-56

"I came to bring fire to the earth...." "I have a baptism with which to be baptized...." Jesus has a great sense of urgency "on the way" to Jerusalem. "Let's get on with it!" he seems to be saying. In Luke 9:21 Jesus uttered his first passion prediction. "The Son of Man must undergo great suffering," he told his disbelieving disciples. In the story of the transfiguration which follows this passion prediction, Jesus spoke with Moses and Elijah about his *exodus* to Jerusalem (9:31). In 9:51 Jesus "set his face" to go to Jerusalem. In 13:31-35 Jesus spoke again about the urgency of coming to Jerusalem, the city that kills the prophets. "He is interpreting his own mission in sharply prophetic terms, and the peril of judgment is deeply felt."[1]

When Jesus speaks about bringing fire to the earth we are to understand that he comes to bring judgment to earth. Fire is associated with God's judgment throughout the Bible. In the Old Testament we see this, e.g., in Zechariah 13:9 and Malachi 3:2-3. Luke also uses the image of fire for judgment (3:9, 17; 9:54; 17:29).

When Jesus speaks of the "baptism with which he is to be baptized" it seems clear that he speaks of his coming death. Mark uses this imagery to speak of Jesus' death in 10:38. We assume that the use of baptism as a metaphor for Jesus' dying was common imagery.

> *Jesus is not merely "wishing" that something might happen. He is caught up in God's will and plan as announced by John that the Messiah would baptize "with the Holy Spirit and with fire ... to gather the wheat ... and burn the chaff with unquenchable fire" (3:16-17). No aspect of the Messiah's mission will fail of fulfillment including the* baptism *and the* fire, *but how it shall all be accomplished*

is still hidden in the will of God. Perhaps even Jesus
does not yet know how all of this will take place.[2]

Robert Tannehill puts it this way:

Fire, a baptism to be suffered, division in place of peace
— Jesus speaks of them not as the unfortunate result of
human blindness but as part of the commission which he
came to fulfill. This extreme language emphasizes the in-
escapability of these experiences if God's plan is to be
realized.[3]

In the Gospel of Luke it is very clear that God has a plan and
that Jesus "must" carry out this plan. There are ways in which *this*
is the gospel message of Luke. The message is that God has a plan
and carries out that plan. Other New Testament writers give more
space to the *nature* of God's plan. God's plan is to come and die
for our sins, for example. It is not so in Luke, and this has long
puzzled students of his Gospel. Tannehill interprets Luke to mean
that Jesus carried out a kind of "prophetic destiny." "A sacred pattern assures those who accept it that events are not meaningless
and chaotic, for they reflect the rhythm of God's work in the world."[4]
This is also "good news"! It is good news most especially to us in
our time when life can really seem meaningless. God as source of
meaning and purpose to human life is a message of good news to
people in our chaotic world.

But God's plan and purpose means that Jesus must die. When
Jesus first spoke such words to his disciples they did not believe
him (9:44-45)! Luke 18:31-34 tells us that well "on the way" to
Jerusalem they still did not understand these things. They couldn't
grasp it.

In verse 51 Jesus announces that he has not come to bring peace
to the world. This word of Jesus stands in clear contrast to other
passages in Luke where Jesus is clearly the One who brings peace
(1:79; 2:14, 29; 7:50; 8:48; 10:5; 19:38; Acts 9:31; 10:36). Luke's
word is true. Jesus did come to bring peace to the earth. When that
word is rejected, however, Jesus' word becomes a fire of judgment.
The disciples are not the only ones who do not get it.

Luke holds before us, therefore, a complex picture of God. God is love! God is wrath! The Bible constantly attests to this twofold word of God. God's twofold word brings *divisions* to human life. We see this reflected in the family divisions spoken of in verses 52-53.

Verses 54-56 speak of the signs of the times. See also 11:29-32. People can read the signs of the weather but they can't seem to read the much more important signs of the kingdom. They cannot grasp or understand what God is up to in a servant who is off to his death in Jerusalem.

> *If you are so clever in predicting the weather, why are you unable to discern the very presence of God's reign in your midst? This is yet one more disclosure of the divine will along with an exposure of human rejection of God's reign. If the whole of Luke's narrative were not confident of God's saving triumph, this haunting question could only demonstrate the validity of divine judgment (see also 13:1-5).[5]*

Homiletical Directions

As with much of the other material in the "Travel Narrative" this week's assigned text is didactic in nature. Jesus is teaching his disciples about his destiny and the destiny of the human race. There is much to teach our people from this text. It does not, however, have many narrative connections. One possible way to put this text in a narrative frame would be to tell those stories which point to God's plan in Jesus Christ. The songs of Gabriel, Mary, and Zechariah in Luke 1 each speak of God's plan for this child who is to be born. The angel announced to shepherds that this child would be the Savior, who is the Messiah, the Lord (2:11). John the Baptist prepared the way of the more powerful one who would baptize with the Holy Spirit and with fire (3:1-21). Jesus quoted from the prophet Isaiah in his hometown synagogue to give shape to his mission.

Things look very bright for this Messiah. But the darkness sets in. In 9:22 Jesus reveals to his disciples that he "... *must* undergo great suffering, and be rejected by the elders, chief priests, and scribes, and be killed, and on the third day be raised." This is a divine *must*. Jesus is under orders, under a plan of God. He *must*. This divine necessity is repeated many times in Luke (13:33; 17:25; 22:37; 24:7, 44).

Under divine necessity Jesus first must suffer! That's what pushes to the surface in today's text. "Let's get on with it!" Jesus is ready to submit to the plan. He is ready to go to Jerusalem. He is ready to die.

If we were to stitch together some of these stories to put today's teaching text in its overall Lukan context we might then end with a word of proclamation. It can go something like this:

"Jesus has a word for us today. 'I came to bring fire to the earth, and how I wish it were already kindled! I have a baptism with which to be baptized, and what stress I am under until it is completed! God has a plan for my life. I must carry out the plan. I must die and then be raised. I must suffer and then see glory. My life has a meaning, a purpose, a destiny when it is in God's hands.

" 'And so it can be for all who put their trust in me. You suffer much in your life in this world. You wonder at times if life is worth the effort, if life has any meaning or purpose or destiny. I am here today to tell you that your life can have meaning. I am here today to tell you that your life can have purpose. I am here today to tell you that your life can have a destiny. Put your trust in me. Your life takes on great meaning when you give it up to me. I am your purpose. I am your destiny.' Amen."

---

1. David L. Tiede, *Luke: Augsburg Commentary on the New Testament* (Minneapolis: Augsburg, 1988), p. 244.

2. *Ibid.,* p. 243.

3. Robert C. Tannehill, *The Narrative Unity of Luke-Acts, Volume One* (Philadelphia: Fortress Press, 1986), p. 252.

4. *Ibid.,* p. 288.

5. Tiede, *op. cit.*, p. 245.

Luke 13:1-9

This week's text, with its appropriate Lenten theme of repentance, is assigned for the Lenten season quite out of context. Luke 13 lies in the middle of Luke's Travel Narrative (Luke 9:51—19:27; see discussion in Chapter 19). The immediate context is one of warnings by Jesus of the impending judgment that is to come. Robert Tannehill puts it this way:

> *Thus in four major statements to the crowd or members of it (11:14-36; 12:13-21; 12:54—13:9; 13:22-30), we find some of the crowd are opposing Jesus and that the crowds are accused of being unresponsive and are threatened with judgment and exclusion. In Luke 11-13 it appears that the previous interest of the crowd in Jesus' teaching and miracles was in many cases a superficial, inadequate response ... Tension is developing in the plot, for the expectations of salvation aroused by the birth stories are being threatened.*[1]

What we have in this passage itself is a kind of *theodicy*. God is on trial here in the questions of "some present." We know from the Old Testament, particularly the Deuteronomic History, that in Israel there was a fundamental trust that good behavior was rewarded by God; bad behavior was punished. One of the proverbs puts it well: "When the tempest passes, the wicked are no more, but the righteous are established forever" (Proverbs 10:25). Two particular instances that have occurred seem to have shaken some of the faithful. Pilate mingled Galilean blood with his sacrifices. A tower in Siloam fell and killed eighteen people. Why? That's the theodicy question. Why would this happen to people? What is God up to in the world? Is our doctrine right about this? Were these people really greater sinners who deserved such punishment?

145

Karl Barth must have loved Jesus' reply to this question! Jesus doesn't answer them at all. Humans don't call God into question. God calls us into question! "Unless you repent, you will all perish as they did." Jesus gives this answer twice.

And then Jesus tells a story about a man who planted a fig tree in his garden. It bore no fruit. He determined to cut it down immediately. Judgment day had come for the fig tree. But the vinedresser intervened. "Give it another year," the vinedresser pleaded. "If it does not bear fruit by then we will cut it down."

Repentance is about bearing fruit! We learned that in Luke's Gospel from John the Baptist. "Bear fruits worthy of repentance" (Luke 3:8). That was the cry of John the Baptist as he prepared the way for Jesus. Now Jesus has come. He, too, calls for repentance. He, too, calls for fruit-bearing lives. And he is gracious in his call to repentance. He is willing to give us time. The vinedresser serves as a kind of Christ figure who argues our case before God! "Sir, let it alone for one more year, until I dig around it and put manure on it."

In Chapter 4 we traced the theme of repentance through Luke's Gospel. The repentance theme in Luke is almost always coupled with the reality of forgiveness of sin. There is a way in which this week's text deals with both repentance (vv. 1-5) and forgiveness (vv. 6-9).

The call to repentance theme is also located elsewhere in the Travel Narrative in 10:13-15 and 11:32.

Homiletical Directions

In Chapter 4 we traced the theme of repentance and forgiveness throughout Luke-Acts. You will need to consult this chapter for the homiletical directions that were recommended there. The repentance theme is also dealt with in Chapter 32 and 33. These chapters deal with the material in Luke 15:1-32. Luke 15 contains three stories of repentance. One story is about a lost sheep, one of a lost coin, one of a lost son. We hear in these stories that there is great joy in heaven when one sinner repents. When sinners repent God throws a party! It is difficult to ascertain, however, just what the sheep or the coin did that constitutes repentance. What happened to the sheep and the coin was *that they were found.* Repentance happens when God finds us. That's a theme worth exploring!

In this Lenten season we follow Jesus' "travel narrative" to Jerusalem and to death. Lent is a season for self-reflection in light of Jesus' journey to Jerusalem on our behalf. This is a season that calls forth repentance and fruit-bearing. According to the parable given for today in verses 6-9 fruit bearing is a *root* problem. The roots need tending, manure must be spread, if the root is to repair and produce good fruit. *Repentance, therefore, is not a fruit problem.* You can't just hang some good fruits on a bad tree and solve anything. You can't just hang some good works on human lives and solve anything either.

Repentance is not a fruit problem; *it is a root problem.* It is the root of who we are that is a problem in God's eyes. So repentance cannot be composed of "I can" statements. "I have sinned God. I am sorry God. *I can do better."* Repentance, rather, must be composed of "I can't" statements. "I have sinned, God. I am sorry, God. I've tried and tried and tried but I just don't produce good fruit. *I can't seem to do better.* I need your Vinedresser to work on the roots of my life. Give me a new life, God. Give me your life. I can't. You can."

"... it is no longer I who live, but it is Christ who lives in me" (Galatians 2:20). This is the confession of a repentant person. This is the solution to the fruit-bearing problems of our lives.

This week's text centers in Christ's call to repentance. Consult Chapters 4, 32, and 33 for homiletical directions for narrative preaching on this Sunday in Lent.

---

1. Robert C. Tannehill, *The Narrative Unity of Luke-Acts, Volume One* (Philadelphia: Fortress Press, 1986), pp. 151-152.

Luke 13:10-17

We have seen that the material in the Travel Narrative consists primarily of Jesus' giving instruction to his disciples and to others. There is very little narrative here. This week's Gospel text marks an exception to this rule. Luke tells us the story of a woman with a spirit that had crippled her for eighteen years. Jesus saw the woman and called her to stand straight and be healed. Jesus did this act of healing even though such "work" was forbidden on the Sabbath.

Acts of healing are extremely rare in the Travel Narrative. Luke 14:1-6 (a text that does not appear in the lectionary) reports another act of healing on the Sabbath. This time the healed person is a man. A woman and a man are healed on the Sabbath. In both cases the Pharisees protest mightily. They have the Law on their side!

But Jesus is the Lord of the Sabbath (Luke 6:1-5). In the passage that immediately follows this, Luke 6:6-11, the story of Jesus' healing of the man with a withered hand is told. They were looking for evidence that would enable them to make an accusation against Jesus (6:7). See also 14:1. The Pharisees were true upholders of the Law. The Pharisees most certainly had the Law on their side. It is clear, however, that for Jesus people are more important than laws. Jesus has the Gospel on his side!

Neither of these Sabbath stories in Luke 6 are included in the appointments for the Lukan year. These texts in Luke 6 and Luke 14:1-6 are texts that most certainly could be put in narrative analogy with this week's text in constructing Sunday's sermon.

There is another kind of parallel narrative to this week's text in 7:36-50. (See Chapter 16.) Here, too, the Pharisees are offended when Jesus befriends a woman — in this case a woman who is a sinner. Jesus acts gracefully toward the women in 7:36-50 and 13:10-17. Women did not count for much in the society of Jesus' time. They count for Jesus! "The Spirit of the Lord is upon me, because ... God has sent me to proclaim release to the captives ... to let the oppressed go free" (Luke 4:18).

David Tiede speaks eloquently about Jesus' healing *touch* with this woman with the bent-over back:

> *... he touched her. This is almost as shocking an act as when he touched the litter of the dead man from Nain (7:14) or when the woman with the flow of blood touched him (8:44-46). Luke's sense for the human dimensions of these encounters is most impressive. We are drawn directly into the drama of the moment and instructed by her appropriate response,* praising God. *As the sermons in Acts will verify (see 2:22-24; 10:38) such healings are mighty works of God, and God is to be praised....*[1]

The crux of the matter with this story is in verse 14. The Pharisees are indignant over Jesus' healing — healing on the Sabbath. The crowd is *divided* (cf. 12:51-53) over Jesus' deed of healing. Jesus' adversaries are put to shame, however, and all the people rejoice (13:17). The Travel Narrative speaks increasingly of division and judgment as Jesus moves on his way to Jerusalem.

In his defense of his healing touch with this woman Jesus points out that she is a "daughter of Abraham." She is an heir of the promise made to Abraham and Sarah. In like manner, Jesus describes Zacchaeus as a "son of Abraham" (19:10). A woman who is bound with a bent-over back and a man who is a tax collector (read sinner!) are recipients of grace because they are heirs of the promise made to Abraham. God's promises are good! They do not fail.

God's promises, however, can be taken for granted. They can be presumed upon. They can be wrenched from the human need of repentance in God's sight. This is John the Baptist's warning as he prepares Abraham's people for the coming of Abraham's heir. "Repent," John cries. "Bear fruit worthy of repentance!" he thunders. "Do not begin to say to yourselves, 'We have Abraham as our ancestor'; for I tell you, God is able from these stones to raise up children to Abraham" (Luke 3:8). The heirs of the promise to Abraham and Sarah are to live in repentance and forgiveness. That's a strong theme of Luke's Gospel. (See Chapter 4.)

Finally, we note that Jesus chose to give life back to this woman because she was bound by Satan. Tiede believes that this is a significant aspect of this story.

> *Jesus is challenging the dominion of Satan, and those who are piously defending the Sabbath have not discerned what is happening. More is at stake here than mere human religiosity. Jesus has suggested that his critics are in danger of aiding Satan in his reign of bondage.*[2]

The context of this story is Jesus "on the way" to Jerusalem where he will encounter all the powers that threaten human life. Luke's Gospel sings out constantly with the note that Jesus has come to put human life back together again (Luke 1:46-55; 4:18-19; 7:18-23). Jesus has come to push back all the powers that threaten human life. Satan is the chief of those who wish to bind and constrict human life. The showdown between life and death lies just ahead — in Jerusalem — on a cross. To quote another New Testament writer, it is there that Jesus "... disarmed the rulers and authorities and made a public example of them, triumphing over them in it [the cross]" (Colossians 2:15).

Homiletical Directions

This text presents rich possibilities for narrative preaching. The first possibility presented for us is the bracket of Sabbath day healing stories that we discussed to open this chapter. We have probably said enough about these four texts to guide your sermon preparation on this topic.

A second vital reality here is the power of God's promise. The bent-over woman is a "daughter of Abraham." As an heir of the promise she is a candidate for Jesus' healing deed. A narrative sermon built around a theme like "heirs of the promise" would work very well with this week's text. Such a sermon should begin with the promise made to Abraham and Sarah in Genesis 12:1-3. This promise governs the material that follows it throughout the Hexateuch. Joshua 21:43-45 and 23:14 announce a kind of fulfillment of the promise made to Israel's ancestors. Land has been promised. Land has been taken. These simple realities give purpose and destiny to the stories of Abraham and Sarah, Isaac and Rebekah, Jacob and Rachel. These simple realities give purpose and destiny to the stories of Joseph and Moses. A promise has been made. A people is on the move from promise toward fulfillment.

Once the land has been taken a new nation that will be a blessing to the nations emerges. Israel is born as a nation. The story of Israel from conquest to David is also a story moving from promise to fulfillment. The nation can now be a blessing to all. David's heir will always rule in this nation (2 Samuel 7:8-16). The Anointed One, the Messiah, will usher in an everlasting kingdom. The promise made to Abraham lives on. An entire people await the fulfillment of God's promises.

Something of this promise-fulfillment sweep of the promise recorded in Genesis 12:1-3 is important to tell in order that we can better understand that the Messiah could come and look gracefully upon a bent-over woman because she was a daughter of Abraham. Likewise, the Messiah could look gracefully upon a sinner like Zacchaeus because he was a "son of Abraham." The stories of the bent-over woman and Zacchaeus ought to be told with this accent. This is what it is like to be people of the promise.

The story of John the Baptist provides a warning to all who would take the promise for granted. Promise never cancels out the need for repentance. In his *Small Catechism* Martin Luther talks of our baptism (a time of promise!) as leading us to a life of *daily repentance.*

The structure of this sermon is: 1) The promise to Abraham and its Old Testament heirs. Something of this story is needed to demonstrate what it might mean to be a "daughter of Abraham." 2) The story of the bent-over woman (Zacchaeus, too?) is told to demonstrate the power of the promise made in Genesis 12:1-3. 3) John the Baptist's warning about taking the promise for granted is told. Promise never replaces the need for repentance. 4) We are sons and daughters of the promise. We are the modern-day heirs of the promise made to Abraham and Sarah. We have heard the promise spoken over our lives countless times. God's promises do not fail! This part of the sermon should probably be in proclamation form so that our people hear Jesus speak promise to them!

A third and very important possibility for preaching on this week's text is to apply it to the deep seated problem of lack of self-esteem. *The bent-over woman is a metaphor of low self-esteem.* People with low self-esteem live truncated lives. This take on this text might well begin with the story of Eve and Adam in the garden (Genesis 3:1-21). Sin has two faces in this story. The story of sin in the face of Eve is *pride.* She wants to be like God. The Christian Church has majored in sermons which deal with *pride as the fundamental human sin.* We humans always want *more.* We want to be like God.

But the Genesis story also tells of the sin of Adam. The story of sin in the face of Adam is sin of *low self-esteem.* Adam didn't want more. He yearned for *less.* Adam couldn't even look God in the eye! He ran for cover in the cool of the day. He knew himself to be naked and he was ashamed of himself. This, too, is sin. If Eve thought too highly of herself, Adam thought too lowly of himself. He was ashamed of himself and thought himself to be a kind of worthless creature. *The sin of low self-esteem is to fail to grasp the reality that we are the worthy creatures of God.* We feel ourselves to be small. *We live bent-over lives.*

As we indicated, the *bent-over woman* is a wonderful metaphor of low self-esteem. Jesus says to this woman: " 'Woman, you are set free from your ailment.' When he laid his hands on her, immediately she *stood up straight* and began praising God." This is the antithesis of Adam! It is as if Jesus had said to this woman: "Stand tall. Look me in the eye. Don't hide your life from me. You are a good creature of God's good creating." Words similar to these can be used as a proclamation for this sermon as we address the many people in our congregation who are like Adam, the many people who live bent-over lives.

The story of the healing of the man with the withered hand in 6:6-11 could be used as a parallel story here. To have a withered right hand was to be a social outcast in Jesus' day. You couldn't work. You certainly couldn't engage in social intercourse with your *left* hand. To have a withered right hand was to have a withered hand and a withered life. "Stretch out your hand," Jesus said to the man (6:10). The man *stretched out his hand and it was restored.*

One of the things Jesus is about in the world is the business of straightening backs and stretching out hands. Jesus has come to enable us to live up to our full created potential. "Stand tall. Stretch yourself out. I have come to make you whole."

---

1. David L. Tiede, *Luke: Augsburg Commentary on the New Testament* (Minneapolis: Augsburg, 1988), p. 250.

2. *Ibid.,* p. 251.

Luke 13:31-35

This week's assigned text comes from the heart of Luke's Travel Narrative: 9:51—19:27. (For comments on the Travel Narrative see Chapter 19.) Next week's text will come from this same chapter of Luke. These texts are assigned for us in the church year without much respect for their context in Luke. We just suddenly jump into the middle of the Travel Narrative. These verses have a definite context.

David Tiede describes that context as follows:

> *This passage stands in the midst of Jesus' journey to Jerusalem ... It is a reminder that the way of the determined Messiah is God's mission which will not, cannot, be deterred. But it is also a prophetic sign that the Messiah is well aware of the resistance and tragic rejection which lie in the path of God's saving purpose.*[1]

Within the Travel Narrative itself we have just come out of a lengthy discourse in which Jesus teaches the disciples many things. In 13:22 a time of teaching is past and Jesus went "on his way" to Jerusalem (cf. 9:51: "... he set his face to go to Jerusalem"). Today's text reveals great *conflict of wills* in Jesus' journey to Jerusalem. We have before us in these few verses, "... the intention of Jesus' adversaries, the determination of the Messiah, the unwillingness of Jerusalem, and the fulfillment of the will of God."[2]

We hear in this week's text that Jesus is on his way to his death in Jerusalem. The first preview we have in Luke that trouble may face Jesus the prophet is in Luke 4:24: "Truly I tell you, no prophet is accepted in the prophet's hometown." (For a discussion of the theme of Jesus as Prophet in Luke's telling of the gospel story, see Chapter 15.) Today's passage makes it very clear that Jerusalem is a place that kills prophets. There are some Old Testament stories about prophets being killed in Jerusalem: Jeremiah 26:20-23; 2 Chronicles 24:20-22. See also Luke 11:47-51. Furthermore, today's text is not the only text in Luke that refers to Jerusalem as the city that stands under God's judgment. See 19:41-44; 21:20-24; 23:27-31.

It was not always so that Jerusalem was cast in such a dark light. In Luke 2:36-38 we heard that when she saw the newborn baby Jesus, the prophetess Anna told one and all that this child had come for the *redemption* of Jerusalem. The story of the child filled everyone with great hope for Jerusalem. But judgment, not redemption, will characterize Jerusalem in this story. Jerusalem passed judgment upon Jesus. Jesus passed judgment upon Jerusalem. Redemption comes only after judgment!

Death for Jesus in Jerusalem is no accident. Jesus himself prophesies of his coming death. "The Son of Man must undergo great suffering, and be rejected by the elders, chief priests, and scribes, and be killed, and on the third day be raised" (9:22). We are not surprised, therefore, that in this week's text Jesus refuses the seemingly friendly counsel of the Pharisees. "Go," they say, "Herod wants to kill you." "Go," Jesus says, "tell that fox that I must be about my mission; *I must be on my way.*"

A "divine must" hangs over Jesus' mission. This is a common theme in Luke. Chapter 26 (Luke 12:49-56) discusses the nature of God's plan, the "divine must" in Luke's Gospel. Jesus' life is lived out according to a kind of sacred plan. Luke's emphasis seems to be that Jesus' life and death fulfill that plan. Luke takes much more care to tell us that the plan is carried out than he does in trying to explain what the plan is. The plan is Luke's point. Most other biblical writers are much more attentive to the *content* of this plan. For Luke the plan must be carried out, and when it is carried out the message of repentance and forgiveness of sins can be preached to the nations. See Luke 24:44-49.

David Tiede refers to a prophetic sense of history that is present in this passage. A prophet cannot be killed anywhere but Jerusalem. This is the place for death to come to the prophet. "Jerusalem, Jerusalem, the city that kills the prophets and stones those who are sent to it!" Jesus must finish his course. He is the prophet. Jerusalem lies just ahead. Jerusalem, therefore, becomes the city where great evil takes place. On the other hand, it is the place where God is to do marvelous things. Human sin and divine intervention meet up in Jerusalem. Prophetic history will be fulfilled.

There is hope in this story for us today. Human sin dwells deep within each and every one of us. Will God have anything to do with sinners such as you and me? The answer is YES. Grace and sin met in Jerusalem long ago. Grace won! So it may be for us. Our sinfulness meets the crucified prophet. Grace wins again. Grace is God's final word on the sinful character of our human hearts.

Jesus' concluding words in this week's text indicate that people will not see him again until the day they say, "Blessed is the one who comes in the name of the Lord." (Cf. Psalm 118:26.) This is precisely what the crowd of disciples shouts on Palm Sunday. At last Jesus enters Jerusalem. The journey is complete. He has finished his course. The crowd sings: "Blessed is the king who comes in the name of the Lord!" (19:38). The time has come. The king rides on to die.

Homiletical Directions

In the first place, we would ask that you read the Homiletical Directions in Chapters 15 and 26 where many of the themes of this week's text are dealt with. These chapters contain most of the narrative possibilities for putting this week's Lukan text in analogy with other biblical stories. From Chapter 15 it is particularly the section about Jesus as a "prophet like Moses" that is relevant to this week's material.

A teaching sermon on this text might follow the outline given above from David Tiede. He speaks of a challenge of wills that collide in Jerusalem. All of these challenges are present in this story. Each willful challenge can be set forth as a point in our sermon: 1) The intention of Jesus' adversaries. 2) The determination of the Messiah. 3) The unwillingness of Jerusalem. 4) The fulfillment of the word of God.

What does this mean for us? See the section above which discusses the encounter of sin, judgment, and grace in Jerusalem. The good news for us here is that a plan is being fulfilled. Sin and grace engage in combat, and grace prevails. Now, therefore, the word of repentance and forgiveness can be preached to all nations (Luke 24:44-49). Jerusalem ultimately means good news for the sinner. Grace prevails. Forgiveness is possible. Our sinful human hearts do not doom us to judgment. Even if you do this as a teaching sermon you may wish to put the good news of God's forgiveness which is part of God's sacred pattern for the world in the first person, present tense language of proclamation.

It might also be important to note that Jerusalem is not just the *end* of something in Luke's telling of the story of Jesus. More importantly, Jerusalem is the *beginning* of something! Luke 24:44-49 indicates that this is so. So does Acts 1:8 ("You will be my witness in Jerusalem ... and to the ends of the earth"). Acts 2 tells of the story of Pentecost that takes place in Jerusalem. The Church is born in Jerusalem. The Church is commissioned to carry on the proclamation of repentance and forgiveness of sin. Grace prevails!

---

1. David L. Tiede, *Luke: Augsburg Commentary on the New Testament* (Minneapolis: Augsburg, 1988), pp. 250-251.

2. *Ibid.,* p. 256.

Chapter 30
Proper 17: Sunday between August 28 and September 3

Luke 14:1, 7-14

Chapter 14 in Luke's Gospel consists of a series of discourses in the setting of a banquet. David Tiede suggests that this banquet context may be assumed through 17:10.

> *Jesus is beginning a discourse on the protocol of the kingdom of God, and the guest list of those "beloved of God" is remarkable ... The Messiah is challenging accepted views of who is "elect" of God, now, in the on-going struggle of the dominion that is emerging, and in the resurrection of the just which is to come.*[1]

We have noted elsewhere that mealtimes are special times of revelation in Luke's telling of the story. There are many mealtime events in the third Gospel: 7:36-50; 9:13-17; 10:38-42; 11:37-54; 22:14-38; 24:28-35. These are some of the most important stories in Luke's Gospel. What is revealed most clearly in today's story — and the stories that bracket it — is the graciousness of God's invitation to God's banquet of life.

Luke 14:2-6 is omitted from the lectionary. It is a story with many parallels to Luke 13:10-17. We made the connections between these stories in Chapter 28. A woman and a man are healed on the Sabbath, causing great consternation to the Pharisees. Such people certainly ought not be healed on the Sabbath. We have rules. We have laws. Rules and laws also appear in the text assigned for today and the parable that follows it (14:15-24). God doesn't seem to pay any attention to such laws when it comes to the deeply felt needs of real human beings. The God of Jesus is a God of the Gospel and not a God of the Law in relation to human need. That's part of the reality of the story in 14:2-6, 7-14 and 15-24.

Tiede discusses the text given for today under the helpful title: "Seating Charts and Guest Lists in the Kingdom." Commentaries agree that the matter of proper seating at an important meal was very important in Jesus' day. Seating assignments had both social and religious connotations. Jesus gives his own seating advice.

> *It would be a total misunderstanding to take Jesus' words as a demand for a Christian "humility" that says "I am nothing" ... A person who attaches no value to him- or herself cannot truly value others ... It is nearer to the mark to say that Jesus would like to free his listeners from the need always to advance their own cause and come out on top or to count the profit ... only the concluding words render these admonitions transparent. They say that it is God alone who gives us identity, honor, and position.*[2]

The precedent-shattering nature of the Inviting One comes to the fore most clearly in verses 12-14. When we humans invite people to a banquet we are not to invite only those who can repay us. Grace is always free. It comes without strings attached. God's invitation is graceful. It invites those who cannot repay.

> *In Deuteronomy 14:29 such an appeal to generous sharing of food with the "Levite and the sojourner, the fatherless, and the widow" had already been linked with God's bless-ing. But when the list goes beyond the poor to include the* maimed, the lame and the blind, *a new level of kingdom protocol is revealed.*[3]

Kingdom protocol indeed! This is a *great reversal*. The exalted are humbled. The humble are exalted. The first are last. The last are first. The symbolism of the list is that it is those who need help who are invited to the banquet. Tax collectors and sinners are welcome as well. Surely, "God has brought down the powerful from their thrones, and lifted up the lowly ..." (Luke 1:52). We identifed this theme and the Lukan passages that carry it through in Chapter 1. The second great reversal theme of the Magnificat is also present in these stories in Luke 14: "God has filled the hungry with good things, and sent the rich away empty" (1:53).

This same theme is pounded home in verses 15-24. A great banquet was prepared and the invitations sent out to those worthy to attend. But the worthy ones shunned the invitations. The householder was angry. "Go out at once into the streets and lanes of the town and bring in the poor, the crippled, the blind, and the lame." This is the same list as that given in 14:13! When Jesus stood up in his hometown synagogue and read from Isaiah he identified precisely this cast of characters as those whom he had come to serve (Luke 4:18-19). The story in 7:18-23 presents the same cast! We are at the very heart of Luke's Gospel here! Jesus Christ has come from God with an invitation to the sinful and needy folk on earth. This is what God is about in Jesus!

Homiletical Directions

The stories in 14:1-24 can be stitched together in one sermon. They can be stitched together under a number of themes. These stories can be told to show how God brings down the powerful and lifts the lowly (1:52). They can be told to show how God fills the hungry with good things and sends the rich away empty (1:53). They can be told to underline the *great reversal* theme in Luke. They can be told in order to lead to a proclamatory invitation to our hearers.

The narrative approach you take will depend somewhat upon your use of the Magnificat, Luke 4:18-19, and Luke 7:18-23 in earlier sermons during the year of Luke. These theme passages from Luke 1, 4, and 7 certainly set up these wonderfully grace-filled stories in Chapter 14. If you can use them again let Story One be an abbreviated version of the Magnificat underscoring the "great reversal" theme. God is to come in Jesus Christ and turn everything upside down with respect to the world's values.

Story Two would make use of either Luke 4:16-21 or 7:18-23. Either one of these stories makes it very clear who Jesus came for. This week's text is not an exception to the main themes of Luke. This text clearly demonstrates that Jesus' ministry is geared to those in deepest human need.

Story Three would be the stories in 14:1-24. The story in verses 2-6 tells us that Jesus invites people to share his power even when

160

it breaks long-standing religious laws. The story in verses 7-12 reveals the "great reversal" that takes place when Jesus invites those in the lowest places to be in the highest places. (Taking the lowest places is something like repentance.) In verses 12-14 the emphasis is on the kind of people Jesus would invite to a banquet — to his banquet! This theme is underscored in verses 15-24.

These are stories of the nature of the Inviting God. This sermon ought to close with the Inviting God speaking to people of today. God's Son Jesus is speaking to us today through these stories. He is saying something like this: "I see you today in the midst of your deep human need. I see you in your sinfulness. I see you and I invite you to share my eternal banquet. I have come to turn everything upside down when it comes to human thoughts about God's kingdom. I have come to reverse the normal order of things. I have come to invite the poor, the maimed, the lame, and the blind to my banquet. I have come to call sinners to my banquet. I have come to call you to my banquet."

---

1. David L. Tiede, *Luke: Augsburg Commentary on the New Testament* (Minneapolis: Augsburg, 1988), p. 261.

2. Eduard Schweitzer, *The Good News According to Luke* (Atlanta: John Knox Press, 1984), p. 236.

3. Tiede, *op. cit.,* p. 265.

Chapter 31
Proper 18: Sunday between September 4 and 10

Luke 14:25-33

In this week's text Jesus fixes his gaze on the multitudes who have followed him and calls them to discipleship. The earlier stories in Luke 14 have been stories of the incredibly gracious character of God who *invites* even the poor, the maimed, the lame, and the blind to the great banquet. The invitation has been extended. People have come. Multitudes follow Jesus "on his way" to Jerusalem. It's time for the multitudes to hear the challenge of following, the challenge of discipleship, which Jesus' disciples have already heard.

This is not the first time that the Lukan Jesus has spoken of the demands of discipleship. What we have here, however, is a good *summary* of what has gone before. The challenge to be disciples focuses on three demands: leave your family, lose yourself, let loose of your possessions. Each of these demands is followed by the refrain: "cannot be my disciple."

"Let anyone with ears to hear listen!" (14:35). We heard the call to listen most prominently in the Parable of the Sower (8:8, 10, 18). Hearing and doing the Word of God is a constant Lukan theme (6:46-49). When one hears the Sower the seed produces fruit!

Word one from the mouth of Jesus has to do with leaving one's family. We have heard this word before (9:59-62). Kingdom priorities and family priorities are sometimes in conflict.

Word two is the word of the cross we are to bear. We have heard this word before (9:23-27). These verses follow immediately upon Jesus' passion prediction (9:22). A Messiah who is "on the way" to Jerusalem, a Messiah who is "on the way" to his cross, invites us to take up our cross as well.

Word three is a word about renunciation of possessions. The matter of possessions dominates Luke's thinking. It was clearly a

162

problem for the church to which he wrote. It is a problem for the church today as well. Already in the Magnificat, Mother Mary has sung of a God who fills the hungry with good things and sends the rich away empty (1:53). Jesus announced to the good folks in his hometown that his ministry would be to the poor (4:18-19). The disciples "left everything" and followed Jesus (5:11, 28). Jesus uttered words of blessing over the poor (6:20) and words of woe to those with riches and possession (6:24). The stories of the rich young ruler and Zacchaeus demonstrate a wrong way and a right way to live with possessions (18:18-30; 19:1-10). (See Chapter 40.)

What are we to make of Jesus' hard words that call to radical discipleship?

> ... it would be incorrect to regard these commands as initiation requirements or ordeals which all who enlist in this kingdom must first perform to qualify. Nothing in the story supports such an understanding. But those who do become Jesus' disciples should know that the securities of family bonds, personal dignity and life, and possessions will be at risk. And the costs of loyalty to this Messiah and his reign will be high.[1]

Eduard Schweizer comments thus:

> Of course not all are called in the same way to the same form of discipleship. But it is equally sure that there is no such thing as a totally middle-class discipleship where there is only preservation of one's heritage and radical renunciation can never flower.[2]

We cannot back away from Jesus' Word that calls us to discipleship. Neither should we conclude that it is up to us to fulfill this word of Jesus. Such a conclusion would lead us only to despair. Jesus' Word stands. With that Word spoken comes also the power to transform us into the kinds of disciples Jesus wants us to be.

163

Homiletical Directions

This week's text leads very naturally into a teaching sermon on Jesus' threefold call to discipleship. Our sermon could also, however, deal with the threefold call and keep a narrative flow. We might begin with the narrative context in Luke 14. If you did not make use of the story in Luke 14:15-24 last Sunday you could use it this week as a narrative introduction. It is the story of a radical invitation and we understand it to be of the nature of Jesus' invitation to us to come to his great banquet.

So we come. We respond to the invitation and come to the banquet. Now we hear what the cost of following Jesus' invitation will be. Jesus' first word is about family. As we tell about family we might remind our hearers of Jesus' similar call in 9:59-62.

Jesus' second call is the call to take up the cross. We can refer here to Jesus' passion prediction (9:22) and Jesus' first call to his disciples to take up the cross and follow him (9:23-27). This week's text provides us with two brief story examples of counting the cost that ought to be told at this point. These stories could be expanded.

Jesus' final call is the call to renounce possessions. In the discussion above we enumerated a number of places in Luke's Gospel where this theme is also enunciated. Some of these stories might be told at this point.

The question that emerges naturally at the conclusion of the telling of these stories is the question of meaning. What does this mean for disciples today? How are we to understand Jesus' words? How are we to be faithful disciples today? One way to bring this sermon to a conclusion would be to make closing reference to the Parable of the Sower. This parable is not appointed for the Lukan year. (See Chapter 13 for an earlier discussion on possible use of the Parable of the Sower.)

The connection to the Parable of the Sower is implicit in Luke 14:35: "Let anyone with ears to hear listen!" Luke 14:35 is not appointed as part of this week's Gospel reading but it belongs together with it. In the Parable of the Sower we hear that the Sower sows the Word. This week's text is about the Sower's call to discipleship. There are many obstacles on the path of those who hear the call to discipleship. The devil may snatch the Word from us (8:12). In times of temptation we might fail (8:13). Finally, the cares and riches and pleasures of life may choke out the life of the seed that is sown (8:14).

In the Parable of the Sower the good soil is described as those who hear the word and hold it fast (8:15). Such soil produces much fruit. The fruit of discipleship comes from the sowing of the word and the "holding fast" of the word that is sown. Pay attention to how you listen (8:18)! Human listening is of great benefit because the Word of the Sower has the power to produce the fruit it demands. When one hears the Sower call to discipleship, the very word of calling has the power to create fruit a hundredfold. Discipleship always begins in the ears. Discipleship always begins with listening. Discipleship tends the Word of God and the Word of God has the power to create the fruit of discipleship it commands!

Jesus' call to discipleship in this week's text comes as a word of judgment upon those of us who have heard this call before. We have not lived up to Jesus' call. We cannot live up to this call to discipleship with our own efforts. Only the transforming power of the Word that is sown in our hearts can create disciples. Our sermon ought to conclude, therefore, with a call to our hearers to cling to the Word that is sown by the Sower. This is a Sower who has graciously invited the poor and the maimed, the lame and the blind, to be part of his kingdom. This is a Sower who has graciously invited us to be part of his kingdom. This is a Sower whose sowing of the Word has the power to create disciples out of all who pay attention to his Word!

---

1. David L. Tiede, *Luke: Augsburg Commentary on the New Testament* (Minneapolis: Augsburg, 1988), p. 207.

2. Eduard Schweizer, *The Good News According to Luke* (Atlanta: John Knox Press, 1984), p. 242.

Chapter 32
Proper 19: Sunday between September 11 and 17

Luke 15:1-10

"The Spirit of the Lord is upon me because ... God has sent me to proclaim release to the captives ..." (Luke 4:18). Over and over again we have come back to this passage which Jesus read from the book of Isaiah to his hometown people in Nazareth. Luke 4:18-19 along with Mary's Magnificat (Luke 1:46-55) and Luke 7:18-23 set forth the underlying themes of Luke's Gospel. Robert Tannehill discusses the subject of "release of sins" at some length.[1] He translates "release" as *forgiveness*. Based on this translation Tannehill proceeds to show how forgiveness of sins is a central theme of Luke's Gospel. The following stories from Luke's Gospel treat this theme: 5:17-26; 5:27-32 (cf. v. 32: "I have come to call not the righteous but sinners to repentance"); 7:36-50. Each of these stories helps to introduce the parables of the lost in Luke 15:1-10. Stories that follow Luke 15 also sing out this theme: 18:9-14; 19:1-10. Clearly the work of Jesus in releasing us from sin lies at the very heart of Luke's Gospel.

In his massive commentary on Luke Joseph Fitzmyer refers to the material that begins with Luke 15 and continues through 19:10 as the "Gospel of the Outcast." Story after story shows God's "... deliberate attempt to show ... concern for those human beings whom people tend to despise or condemn." He cites the story of the dishonest manager (16:1-8a), the dishonest judge (18:1-8), the rich man and Lazarus (16:19-31), the ten lepers (17:11-19), the Pharisee and the toll-collector (18:9-14) and the story of Zacchaeus (19:1-10) as related stories of God's concern for the outcast.[2] These stories in Luke 15 are, therefore, the heart of the matter for Luke.

The material from 15:1—17:10 appears to reflect a single occasion. It begins with the murmuring of the scribes and Pharisees. This challenge of the Pharisees to the teachings of Jesus also ties this passage to many other passages in Luke. The Pharisees were

166

always asking challenging questions trying to "catch" Jesus. They challenge him when he eats with tax collectors and sinners (see also 5:29-32); when he heals on the Sabbath (6:6-11; 13:10-17; 14:1-6); when he eats in a Pharisee's house (7:36-50; 11:37-54; 14:1-24); and when a Jewish leader asks Jesus what he must do to inherit eternal life (10:25-37; 18:18-23).

The murmuring of the scribes and Pharisees is about table fellowship which was a critical issue in Jesus' day. To eat with another person was a sign of deep fellowship. One only ate with a select group of properly qualified people. In the eyes of the Pharisees, however, Jesus ate with all the wrong people. That's what the Pharisees thought. It's probably also what the elder brother thought about the prodigal son. Jesus answers the charge by telling stories! He tells three stories about One who welcomes sinners and eats with them! He tells stories about God.

One of the strong themes of these three stories (including the prodigal story) is the theme of repentance. A shepherd finds the one sheep out of 100 that was lost. He decides to have a party to celebrate the joyful occasion. Jesus' closing comment on this story is: "Just so, I tell you there will be more joy in heaven over one sinner who *repents* than over 99 righteous persons who need no repentance." Who repented? The sheep? The only possible action in this story which could constitute repentance is the *finding of the lost. Repentance, therefore, may be defined as our acceptance of being found.*[3]

Jesus' second story underscores the same reality. The lost coin is found. That's the central thing that happens in this story. The lost coin is found. This time it is a woman who plays the role of God who rejoices when the lost is found. She throws a party. And Jesus says: "Just so, I tell you, there is joy in the presence of the angels of God over one sinner who *repents*." Again, there is only one action here that can be construed as repentance. The lost is found!

This theme of repentance carries over into the story of the Prodigal Son. Though this story is appointed for next week it is difficult not to connect it to the stories that precede it. We'll have more to say on the Prodigal Son in the next chapter, however. It is

Kenneth Bailey's conviction that one of the purposes of these back-to-back-to-back stories is to give a new definition of repentance. He maintains that the rabbis of Jesus' day understood repentance to have three components: 1) Confession of sin. 2) Compensation for the evil done. 3) Sincerity in keeping the law previously broken.[4] Bailey goes on to say that the Prodigal Son intended to carry out this threefold model of repentance. When this young man "came to himself" he decided that his best course of action was to return home. Upon his arrival at home he would make a confession of his sins: "Father, I have sinned against heaven and before you; I am no longer worthy to be called your son...." That's the first stage of repentance.

The second thing the son would do on his arrival home is to make clear his plan for compensation for the evil he has done. "Treat me as one of your hired hands." Bailey argues that in its Middle Eastern context this can only mean that the son has come up with a plan for compensation. He will become a hired worker and pay off his debts! Then he can be a son again! That's the second stage of repentance.

The third stage of repentance is implied in the attitude of the Prodigal. He would, in *sincerity*, throw himself on his father's mercy and plan to work off his debts. So far, so good. So far, this is a traditional story of the need for repentance. BUT! The son hardly got a chance to make his speech. His father ran out and embraced him before he could get a word out of his mouth. *The lost was found!* The dead was alive (15:24)! The son realized what had happened to him in this incredible moment of grace. He was found. He was a son again. He was alive again. He threw away his traditional plan of repentance. He didn't need it! All he said now was: "Father, I have sinned against heaven and before you; I am no longer worthy to be called your son" (15:21).

This prayer of repentance only acknowledges that he was lost. There is no compensation plan now. He won't have to pay off his debts by being a hired hand! He won't have to earn his place at the Father's table. The Father has welcomed him home and restored him to sonship. Let's have a party! That's the kind of God that the God of Jesus is. God throws a party when lost sinners are found.

Homiletical Directions

We have mentioned above a number of passages that are related to these three stories of repentance and forgiveness. These passages suggest many narrative connections that can be made by connecting the stories in Luke 15 with other Lukan stories. We will confine our remarks for preaching to a sermon with the theme of repentance which makes use of the three stories of the lost being found in this chapter of Luke. The material for such a sermon is given above.

There is a variety of ways that you may choose to set the context for the stories appointed for this week. Having set the context for these stories, tell them one by one with a focus on repentance. It is clear in the stories of the lost sheep and the lost coin that the repentance which God celebrates in heaven is quite different than either rabbinic or contemporary notions of repentance. What happens in these stories is that the lost is found. That's how repentance is defined in these stories. Repentance is our acceptance of the reality that God has found us in Jesus Christ. This means, of course, that we acknowledge our own "lostness."

The Prodigal Son story needs to be told with more breadth than the sheep and the coin stories. Keep the focus on repentance. Use Bailey's rabbinic definition of repentance to contrast with what happens in this story as we have recounted above. The Prodigal experienced the incredible power of grace in this story. He experienced the forgiveness of his sins. His father announced: "Quickly, bring out a robe — the best one — and put it on him; put a ring on his finger and sandals on his feet. And get the fatted calf and kill it, and let us eat and celebrate; for this son of mine was dead and is alive again; he was lost and is found!" (15:22-24). The father's announcement changed everything for the Prodigal! He was alive again. The lost had been found. In light of his acceptance, he repented. He acknowledged that he was lost. He celebrated that he was found. God throws a party when lost sinners repent!

After telling these three stories with a focus on repentance we need to call upon our hearers to think over their own lostness. Do this in some concrete way in the midst of the sermon. A time of silence to think about lostness. A sheet of paper provided to write down a few thoughts. A sentence prayer composed by each hearer

169

which speaks to God of lostness. Part of the reality of repentance in the Bible stories in Luke 15 is the recognition of our lost condition.

After this time of personal reflection it is time to announce the gospel word. The stories themselves give us the language to speak for God. The God of Jesus says to lost persons today through these stories: "I have come to find those dead in sin. I have come to find the lost. I have come to find you, just you! When I find you my heart overflows with joy. When the lost are found everyone in heaven gathers for a party."

We hope it is Party Sunday in your church. Party Sunday is the day of Eucharist! "Join me at my table," the God of Jesus says. "Join me at this mealtime-party. Let us eat and celebrate. This is still the place on earth that I 'welcome sinners and eat with them.' "

P.S.: What might it do for our evangelism efforts if people knew that our church is a church that throws a party whenever the lost are found?

---

1. Robert C. Tannehill, *The Narrative Unity of Luke-Acts, Volume One* (Philadelphia: Fortress Press, 1986), pp. 103-109.

2. Joseph Fitzmyer, *The Gospel According to Luke, X-XXIV* (New York: Doubleday, 1985), p. 1072.

3. I am indebted to Kenneth E. Bailey's book, *Finding the Lost: Cultural Keys to Luke 15* (St. Louis: Concordia, 1992), for its discussion of repentance in the Luke 15 stories. I highly recommend this book for its incredible insights into this Lukan chapter.

4. *Ibid.*, p. 138.

Luke 15:1-3, 11b-32

We come now to the story in Luke in which the heart of the Christian faith is explicated in story form. Luke 15 is treated as a whole in Chapter 32. Please refer to this chapter for a discussion of the context of Luke 15 within Luke's Gospel. In Chapter 32 it is suggested that for Proper 19 it would be well to tell all three stories of the lost that are contained in Luke 15. The focus of such a sermon would be on the new understanding of repentance which these stories contain. You might determine that the repentance theme suggested there is appropriate for preaching during Lent. We reviewed the theme of repentance in Luke's Gospel in Chapter 4.

Homiletical Directions

Who was it that taught us that the sermon points that we might make on this parable are more important than the story itself? Why should we take this incredible story and turn it into lessons of our own devising? Our suggestion is that the sermon for this week *be a retelling of the Prodigal Son story*. The open-endedness of the story invites our hearers to participate in the parable by inviting each to provide his/her own ending to the story.

Kenneth E. Bailey has written a marvelous book in which he seeks to provide Middle Eastern insights into the understanding of this story. Bailey has worked in the Middle East most of his life. He understands its culture. He has a grasp of the languages so that he has access to "eastern" attempts at understanding this parable over the course of the church's life. His goal, he writes, is to rediscover the original cultural assumptions behind this story. Our task here is to share some of these insights in order to enhance your telling of the Prodigal Son story. The amplifications given here can simply be woven into your telling of the tale.[1]

There are three main characters in this story: the father, the elder son and the younger son. It is a surprise in a Middle Eastern story that the younger son speaks *first*. He is out of his place already! *What* he speaks is even more astonishing. He is basically telling his father to "drop dead." All Eastern commentators on this story acknowledge that the son's request is totally illegitimate. It is an unthinkable request. A father only gives the inheritance in death.

The father should explode with anger at such an inappropriate request. He does not explode. He grants a request that was completely unimaginable in his time. Such is the nature of the father in this story. This is a very unusual father! "He is willing to grant ultimate freedom; the freedom to reject the love offered to him (the Prodigal) by a compassionate father" (Bailey, p. 118). And the father did it. He divided his *life* with his sons.

The son promptly goes out and squanders his property in dissolute living. Eastern commentators do not take this to mean a necessarily immoral lifestyle on the part of the son. He is a spendthrift to be sure. He spends money like it is going out of style. We often talk about the Prodigal as being engaged in all kinds of immoral activities. Eastern commentators do not read it that way. It is the Elder Brother who suggests that the Prodigal has spent his money on prostitutes (v. 30). The Elder Brother is not a very reliable source of information on the matter!

The younger son soon began to be in deep need. What to do? Returning home was not a likely option at this point. Such a return would bring great shame on his father, on his brother, and on his whole community. Shame was to be avoided at all costs in the culture of the time.

In his desperation the Prodigal attaches himself to a *Gentile*. We know he is a Gentile because he raises pigs. How desperate he was! He sought pleasure and found pain. He sought freedom and got bondage. The son must now do things with pigs that were unthinkable and deeply offensive to his family and community. Bailey suggests that what is broken here is *relationships* more than laws. It is the broken relationships with his family and community that have led him down the pathway to shame.

172

In verse 16 the Prodigal reaches the low point. He wishes he were a pig! At least the pigs had something to eat.

And then the young man "came to himself." We usually think of this as his moment of repentance. But that is not the meaning of repentance that these stories of the lost in Luke 15 convey. Repentance in these stories occurs when the *lost is found.* (See Chapter 32 for a discussion of repentance.) Bailey notes that Arabic translations of these words read that the Prodigal "got smart." He got smart in the sense that he now was ready to look out for himself. He had a plan. He knew that his father had many hired hands who had bread enough and to spare. He'll go back home. He knows he can't go back as a son. He won't go back as a slave. So he will go back as a hired hand. "He will not live at home, and not join the family. He will pay his own way. First he must convince his father to support the plan" (Bailey, p. 133). The Prodigal's plan, that is, is to *earn his restored status.* "Give me a second chance. I'll earn it back and repay you. I'm not now worthy to be called your son, but I will be if you give me a chance" (Bailey, p. 133).

It is hard to read this interpretation by Bailey and not think of Martin Luther's determination to *earn his restored status with God.* The Prodigal Son story would make a good Reformation Sunday story!

In Chapter 32 we set forth Bailey's suggestion that the three elements of rabbinic repentance were: 1) Confession of sin. 2) Compensation for the evil done. 3) Sincerity in keeping the law previously broken. The Prodigal's plan fits the norms of traditional repentance. The Prodigal will *fulfill the law of repentance and be restored.* He will, that is, if the father will be satisfied with the son's proposal to enter a master-craftsman relationship with his son. Will the father accept this plan? NO! The father has been watching the distant road as it approaches the village where the people lived. People went forth from the village each day to work in their fields. The father watches that road. He knows that if the son returns the village will treat him with contempt. He is determined *to reach the boy first.* "He alone can protect the boy from the hostility of the town" (Bailey, p. 143).

When the father sees the boy coming he has compassion and runs to meet him. He *runs*! No Middle Eastern gentleman would ever run in public. This is the only story of its kind in the Gospels where a man runs in public. In order to run, a man had to gather up his robe and expose his legs. This was a great shame in this culture. The father, therefore, exposes himself to shame. He dismisses the fact that this will dishonor his family. And he runs! Bailey notes that Arabic translations of this story refuse to translate this running! They avoid this because it is clear that the father here is *acting as God acts towards prodigals*. Running in public is too humiliating to attribute to a person who symbolizes God. "... in a humiliating public demonstration [the father] takes upon himself the form of a servant and runs down the village street to the boy ... he wants to reach the boy before the boy reaches the village" (Bailey, p. 146).

Bailey calls this a *costly demonstration of unexpected love*. He thinks of the father here as a *suffering servant*. He endures humility. His love is made visible in public. "I am convinced that at this point Jesus is talking about himself and about the meaning of his suffering" (Bailey, p. 148).

We have the image here of the Running God. God running in public. How humiliating! This image goes on in its development The father *kisses his son*. In public! A mother might do this. A father — never! Jesus portrays God here as a *mother* in the manner of Isaiah 66:10-14.

The God symbolized in this story is clearly a God of *powerless love.*

> *... this almighty father has no power at all. He has decided once and for all in favor of love and knows that if he acted in this fashion, he would have lost his sons forever ... Within five minutes, in Jesus' parable, the father is standing outside in the dark, where he could catch pneumonia, facing his elder son with no means but words to express what is in his burning heart. In Jesus' narrative the kingdom of God becomes real. But a few weeks or months later he will hang on the cross, equally powerless, mocked by all....[2]*

The son accepts what the father offers. He omits his *plan* from his well rehearsed speech. In verse 18 the son is talking about being treated as a hired hand. That's the speech he practiced. The speech he delivered (v. 21) omits this plan altogether. He won't have to earn his way back to a restored status of sonship. The father simply gives him back his sonship as an act of grace. The son accepts. *He repents: he accepts being found!*

A change of clothes is called for by the father. The son had come home in rags. The father wants no one to see him dressed so poorly. Rather, the Prodigal gets the best robe, the father's robe! The son is thus honored. He receives a ring as a symbol that he is trusted. He puts on sandals and with them his self-respect. A mighty reversal has taken place. "God has brought down the powerful from their thrones *and lifted up the lowly* ..." (Luke 1:52).

The father proceeds to throw a banquet as an act of formal reconciliation that involves the whole village. They kill the fatted calf for the occasion. Since fatted calves are killed only for those with greatest respect, Bailey concludes that *the banquet is in honor of the father and the reconciliation that has been achieved.* Just as the shepherd's party was not in honor of the sheep nor the woman's party in honor of the coin, so this party is *in honor of the One who finds!*

Finally, there is the matter of the Elder Brother. This series of stories began in reply to the words of the Pharisees and scribes: "This fellow welcomes sinners and eats with them" (15:2). The Elder Brother now speaks on their behalf. See especially verses 29-30. The Elder Brother now brings shame on his father by refusing to attend the banquet of reconciliation. It is probably the public nature of this reconciliation that affronts the Elder Brother. He prefers the righteousness of the Law. "I have never disobeyed your command" (v. 29). He sounds just like the Pharisee praying in the temple (Luke 18:11-12).

Bailey lists many similarities between Prodigal Son and Elder Brother. The key realities are that both sons insult their father and break the relationship. Each seeks to manipulate his father. Each finds a primary community apart from home. The Prodigal looks for community in the far country, the Elder Brother with his "friends" (v. 29). Yet for each son the father makes a public and costly demonstration of unexpected love. In the father's eyes *both sons are equally welcome at the banquet.* The one who broke the law and the one who kept the law are welcome only by the grace of the father.

Bailey points out structural similarities between the story of the Prodigal and the story of the Brother. The most important structural similarity is that the father's speech to each brother concludes with the same words: "This son of mine was dead and is alive again; he was lost and is found!" (v. 24). "This brother of yours was dead and has come to life; he was lost and has been found" (v. 32). There is one momentous difference, however. After the father's words in verse 24 we hear, "They began to celebrate." We know how this story ends. In verse 32, however, the story just stops. But it does not stop! *Everyone awaits the response of the Elder Brother.*

In other words, the story of the Prodigal Son is *open-ended.* The audience must finish the story! How do we respond to the father's invitation? The scribes and Pharisees end this story by killing Jesus. What shall *we* do with Jesus? The sermon can end just there. Challenge those who hear the story to finish it themselves!

God says to each and every one of us through this story: "You were dead and now you are alive. You were lost and now you are found. You were alienated, now you are invited to the reconciliation banquet. This God of powerless love awaits the honor of your reply."

---

1. Kenneth E. Bailey, *Finding The Lost: Cultural Keys to Luke 15* (St. Louis: Concordia, 1992). Chapters 3 and 4 deal with the story of the Prodigal Son and the Elder Brother.

2. Eduard Schweizer, *The Good News According to Luke* (Atlanta: John Knox Press, 1984), p. 250.

Chapter 34
Proper 20: Sunday between September 18 and 24

Luke 16:1-13

We have made reference to these verses in Chapter 11 and in Chapter 24. It would be helpful if you would review these chapters that help to put this week's text in its broader Lukan context. In our comments on the Parable of the Sower we have also noted that among the fundamental temptations that keep us from hearing the word of God (the seed that is sown) are the cares and riches and pleasures of life. See Luke 8:4-15, v. 14. In Chapter 31 we dealt with the material in Luke 14:25-33 in which Jesus called his disciples to leave family, lose self, and let loose of all possessions (v. 33). The matter of wealth and possessions and the concern for the poor are clearly fundamental themes in Luke's Gospel.

Jesus' story begins with the introduction of a steward who was *squandering his master's property.* There is a link here to the story of the Prodigal Son which has preceded it. The Prodigal was also reported to be one who *squandered his* [father's] *property in dissolute living* (15:13).

This is a difficult text! The standard commentaries will help you to come to terms with its meaning. We will just make a few comments. Eduard Schweizer makes the helpful point that what is praised in the manager is his sagacity. The unrighteous steward (v. 8) is praised! The fact that he is unrighteous,

> *... makes the praise accorded to him even more striking. The point is therefore neither the demonic effects of wealth nor the right use of property but the sagacity of the steward. He is smart because he knows what is coming and adapts to it. Thus the parable understands the present as the possibility of adapting to the future ... the parable holds up the man of this world as a model for the sons of light.*[1]

177

Joseph Fitzmyer speaks similarly:

> *What is the point of this parable? ... The master's approval bears on the prudence of the manager who realized how best to use what material possessions were his to ensure his future security. The "dishonest manager" thus becomes a model for Christian disciples, not because of his dishonesty, but because of his prudence.*[2]

Luke 16:11 appears to support these views and serves as a helpful interpretive key to this complex story. If we cannot be trusted to manage well the affairs of this world that are entrusted to us, how can we be entrusted with the management of true riches? This is not to say that the two realities are like each other. They are not. We cannot serve both of these realities. We cannot serve God and Mammon. Schweizer writes that "Mammon" originally meant "that in which one trusts." We can't trust two things. We must have only one source of our ultimate concern! We must not commit *idolatry.* The First Commandment is at stake here.

Homiletical Directions

We have made reference above to other chapters in this book where this week's text is set in narrative context. The Homiletical Directions in those chapters may prove useful for your sermon work on this week's text.

The theme of idolatry is raised in this text. Idolatry is a constant theme in the Bible and could certainly be the theme of a narrative sermon for this week. In his *Large Catechism* Martin Luther wrote as follows on the First Commandment:

> *A god is that to which we look for all good and in which we find refuge in every time of need. To have a god is nothing else than to trust and believe him with our whole heart ... If your faith and trust are right, then your God is the true God ... if your trust is false and wrong, then you have not the true God. For these two belong together, faith and God. That to which your heart clings and entrusts itself, is, I say, really your God.*

A narrative sermon on idolatry could begin with the First Commandment and its narrative context in the Old Testament. See Exodus 20:1-17 or Deuteronomy 5:1-21. This could be followed up with the *Shema* (Deuteronomy 6:4-9). This confession that God is *one* and that we are to serve God with *all* our heart, soul, mind, and strength is Israel's fundamental confession.

A wonderful narrative which challenges Israel to choose between God and idol gods is Joshua's speech to his people in Joshua 24. Joshua's sermon sets the context of God's gracious deeds for Israel that call her to serve only this God. "... choose this day whom you will serve, whether the gods your ancestors served in the region beyond the River ... but as for me and my household, we will serve the Lord" (Joshua 24:15).

Isaiah 44 represents a different historical context than the book of Joshua. The message of this chapter is also a call to choose the true God or an idol. The description of an idol in 44:9-20 is a comical look at idols that we probably never have a chance to narrate.

This sermon could close by presenting Jesus' call in this week's text. "You cannot serve two masters. You cannot serve God and wealth." The "Why?" question arises here. Why serve God? Why not serve Wealth? Wealth certainly qualifies as an idol in our culture! It might be well to cite the *promises that Wealth makes* at this point.

Close by reciting *the promises that God makes* which speak to the "Why?" question. These promises can be taken from the Old Testament passages at which we have looked. "I am the Lord your God, who brought you out of the land of slavery ..." (Exodus 20:1). This is the reason, this is the context, in which God asks for a minimal response of obedience from Israel.

The speech of Joshua (Joshua 24) recites a panoply of God's gracious deeds of deliverance. Isaiah 44 is filled with wonderful passages calling people to serve God, not idols: "I am the first and I am the last; besides me there is no god. Who is like me? Let them proclaim it ... Is there any god besides me? There is no other rock; I know not one" (Isaiah 44:6-8). "I formed you, you are my servant; O Israel, you will not be forgotten by me. I have swept away your transgressions like a cloud and your sins like a mist" (Isaiah 44:21). "I am the Lord, who made all things, who alone stretched out the heavens ..." (Isaiah 44:24.) See also 44:25-28.

This sermon might close with an appropriate prayer to God for guidance in choosing this day whom we shall serve.

---

1. Eduard Schweizer, *The Good News According to Luke* (Atlanta: John Knox Press, 1984), pp. 254-255.

2. Joseph Fitzmyer, *The Gospel According to Luke, X-XXIV* (New York: Doubleday, 1985), p. 1098.

Chapter 35
Proper 21: Sunday between September 25 and October 1

Luke 16:19-31

The assigned Lukan text for this week is another uniquely Lukan story which is so very well known. In Chapter 1 we talked about two themes from the Magnificat which flow through the Gospel of Luke. One of these themes is: "God has scattered the powerful from their thrones, and lifted up the lowly ..." (Luke 1:52). The other is: "God has filled the hungry with good things and sent the rich away empty" (1:53). Both of these themes can be understood to be part of a larger theme of *reversal*. The gospel that is incarnate in Jesus Christ turns the world upside down!

There is also a reference to other Lukan stories in the plea to "Father Abraham" by the rich man (16:24). Luke consistently refers to "Abraham" when he thinks of ways in which the people of Israel trusted and/or abused the promises of God (3:8; 13:16; 19:9).

Homiletical Directions

In Chapter 1 we cited stories in Luke which carry out these themes of reversal. We included the story of the rich man and Lazarus under both themes. The Lazarus story, therefore, can be stitched together with these other Lukan stories to demonstrate the reality of the reversal of powerful and lowly or the reversal of rich and poor. This week's text affords a wonderful opportunity to work with one or the other of these dominant Lukan themes by telling a series of Lukan narratives.

We have discussed many of these reversal stories in Luke in earlier chapters of this book. The Homiletical Directions in Chapters 11, 16, 24, and 30 may be consulted for ways in which Luke's reversal stories can be stitched together.

Luke 17:5-10

These verses of instruction to the disciples close a discourse of Jesus that began in 15:1. It would probably be best to include 17:1-4 as part of this week's assigned text so as not to truncate this brief section of teaching on Jesus' part.

> *Four sets of isolated sayings of Jesus now bring the second part of the travel account to a close: 17:1-3a, on scandals and stumbling blocks; 17:3b-4, on the duty of Christian forgiveness; 17:5-6, on the power of Christian faith; and 17:7-10, on the inadequacy of Christian service.*[1]

These brief instructions that Jesus gives to his disciples are fairly transparent in meaning. There are no hidden agendas here. As small pieces of instruction they do not live in narrative analogy with many other parts of Luke's Gospel. One exception to this might be Jesus' call to his disciples to be the kind of people who forgive others who repent. Repentance and forgiveness are major themes in Luke's Gospel. For a discussion of these themes see Chapters 4 and 32.

In verse 5 the disciples abruptly ask Jesus to "increase our faith." This notion that faith can be increased is a new note in Luke's story. In 8:22-25 we have a story in which the disciples were caught in a windstorm out on the lake. Their lives were in danger. They awoke their master and cried, "Master, Master, we are perishing." Jesus awoke and calmed the wind and the waves. In the calm Jesus said to his disciples, "Where is your faith?" We are made aware through this narrative that Jesus and his disciples have talked about the disciples' lack of faith. Their request to "increase our faith" in 17:5, therefore, has some narrative background. In Luke 22:32 Jesus offers to pray for Peter's faith. On the road to Emmaus

Jesus acknowledges that it is hard for this generation to *believe* that it was necessary that the Messiah should suffer (24:25).

David Tiede makes the following point about "faith" in Luke's Gospel:

> *In Luke, faith is always faith in God or God's Messiah Jesus (see especially 5:20; 7:9; Acts 20:21; 24:24; 26:18), and it is closely correlated with the presence of the Holy Spirit (Acts 6:5; 11:24). Faith is a power because it is the link to the power of God.*[2]

Tiede interprets Jesus' reply to the disciples that their faith might be like a grain of mustard seed as a sign of assurance. One needn't have *great* faith. Neither the disciples nor we ourselves should be consumed, as some people are, that our faith be *more* than we can presently see. Belief in Jesus is the heart of the matter. In centering our life in Jesus we ought to pray constantly that our Lord would *increase our faith.* Such is the attitude of Christian prayer. This prayer is always informed, however, by the assurance that a mustard-seed-sized faith has much power!

The closing verses of this week's text indicate that our good works, so to speak, only fulfill our duty as Christians. "We have only done what we ought to have done." For that we can get no *credit*!

> *In the context of this discourse, these words reinforce the assurance Jesus has just given his apostles. The question has been, "How can we do what has been commanded?" The answer is, "Through the power of God at work in faith." Thus those who do* what is commanded *cannot boast of their own achievement. Not only have they only done what was commanded (vv. 7-10), but they are dependent on God all the while.*[3]

Homiletical Directions

As we have indicated above, there is very little of narrative analogy for these verses. This fourfold instruction of Jesus (17:1-10) lends itself very well, however, to a teaching approach. Jesus has four words of instruction for disciples of every age. A four point didactic sermon would be a good way to treat this instruction of Jesus.

---

1. Joseph Fitzmyer, *The Gospel According to Luke, X-XXIV* (New York: Doubleday, 1985), p. 1136.

2. David L. Tiede, *Luke: Augsburg Commentary on the New Testament* (Minneapolis: Augsburg, 1988), p. 294.

3. *Ibid.,* p. 295.

Chapter 37
Proper 23: Sunday between October 9 and 15

Luke 17:11-19

This week's familiar story of the ten lepers begins with a travel marker. We hear that this story took place "on the way to Jerusalem...." We are reminded that this material is all part of the Travel Narrative which began in 9:51 with the words: "he set his face to go to Jerusalem." Other travel markers occur in 13:22, 18:31, and 19:11. The Travel Narrative ends in 19:27. In 19:28 we are informed that travel time is over: "Jesus went on ahead, going up to Jerusalem."

The setting for this story is the land between Samaria and Galilee. Ten lepers met Jesus. "Have mercy upon us," they cried. We expect Jesus to speak a word or effect a touch of healing. Jesus does not do so. His word seems to be only a word of direction: "Go and show yourselves to the priests." The ten lepers headed off for the priest and as they went they were cleansed.

Jesus' command to go to the priests comes right out of the pages of Jewish law. Leviticus 14 details the instruction for the law of the leper on the day of cleansing. It was the task of the priests to pronounce the leper clean. This announcement was necessary in order to restore the leper to the community from which he/she had been isolated.

We assume that the nine lepers, at least, did follow the law. They went to the priests as they had been directed. Perhaps they knew of the right of the priest to pronounce them clean. Jesus' word, therefore, must have filled them with great joy. There was only one good reason to go to the priests. The priests would certify their healing and cleanness. Jesus' word was more than a word of direction. In sending them off to the priests he was, in effect, announcing their healing.

This author, in his youth, once preached a Thanksgiving Day sermon making use of this text. The theme was "Where are the nine?" Only one leper returned to give God thanks. Where are the nine? And where are the nine today? So the sermon went. There is nothing in this text, however, that suggests that the nine were not thankful. They went to the priests. They did their religious duty. Surely they were thankful. But one of them recognized that Jesus was the source of healing. He returned to Jesus in order to *give thanks and praise to God.* And then the shocking line: he was a Samaritan. "Get up and go on your way," Jesus said to the Samaritan who had fallen to his knees, "your faith has made you well." As this story defines it, faith is the recognition of the One who has made us well. Faith returns to Jesus and accepts, praises, and gives thanks for what the Savior has done.

In his narrative commentary on Luke, Robert Tannehill identifies several stories in Luke as "quest" stories. Quest stories, says Tannehill,

> ... *attack stereotypes and prejudices by presenting a series of remarkable individuals who combine characteristics which seem incompatible according to the stereotypes: gratitude and Samaritan, great love and sinful woman (7:36-50), outstanding faith and Gentile (7:2-10).*[1]

These Quest stories, according to Tannehill, are about people in *quest* of help from Jesus. In each of the stories Jesus effects a dramatic reversal of fortune. We remember the *reversal* theme from Mary's Magnificat. It runs throughout Luke's Gospel. According to Tannehill these Quest stories almost always portray Jesus reversing the fortune of oppressed and excluded persons. Jesus speaks his powerful word and there is a reversal in the lives of those who are turned around. These stories also tell us of the *faith* of the one who has made the Quest. Often this faith is exemplified in the very fact that they overcome great obstacles just to fulfill their Quest and come to Jesus.

The first story that Tannehill identifies as a Quest story is in 5:17-26. Friends of a paralytic bring him to Jesus for cure. His fortunes are reversed. A second Quest story is the story of the centurion who had a slave who was at the point of death. The centurion understood the power of a word. He believed that Jesus' word had the power to reverse the fortunes of his slave. Jesus saw a faith in the centurion that he did not see even in Israel. A third Quest story is the story of the sinful woman in 7:36-50. Tannehill cites the story of the ten lepers as a story in the Quest category. In 18:18-23 we have the story of the Quest of the rich ruler. This is a different kind of Quest story in that the ruler has everything. He is not an oppressed or excluded person. His fortunes are also reversed, however. "God has filled the hungry with good things and sent the rich away empty" (Luke 1:53). Another Quest story is the story of Zacchaeus (19:1-10). Finally, Tannehill puts the thief on the cross in the category of a Quest story (23:39-43). He came to Jesus in quest of life itself. And what a reversal he experienced! "Truly I tell you, today you will be with me in Paradise."

Homiletical Directions

We have said nothing so far about the Samaritan theme that is present in this week's text. We outlined this theme in Chapter 21 when we discussed the story of the "Good Samaritan." In Chapter 21 we proposed a sermon on the graciousness of God's love for the outcast and oppressed, for us!

The Samaritan stories (see Chapter 21) can also be stitched together as a *mission* sermon. Put together these stories about the outcast Samaritans which climax in the "Samaritan Pentecost" as told in Acts 8:4-17. These stories are a challenge to us as we recognize the outcast ("Samaritan") people in our community and in our world. These persons are our mission field. Jesus brought salvation for the outcast, oppressed, and excluded. The mission challenge is before us.

Another possibility for stitching narratives together would be to work with the stories we have identified as Quest stories. You can't tell them all, but you can tell three or four of them. Tell those that you choose as stories of people who come to Jesus. Tell them as stories in which oppressed and excluded people come to Jesus. Tell them as stories full of the surprises that occur when people encounter Jesus: a centurion is commended for great faith; a Samaritan is commended for giving praise to Jesus; a dying thief receives the gift of eternal life, and so forth. Tell these stories as stories which demonstrate the kinds of *reversals* that happen when people on a Quest encounter Jesus Christ. Jesus acts. Jesus speaks and people's lives are *turned around.* This is a great series of stories!

This sermon could close with an acknowledgment that people in this church today are also people on a Quest. The fact that they are in your audience indicates that they believe Jesus has something to do with their Quest. Jesus has a word for Questers. "Come to me," Jesus says, "whoever you are, whatever your background, however excluded you may have felt in your life. Come to me. I have a word for you. I heal the sick. I welcome the outcast. I give eternal life to people who may be breathing their last worldly breath. I will to turn your life around. To all who believe in me I have this simple word: 'Get up and go on your way; your faith has made you well.' " Amen.

---

1. Robert C. Tannehill, *The Narrative Unity of Luke-Acts, Volume One* (Minneapolis: Fortress Press, 1986), p. 119.

Chapter 38
Proper 24: Sunday between October 16 and 22

Luke 18:1-8

The appointed Lukan text for this week is given to us without its context. Last week's text, the story of the ten lepers, ended in Luke 17:19. This week's text begins in 18:1. Luke 17:20-37 has been omitted from the lectionary. These verses are vitally necessary, however, if we are to understand the nature of Jesus' parable in 18:1-8.

In 17:20 the Pharisees ask Jesus a question. "*When* is the kingdom of God coming?" This question of the Pharisees controls the discussion that follows through 18:8. Jesus reproved the question of the Pharisees and then proceeded to utter prophetic words about the future.

Jesus' word of reproof here is one of the best-known sayings of Jesus and is quoted endlessly by those who want to identify their religious view with those of Jesus. Jesus' simple word is: "The kingdom of God is *among* you." Gnosticism both yesterday and today has endlessly quoted these words of Jesus to prove that the "spark of the divine" is really inside us. The widely approved way of translating these words from Luke is: "The kingdom of God is *within* you."

Religious teachers affirm that we are gods if only we awaken to the divine potential *within* us. This religious notion, this Gnosticism alive-among-us, is the underlying teaching of most of what passes for spirituality in our culture today. It is the basic teaching of most of today's cults. The modern spiritual message is that it is a good thing to "be like God." Genesis 3:5 presents this "will to be like God" as the fundamental human temptation. Saint Paul celebrates a God incarnate in Jesus Christ, "who, though he was in the form of God, did not regard equality with God as something to be exploited, but emptied himself...." See Philippians 2:5-11.

189

The New Revised Standard Version of the Bible translates this verse as we have quoted above, "The kingdom of God is *among* you." The footnotes acknowledge other possible translations. In their context Jesus' words are the answer to the question of the Pharisees about when the kingdom will come. "It has come *now*." That's Jesus' reply. "The kingdom is among you. It is as close to you as you are standing to me. The kingdom is present in me."

> *It is now here in the presence and person of the Messiah Jesus. To ask about when it will come is to miss the point that God's reign has been inaugurated in Jesus.*[1]

Jesus turns next to instructions for his disciples. He speaks to them of the eschatological coming of the kingdom. The kingdom is both here and now in Jesus' presence and still to come as a public revelation of judgment on the earth. Standard commentaries can give you background on this eschatological section. We note Jesus' passion prediction in 17:25. There are five such passion predictions in Luke: 9:22, 44; 12:50; 13:32-33; and 17:25. Luke 9:22 is the first of Jesus' passion predictions. It is followed by Jesus' call to his disciples to take up the cross daily and follow him (9:23-24). The true disciple of Jesus gives up life in order to find life. This note is also sounded in 17:33.

Jesus' eschatological sayings to his disciples are dominated by themes of judgment. This week's text appears in this judgment context as a word of comfort to disciples who may grow weary of waiting for Messiah to come. Verse 17:22 hints at this kind of weariness, this kind of losing heart. So, "Jesus told them a parable about their need to pray always and not to lose heart." In order to encourage the disciples not to lose heart he tells them a parable about a *widow, a woman who does not lose heart*!

> *Luke has set the parable of the unrighteous judge (vv. 2-5) into the context of this discourse on the coming of the Son of man in order to encourage the faithful to continue in prayer (v. 1), to assure them that they are not dealing with a judge who will delay their pleas in indifference (vv. 2-7), and to raise the sharp concluding question about*

190

whether they will have kept the faith when the Son of man
comes (v. 8). In Luke's narrative, therefore, the passage
as a whole is integrated with the eschatological discourse
which precedes it.... [2]

It is worth noting that the woman in Jesus' parable is a widow. Widows are signs of the kind of societal outcasts who merit special attention from Jesus. Luke speaks often of widows: 2:37; 4:25-26; 7:12; 20:47; 21:2-3. Widows in the time of Jesus would normally have lived in a precarious financial state due to the loss of their "breadwinner."

When is the kingdom of God coming? That was the question of the Pharisees. Jesus' answer was that the kingdom is both present in his life and yet to be revealed in public for all to see. We are not to be discouraged or *lose heart* as we live out this paradoxical Christian reality. We should, rather, look to the example of a woman who did not lose heart. Her persistence evoked a response even from an unrighteous judge. God is not unrighteous. God will come and grant justice to the righteous ones. God will grant justice to those who stand firm in their faith. *Faith is strengthened through prayer!* Will the Son of man find faith on earth when he returns? He will if we have been faithful in prayer that our faith not lose heart.

> *If the helpless widow's persistent prayer accomplishes so*
> *much with a dishonest judge, how much more will the*
> *persistent prayer of Christian disciples! To this extent*
> *the parable carries the same message as that of the*
> *parable of the persistent friend (11:5-8) ... continual*
> *prayer ... continues to mark the existence of disciples until*
> *the Son of Man is revealed (17:30). The rest of the Lucan*
> *story will exemplify what is meant: Jesus on the Mount of*
> *Olives (22:41); the prayer of the Christian community*
> *during the imprisonment of Peter (Acts 12:5).* [3]

We have been taught well by Jesus how we should pray in the Lord's Prayer: "Your kingdom come on earth as it is in heaven." We are reminded of Martin Luther's explanation of this petition of the Lord's Prayer in his *Small Catechism*: "God's kingdom comes indeed without our praying for it, but we ask in this prayer that it may come also to us."

Homiletical Directions

Jesus' parable of the Persistent Woman is not a passage with narrative analogies in many other parts of Luke's Gospel. Narrative context is another matter. It is hardly possible to preach on this text without setting Jesus' parable in the context of the question of the Pharisee about *when* the kingdom of God was to come. If we choose to focus on the witness of the assigned text we will at least need to tell the story in 17:20-37 as an introduction to the text.

Luke 17:21, "The kingdom of God is among you," is not part of our textual assignment. That's too bad. We desperately need to deal with this text in some context in our preaching. As indicated above, this is the passage that modern-day Gnostics always quote when they wish to identify their spirituality with the spirituality of Jesus. The best book on gnostic religion in America today is by Harold Bloom. Bloom identifies himself as a Gnostic Jew. He argues that Gnosticism is the religion that grows most naturally out of the American soil. He identifies almost every American cult and new religion as gnostic.

> *(Gnosticism is centered) in two absolute convictions: the Creation, of the world and of mankind in its present form, was the same event as the Fall of the world and of man, but humankind has in it a spark or breath of the uncreated, of God, and that spark can find its way back to the uncreated, unfallen world, in a solitary act of knowledge.*[4]

It is of vital apologetic significance that we in the church combat this gnostic myth which is leading so many of our people into a spirituality centered in the "within" of the self. This myth is everywhere among us. If you are unaware of this, it would be wise to do some reading on the subject (start with Bloom!) and put this topic on your future teaching or preaching list of things to do.

Once we have set a narrative context for the assigned text for this week our sermon can take a didactic character. Explain the points made by the parable in relation to the whole question of *when* the kingdom of God is coming. The summary of the teaching of this text by David Tiede (see footnote #2) can guide you in constructing the points to teach on this matter.

---

1. David L. Tiede, *Luke: Augsburg Commentary on the New Testament* (Minneapolis: Augsburg, 1988), p. 300.

2. *Ibid.,* p. 304.

3. Joseph Fitzmyer, *The Gospel According to Luke, X-XXIV* (New York: Doubleday, 1985), pp. 1177-1178.

4. Harold Bloom, *The American Religion: The Emergence of the Post-Christian Nation* (New York: Simon & Schuster, 1992), p. 27.

Luke 18:9-14

"Two men went up into the temple to pray...." These are very familiar words. This week's text is a very well known text from the Gospel of Luke. It is well known for good reason. This story of a Pharisee and a tax collector reminds us of the stories of the "lost" in Luke 15 in its ring of gospel clarity. God's love for sinners in Jesus Christ is portrayed in this story in a powerful way.

David Tiede sets the context for this week's text as follows:

> The larger context is that of the third and final phase of Jesus' journey to Jerusalem (17:11—19:27), and this phase moves with a rhythm of stories, sayings, and healings, punctuated three times with prophetic warnings and predictions (17:22—18:8; 18:31-34; 19:11-27) ... The controlling motif of the larger context continues to be crucial: Jesus is instructing his disciples in the way of the kingdom as he travels toward his fateful arrival in Jerusalem. Thus this second cycle of stories in 18:9-34 again moves from stories which reveal the character of God's kingdom (vv. 9-30) to prophetic warnings that God's way of ruling will be beyond human understanding (vv. 31-34).[1]

This week's text follows immediately upon the parable of the woman who prayed without losing heart (18:1-8). Luke 18:9-14 is also about prayer.

We are in the Reformation season of the year and it is fitting that this text deals so clearly with the reality of justification. Jesus is well acquainted with those who seek to justify themselves. We remember the lawyer who answered Jesus' question about that which is written in the law. If love of neighbor were the key to inherit eternal life, this lawyer wanted to know exactly which neighbors he should serve: "... wanting to *justify himself,* he asked Jesus, 'And who is my neighbor?' " (Luke 10:25-37).

In Luke 16:14-15 Jesus upbraids the Pharisees. "You are those who *justify yourselves* in the sight of others...."

This week's text begins with this same note of self-justification. "He also told this parable to some who *trusted in themselves* that they were *righteous* ..." (18:9). In each of these contexts a form of the word *dikaios* is used. This word can be translated as righteousness or as justification. A form of *dikaios* appears again in verse 14: "I [Jesus] tell you, this man [the tax collector] went down to his home *justified* rather than the other...."

Another clue to the nature of the prayer of the Pharisee is that he prayed "with himself" as some translations have it. Evidently this Pharisee loved to hear himself pray. We are reminded here of Matthew's Gospel where Jesus speaks a word of judgment upon those who practice their *righteousness* in public (Matthew 6:1-8).

The tax collector, on the other hand, threw himself on the mercy of God. His body language is typical of Semitic humility and contrition. "He has understood the dynamic character of God's reign and its ultimately gracious character ... the point is that this is how the reign of God works, and the primary force of the story is to correct misunderstandings."[2]

This story turns everything in the world of standard religion upside down. There is a great *reversal* here. A self-professed righteous person is sent away empty. A tax collector (the very word meant *sinner*) is sent away *justified.* He is justified by a word of Jesus. He has prayed the prayer that is the everyday stuff of life in Christian posture towards God: "God, be merciful to me, a sinner." And then Jesus spoke a word of justification. "This man went home justified." That's what Jesus said. And that's what happened. A sinner became righteous. A tax collector became a saint. A man crying for mercy became justified. All of this is possible when Jesus speaks his justifying word.

Jesus' justifying word is a word that turned things upside down. In this story of the Pharisee and the tax collector a *great reversal* took place. This is a common theme in Luke. It began in the Magnificat. Mary sang of what Jesus would do. Did she sing this song to Jesus? Perhaps. "God has brought down the powerful from their thrones, and lifted up the lowly; God has filled the hungry with good things, and sent the rich away empty" (Luke 1:52-53). See Chapter 1 for a listing of the stories which carry out this theme of reversal in Luke's Gospel.

Homiletical Directions

A first possibility for a narrative sermon on this text in the season of Reformation would be to deal with the theme of *reversal.* Since we are in the Reformation season it might be well to note that Martin Luther also experienced a dramatic reversal when it was revealed to him that the *dikaios* of God came to humans not as *active righteousness* that we are to *achieve* but as *passive righteousness* that we are to *receive* as God's gift. Said Luther of this revelatory discovery: "Then I had the feeling that straight away I was born again, and had entered through the open doors into paradise itself. The whole scripture revealed a different countenance to me." Luther's life had been turned around; everything was reversed for him! There are parallels between Luther's experience of *God's justification* and the experience of the tax collector who went down to his house justified.

A sermon on the reversal theme would tell two to four of the stories in Luke which depict the reversal theme. The last story told would be the story of the Pharisee and the tax collector. The story of Martin Luther might be told as well under the theme of reversal. At any rate, this sermon should close with Jesus speaking a word of justification to the sinners in our pews. Jesus' word for us in these stories is: "I have come to hear and respond to the prayers of sinners who cry for mercy. I have come to make sinners righteous. I have come to make you righteous. I have come to give you the gift of being justified in God's eyes. Sinners, you are justified! My word makes it so."

A second narrative possibility would be to tell only the story of this week's assigned text. Tell first the story of the Pharisee. Give some background on his life. Tell his story using language we might use today for describing a person who seeks to justify him/herself. How do self-righteous persons behave among us? Fit these descriptions to the Pharisee. Jesus' word to this man was and is that he does not go home justified.

Next tell the story of the tax collector. Again, give background details out of your creative imagination on this person. Weave in language we use today to describe sinful persons. Dwell for some time on the prayer this man prays: "God, be merciful to me, a sinner." This is the prayer that God longs to hear. This is the prayer that ought to characterize the daily life of all God's people. This story ends with a word of Jesus that brings a great reversal. A sinner is made just. A sinner becomes righteous. Jesus says so and Jesus' word does what it says!

It is recommended that this way of telling the story end in the same kind of word of proclamation that we proposed above. Jesus' word is the crux of the matter! Jesus spoke and a man was made just. So we speak for God, so we speak for Jesus, and people are made just, as the Holy Spirit takes our words and plants them in the mind and heart of those who hear.

---

1. David L. Tiede, *Luke: Augsburg Commentary on the New Testament* (Minneapolis: Augsburg, 1988), pp. 306-307.

2. *Ibid.,* p. 308.

Luke 19:1-10

"This story is a Lukan masterpiece, a wonder story of the first order. Here God and the Messiah Jesus accomplish what is humanly impossible (18:27) — a rich man is saved!"[1]

What a wonderful happening it is that this great story of God finding sinners should fall on or near Reformation Sunday. There are ways in which Zacchaeus is a "model of the Reformation." Just prior to this story (18:18-30) is the story of a rich ruler who wants to know what he must *do* to inherit eternal life. The would-be-doer is sent away from Jesus. The story of Zacchaeus completes the story of the rich ruler. The Messiah *finds* a sinner "out on a limb" and invites him to come to his own house for a salvation party. Only with God is salvation, eternal life, possible! The themes here echo the stories in Luke 15. The themes here echo the reality of salvation by grace alone.

We have spoken many times about the theme of poverty and riches in Luke's Gospel. The theme verse for this emphasis is Luke 1:53. See Chapters 1 and 11 for commentary on this theme and citation of the many stories in Luke that take up this theme. The story of Zacchaeus is a kind of climax to these stories of the reversal of rich and poor. Remember, this is a centrally important topic for Luke. We have heard it expounded upon time and time again. When we come to the Zacchaeus story in Luke 19 we come very near the end of the Travel Narrative which has touched on this subject several times. Only the story in 19:11-27 remains before we come to the end of the Travel Narrative. The Zacchaeus story, therefore, is very strategically placed in Luke's Gospel. It is the climax of Luke's teaching on poverty and wealth.

The Zacchaeus story comes on the heels of the story of the *rich* ruler who was *sent away empty*. But! Zacchaeus reverses the reversal. All the rich ones get sent away empty in Luke's story. This is not so with Zacchaeus! Zacchaeus is *not sent away empty.* Zacchaeus is *found.* Zacchaeus repents. Zacchaeus gives of his goods to the poor and to those whom he has defrauded. Many commentators feel that Zacchaeus is Luke's *model of a rich Christian.*

Tannehill includes the Zacchaeus story with the "quest" stories that he identifies. See Chapter 37 for a discussion of these quest stories.

The Zacchaeus story is a pivotal text in Luke. It has importance on many levels. One of the key relationships of this story to other Luke stories is its relationship to the story of the rich ruler in 18:18-30.

> *The story of Zacchaeus is placed late in the narrative of Jesus' ministry, shortly before his arrival in Jerusalem. This is useful for two reasons. First, there is a link with the story of the rich ruler ... (both he and Zacchaeus are described as "rich") ... The story of Zacchaeus provides an answer to the question of whether and how a rich man can be saved ... Second, 19:10 provides a retrospective summary of Jesus' saving work. The connection between 5:32 and 19:10 suggests they form an inclusion.*[2]

Tannehill refers here to Luke 5:32: "I have come to call not the righteous but sinners to repentance." By "inclusion" he means to say that 5:32 introduces the theme of Jesus' ministry to sinners and the Zacchaeus story closes this theme. Zacchaeus is a sinner who repents.

Homiletical Directions

The story of Zacchaeus has many narrative connections within Luke's Gospel. This gives us a variety of sermon possibilities. First, we could tell the stories of the rich being sent away in Luke's Gospel climaxing in the story of this rich man who is not sent away. Second, we could relate the story of Zacchaeus to the "quest" stories in Luke. Third, we could begin with the passage in Luke 5 where Jesus announces his mission to call sinners to repentance and follow that theme through Luke's Gospel climaxing in the wonderful story of Zacchaeus. The story of Zacchaeus is much, much more than the theme of a popular Sunday School song. It is an integral passage to Luke's entire Gospel. We could spend several Sundays on this text alone!

There is a fourth theme within the Zacchaeus story which is worthy of sermonic attention. A sinner is *found*. A sinner *repents*. *Justification* happens. The justified sinner turns immediately to matters of *justice*. The Zacchaeus story is a wonderful story of the relation of justification and justice. This theme also deserves our attention.

As a Reformation sermon we will give our fuller attention here to the relationship between the story of the rich ruler (18:18-30) and the rich tax collector. The theme of 18:18-30 is a constant Lukan theme. A *rich* man is sent away empty. He could not sell what he had to give to the *poor*. Sadly, he walks away from Jesus. Jesus notes how difficult it is for those who are rich to enter the kingdom of God. The crowd was incensed. They were dumbfounded. They knew this man. He was wonderful. Every civic accolade possible had been heaped upon this righteous man who had kept all God's commandments. How could Jesus turn such a person away? "Then who can be saved?" the crowd gasped. This is a Reformation question! "What must I do to inherit eternal life?" "Who can be saved?" These were Martin Luther's questions. These are universal human questions.

Jesus answers this theological question of the crowd with a theological answer. "What is impossible for mortals is possible for God." This answer is unlike most of Jesus' answers. Jesus didn't usually answer questions with theological abstractions. Be patient. The answer is coming. Zacchaeus is the answer to the question of who can be saved. Zacchaeus? How can that be possible? He is a rich man, after all (v. 2). All things are possible for God.

In the sermon it would be well to make a list of the characteristics of Zacchaeus and the rich ruler. The ruler kept the commandments. Zacchaeus had probably broken most of them. The ruler wanted to know what he could do to be saved. He was a religious man.

Zacchaeus was just curious. He got out on a limb (is there a metaphor here?) to satisfy his curiosity. The ruler was a very good candidate for salvation. Zacchaeus was a bad candidate for salvation. If it were up to us we would choose the ruler every time!

The gospel, however, turns everything upside down. Jesus chooses Zacchaeus. We choose the ruler. Jesus chooses Zacchaeus. Salvation does not happen when we choose. Salvation happens when God chooses. "Zacchaeus," Jesus said, "you come down." Jesus goes then to have a party with a sinner. The crowd murmurs. The crowd murmured about the rich man, too. They thought he was a good candidate for salvation. They didn't think Zacchaeus was a good candidate at all. "And all who saw it began to grumble and said, 'He has gone to be the guest of one who is a sinner.'"

Who then can be saved? That was the open question of the story of the rich ruler. At first Jesus gave a theoretical answer. With God all things are possible. Jesus' deeds spoke more clearly than his words in this case. Who can be saved? Zacchaeus can be saved. Sinners can be saved. We can be saved!

Jesus has a word for all people whose lives are "out on a limb." Jesus has a word for sinners. Jesus says to us through this story: "Come on down from your limb. I'm coming to your house today. Let's have a party! Today I have done what humans cannot do. Today salvation has come to your house. I have come to seek and to save the lost. I have come to seek and to save sinners like Zacchaeus. I have come to seek and to save sinners like you!" Amen.

---

1. David L. Tiede, *Luke: Augsburg Commentary on the New Testament* (Minneapolis: Augsburg, 1988), p. 319.

2. Robert C. Tannehill, *The Narrative Unity of Luke-Acts, Volume One* (Philadelphia: Fortress, 1986), p. 107.

Chapter 41
Palm/Passion Sunday

Procession with Palms: Luke 19:28-40
Liturgy of the Passion: Luke 22:14—23:56 or Luke 23:1-49

"After he had said this, he went on ahead, *going up to Jerusalem*" (Luke 19:28). We're at the destination at last. The Travel Narrative is over. Jesus enters Jerusalem to meet his destiny. We should perhaps remind ourselves of the markers along the way in Luke keeping the focus on Jerusalem. The way to Jerusalem was first mentioned in the Transfiguration story (9:28-36). Before the disciples' eyes Moses and Elijah are engaged in conversation with their transfigured Master. Moses and Elijah "... appeared in glory and were speaking of his *departure* (Greek: *exodus*), which he was about to accomplish at Jerusalem" (9:31). Throughout the Travel Narrative there are constant markers that the story is taking us to Jerusalem: 9:51, 53; 13:22; 17:11; 18:31; 19:11.

Jerusalem was the city of Jesus' destiny. It was also to be the city of his great suffering. There are at least six *passion predictions* in Luke's story. The first of these predictions is in Luke 9:22: "The Son of Man must undergo great suffering, and be rejected by the elders, chief priests, and scribes, and be killed, and on the third day be raised." There are several other passion predictions in Luke's story: 12:49-50; 13:33-34; 16:31; 17:25; 18:31-33; 19:14. It is very clear, therefore, that Jerusalem lies before Jesus as the city of his great suffering and pain. This is the plan. "Was it not necessary that the Messiah should suffer these things and then enter into his glory?" That's Jesus' word about God's plan as he spoke to disciples on the road to Emmaus on the day of his rising (24:26). Now that the *plan is complete* disciples can be commissioned to go to all nations with the message of repentance and the gracious forgiveness of sins (24:44-49).

In Jerusalem the whole plan will go public! All the world shall see. All the world shall know. All the world shall become a mission field for the message of repentance and forgiveness. According to Robert Tannehill:

> ... there are three scenes just before and shortly after the arrival at Jerusalem which provide previews of what will happen there. They indicate that the king will be rejected by his citizens and that this will bring disaster upon the city as a whole, both the leaders and the people. These three scenes are the parable of the pounds (19:11-27), Jesus weeping over Jerusalem (19:41-44), and the parable of the vineyard tenants (20:9-19).[1]

The parable of the pounds follows immediately upon the story of Zacchaeus (19:1-10). Jesus told this parable to his followers because he was near to Jerusalem! Jewish expectations of the Messiah and the Messiah's entrance into Jerusalem were expectations of glory. All those in Jesus' entourage must have expected a glorious entrance into the city of David. The parable of the pounds is precisely a warning about what to expect in Jerusalem. The people expect glory! Jesus' parable warns of the cross! In what is clearly a kind of allegorical parable the nobleman in this story represents God. The citizens of the city do not want the nobleman/God to "rule over us" (19:14). The nobleman/God has enemies "... who did not want me to be king over them ..." (19:27). King Jesus will enter Jerusalem, but he will be met by many who do not want him to be their king. Jesus' days in Jerusalem, therefore, will not be simple days of glory. The passion predictions are true. King Jesus rides on to die.

The story of Jesus weeping over Jerusalem (19:41-44) and the parable of the tenants in the vineyard (20:9-19) make very similar points. These three stories set a context of dread around the story of Jesus' entry into the city.

As for the Palm Sunday text itself, its clearest parallel is the story of the coronation of Solomon told in 1 Kings 1:32-40. Jesus' entry into Jerusalem must surely have called forth this story from of old in the minds of all who watched on that first Palm Sunday. The parallels between the two events suggest clearly that Jesus' entry into Jerusalem was the coming of the King, the coming of Israel's long-awaited Messiah!

On that first Palm Sunday the multitude of the disciples praised God joyfully with a loud voice and cried, "Blessed is the king who comes in the name of the Lord!" (19:38). See the reference in 13:35. They cried out further: "Peace in heaven, and glory in the highest heaven!" There is a play on words here with the words that the angels sang to the shepherds: "Glory to God in the highest heaven, and on earth peace among those whom God favors!" (Luke 2:14).

Homiletical Directions

It is indeed difficult to come up with a new approach for a Palm Sunday sermon. We've rehearsed this story so many times that there may seem little left to be said. The contextual approach that we suggested above might be a possibility, however. Introduce "Jerusalem" through the stories in Luke 9 where Jesus utters his first passion prediction and where Elijah and Moses speak with Jesus of his *departure* (exodus) to Jerusalem. The Travel Narrative is full of references to Jerusalem as the destiny of King Jesus. Build up the suspense, as Luke does with his constant reminders that we are on the way to Jerusalem and his constant repetition of passion predictions which put us on notice that Jerusalem will be a city of suffering for Jesus. There is a *plan* here to go to Jerusalem and to suffer.

The three stories identified by Tannehill stand in closest relationship to Jesus' entry into Jerusalem. The parable of the pounds is a warning that the king will not be welcome (19:11-27). Jesus' words and tears for Jerusalem also make it clear that Jerusalem is a city in which unspeakable things happen (19:41-44). The parable of the tenant and the vineyard also makes it clear that "the beloved son" will be rejected by the people. Tell these three stories as stories which cradle the Palm Sunday story and help to give it meaning.

If we make use of these stories it will probably not be necessary to retell the Palm Sunday story. It has been read. It is well known. Our task this year is to tell the stories that help to bring the meaning of this story to light. What we know from the passion predictions and from the three stories in Luke 19 and 20 is that Palm Sunday is a story on the way to the suffering and death on the cross.

We only know for sure how the story ends by peeking ahead at Luke 24. On the road to Emmaus Jesus reminds his disciples that he had to *first* suffer *then* enter his glory (24:26). It was necessary for the Christ to suffer. Jesus repeats these words in 24:46. The Messiah had to suffer. The Messiah had to suffer in order to carry out God's *plan*. Only then can the disciples be *sent forth from Jerusalem* with a message of repentance and forgiveness. So the disciples wait in Jerusalem. On Pentecost, in Jerusalem, they are filled with the power of the Holy Spirit so that they may be witnesses to Jesus Christ to the ends of the earth. (See Acts 1:8.) Empowered by the Spirit they will preach the message of repentance and forgiveness. (See Acts 2:38.)

This is our commission as well. As modern-day disciples we, too, have been to Jerusalem. We have been empowered by the Holy Spirit and it is our turn to carry out God's *plan*. Today we are the messengers sent by Christ to call people to repent and to announce forgiveness. On that note the sermon can end. Call people to repentance. Announce to them the word of forgiveness. In this action Palm Sunday's promise is fulfilled among us.

If you choose to use the Passion Sunday texts instead of the Palm Sunday text we would advise a story-telling approach. If there is to be a Passion Sunday let it be a Sunday to tell, not explain, the contents of Luke 22 or of Luke 22 and 23. In *Preaching Mark's Gospel* we made the suggestion that Passion Sunday be a day for the telling of the passion story using every form of story telling we can muster. Tell the stories in Luke 22 or 22 and 23. Some of the stories can be told from memory by good orators. There are musical pieces which would give expression to some of the stories. Appropriate hymns can be sung. Other stories could be dramatized by members of the congregation. Others of them could be told as stories to the children. Some stories could be set into choral readings. Others might be told with a rap beat. The possibilities are many! Use your imagination.

Should you choose to tell the Lukan passion story there are certain themes that dominate the story which might be underscored in the telling. Luke tells the passion story in such a way that it is unmistakably clear that what takes place here *is the fulfillment of the plan of God.* Judas appears at the outset of the story. The "opportune time" for betrayal is at hand. (Cf. Luke 4:13.) Luke introduced us to Judas the traitor long ago (6:16). "For the Son of Man is going *as it has been determined,* but woe to that one by whom he is betrayed" (22:22).

Judas introduces us to a story that is carried out according to the plan of God. This theme occurs repeatedly in the story (22:29, 37, 42, 53). In the Easter story Jesus reveals again that the plan of God has been fulfilled in his passion (24:25-27, 44-49). As we have noted above, God's plan is that repentance and forgiveness of sins is to be proclaimed in Jesus' name to the ends of the earth. Here, too, we note that the sacrificial motif is not prominent in Luke. Luke does not focus our attention on Jesus' sacrificial death. Luke paints a broad picture of a passion that in all its parts carries out the plan of God.

In Acts 4:24-28 we hear a clear Lukan summary of the work of Jesus whom God anointed "to do whatever your hand and your plan had predestined to take place." In these verses Luke cites Psalm 2 as a way of talking about the necessity of the Royal One to suffer at the hands of rulers and nations. Many scholars believe that Luke models his passion story as a fulfillment of Psalm 2.

Luke portrays Jesus as a person struggling with his destiny. Jesus' prayer at the Mount of Olives captures this struggle as Jesus prays for the cup to be taken from him (22:39-46). Ultimately, however, Jesus entrusts his spirit, his very self, into the *hands* of God. "Father, into your *hands* I commend my spirit" (23:46).

The passion story is one of the most powerful human stories ever told. One of the options open to us as preachers is to tell this story each year to our people. Make it a tradition in our congregations. Each year more and more pieces of the story could be told in a variety of ways. We might finally mount a full-blown pageant! The pageant will differ from year to year as we move from Luke's story to Matthew's story and so forth. The goal is to tell this passion story in all of its power. The goal of good story telling is participation. We set forth to tell this story in all of its power so that those who hear might be grasped by the power of the story of the One who announced early in his ministry that "... the Son of Man must undergo great suffering, and be rejected by the elders, chief priests, and scribes, and be killed and on the third day be raised" (9:22).

---

1. Robert C. Tannehill, *The Narrative Unity of Luke-Acts, Volume One* (Philadelphia: Fortress Press, 1986), p. 159.

Luke 20:27-38

Today's text comes to us rather radically ripped from its Lukan context. Proper 26 offered the wonderful story of Zacchaeus. Just a week ago, therefore, we were in the closing moments of the Travel Narrative. The grand climax of the Travel Narrative, of course, is the entry into Jerusalem. Palm Sunday, however, is far behind us now. We would encourage you to re-read the Palm Sunday material (Chapter 41) as you think about the context for this week's Gospel reading. The pericope assignments have moved us from 19:1-10 to 20:27-38. It is important to remind ourselves of what is missing as we move from Proper 26 to Proper 27.

After Jesus entered the city of Jerusalem on Palm Sunday he went directly to the temple (Luke 19:45, 47). The closing verses in Luke 19 set the context for Luke 20. "The chief priests, the scribes, and the leaders of the people kept looking for a way to kill him; but they did not find anything they could do, for all the people were spellbound by what they heard" (19:47-48). David Tiede in his Lukan commentary gives this heading for the material in 20:1—21:4: "Conflicts While Teaching In The Temple." Robert Tannehill summarizes as follows:

> The persistent efforts of the Sanhedrin to find a way of re-
> moving Jesus in spite of the people's support is an impor-
> tant unifying thread in the narrative from 19:47 until
> Jesus' arrest.[1]

Luke 20:1-8 is the first attempt by the temple leaders to trap Jesus in his words. The chief priests and the scribes and the elders ask Jesus about the nature of his authority. If Jesus answered that his authority was from God they would accuse him of blasphemy. If he answered that his authority was mere human authority the crowds would be disenchanted with him. The trap doesn't work. Jesus parries question for question. "Did the baptism of John come from heaven or was it of human origin?" he asked them. They had no answer for Jesus. Round one goes to Jesus!

Before we come to round two in the verbal wrestling match between Jesus and the temple authorities we encounter a kind of allegorical parable on the lips of Jesus. "A man planted a vineyard and leased it to tenants...." When the master of the vineyard sent for his share of the produce his servant was sent away by the tenants. The master finally sent his "beloved son." "This is the heir; let us kill him so that the inheritance may be ours." That's the response of the tenants. We read this to mean that when the Master of the human race sent his "beloved" son he was killed by the very persons who should have received him with joy. The scribes and chief priests got the point. They "realized that he had told this parable against them, they wanted to lay hands on him at that very hour, but they feared the people" (20:19). These conversations between Jesus and the temple leaders are not just interesting debates. Life and death hang in the balance.

Round two brings us to a conflict about the relative authority of God and Caesar (20:20-26). Once again Jesus proves the superior debater in a life-and-death quarrel of wits. "Then give to the emperor the things that are the emperor's, and to God the things that are God's" (20:25). Jesus' words confounded them. Their rage mounted. "And they were not able in the presence of the people to trap him, by what he said; and being amazed by his answer, they became silent" (20:26).

Round three. This is the text assigned for this week. Now it's the turn of the Sadducees to question Jesus. The Sadducees did not believe in the resurrection. They had good reason. God hadn't done any resurrections as yet. God raising the dead was a deed for the future of Jesus. So the Sadducees were not stupid. They thought that resurrections were unbiblical and they tried to get Jesus to agree by presenting their hypothetical case of a woman who had seven husbands and no sons by any of them. "In the resurrection, therefore, whose wife will the woman be?" (20:33). Jesus was up to their challenge. Even the Sadducees admitted such. " 'Teacher, you have spoken well.' For they no longer dared to ask him another question" (20:39-40).

Round three in this debate also goes to Jesus! These stories that occur on the brink of Jesus' death are delightful nonetheless. As Tiede puts it, "These are stories which early Christian communities would have treasured as disclosures of the triumph of messianic teaching over the attacks of the temple leadership."[2]

In 20:41 the tables are turned and Jesus starts to ask the questions!

Homiletical Directions

In the first place, we must note that the stories we have looked at above are made for teaching. They are conflict stories between Jesus and the Jewish religious leaders in the days leading up to the move on the part of the religious authorities to kill the Messiah. A teaching sermon could set the narrative context of conflict for these three dialogues with Jesus and then proceed to make Jesus' points in each of these stories clear in our exposition. Jesus taught. We teach. We seek to explain for faith today the true nature of Jesus' authority (20:1-8), how we should regard God and the emperor (20:19-26), and how we ought to think about the resurrection of the dead (20:27-40). Standard commentaries explicate the *meaning* of these stories very well.

A narrative alternative for dealing with these three stories would be to focus on the *nature of the conflict* rather than the content of the teaching. The issue for the sermon would be this series of conflicts as the Jewish religious leaders seek to trap Jesus so that they can undermine his popularity with the people and see to it that his days are numbered on this earth. We would tell these three stories but not with the intention of explaining them. Our intention would be to lay out the nature of the conflict. Life and death are engaged in these conversations. Tell the stories. Build the conflict. Life vs. Death.

It is probably best that our sermon not just deal with the nature of the conflict. We may need to jump ahead of ourselves a bit and anticipate the end of the conflict. The religious leaders won! At least that's how it looked for a while. They did get him crucified.

The religious authorities unwittingly carried out God's plan! That plan is reiterated over and over again in Luke's Gospel beginning with 9:22: "The Son of Man must undergo great suffering, and be rejected by the elders, chief priests, and scribes, and be killed, and on the third day be raised." We refer you to Chapter 41 for a discussion of God's plan that the Messiah must suffer. Predictions of Jesus' passion occur regularly in this Gospel. Suffering and death are part of the plan. As discussed in Chapter 41 the plan is explained in Luke 24. Twice in Luke 24 the newly risen Jesus indicates that *it was necessary that he should suffer* (24:26, 46). Jesus' suffering is completed and now the message of repentance and forgiveness of sins may be "proclaimed in his name to all nations, beginning from Jerusalem" (24:47).

The Homiletical Directions in Chapter 41 offer possibilities for preaching on this story of suffering that is the plan of God, brought about by the religious leaders, and proclaimed by us as the hope of the world.

---

1. Robert C. Tannehill, *The Narrative Unity of Luke-Acts, Volume One* (Philadelphia: Fortress, 1986), 189.

2. David L. Tiede, *Luke: Augsburg Commentary on the New Testament* (Minneapolis: Augsburg, 1988), p. 336.

Chapter 43
Proper 28: Sunday between November 13 and 19

Luke 21:5-19

With this week's text we come to material that is focused on the future. It is material that draws very heavily on the apocalyptic material in Mark 13. Images from Old Testament apocalyptic material also abound in this material. A good cross-reference Bible will give these notations.

Joseph Fitzmyer has a helpful outline for the material in Luke 21:

> *The discourse proper falls into two main parts:*
> *a)* *vv. 8-24:* What will precede the end of Jerusalem?
> *It is subdivided:*
> *(i) vv. 8-11, The Signs before the End.*
> *(ii) vv. 12-19, Admonitions for the Coming Persecution.*
> *(iii) vv. 20-24, The Desolation of Jerusalem.*
> *b)* *vv. 25-36:* What will precede the end of the world?
> *It is subdivided:*
> *(i) vv. 25-28, The Coming of the Son of Man.*
> *(ii) vv. 29-33, The Parable of the Fig Tree.*
> *(iii) vv. 34-36, Concluding Exhortation to Vigilance.* [1]

This week's text takes up part a), points (i) and (ii), of this outline. The verses in the remainder of the outline are appointed for the First Sunday in Advent.

We note that Luke 21 moves in an entirely different direction than the preceding verses. In Luke 20 Jesus is under siege from the Jewish religious leaders as they seek to entrap him in his words in order to diminish his standing in the eyes of the populace and to give them an opportunity to bring charges against Jesus so they might be rid of this religious nuisance once and for all. At the end of Luke 20 Jesus himself asks a question about the relationship between the Messiah and David. Luke 21 opens (vv. 1-4) with the story of the widow's mite. This story of a widow who had nothing and gave everything stands in marked contrast to the beginning of this week's appointed text which speaks of the noble stones of the beautiful temple. Poverty and opulence live side by side here. We know one thing for sure. Luke is on the side of the poor widow.

The story of the widow and today's text both take place in the temple. The temple, as we have seen, was Jesus' destination as "he set his face" to go to Jerusalem. The temple becomes the location for Jesus' final extended discourse.

> *In Luke's presentation, this discourse rivals the Sermon on the Plain (6:20-49) for length and significance. It gathers up themes from Jesus' earlier prophetic discourses about readiness for the coming day of the Son of Man (12:35-39; 17:20-37; see also 18:8). It also pronounces Jesus' verdict on the temple and city as divine judgment which fulfills prophetic warnings....[2]*

Luke 21:5-9 speaks of the coming destruction of the temple. The disciples wonder if a sign will light their way in grasping the import of a destroyed temple. Jesus warns against signs. His warning still holds today. There are always those among us who insist that the signs point to this or that reality for God's people. Jesus will have none of it. He assures his disciples simply that the destruction of the temple is *part of the plan of God.* There are many passages in Luke which speak of the dire future of Jerusalem as well: 13:1-9, 34-35; 19:27-28, 41-44; 20:9-18; 23:28-31.

Jesus then tells his disciples that they are not to be *terrified* by the things that are coming. "These things must take place," he tells them (21:9). We recognize this "divine *must*" from its usage in Luke. See Luke 2:49; 4:43; 9:22; 22:37; 24:7, 44. The destruction of the temple does not mean that God's agenda for the world has gotten out of control. Temple destruction, rather, is part of God's design in bringing salvation to the world. So, do not fear!

In Luke 21:10-19 the suffering that the disciples must bear is understood as fulfillment of Jesus' own words of prophecy. People are to understand what such calamitous events mean not just for their future but for their present lives.

> They mean that Jesus' prophetic words here and in 12:11-12 are coming to fulfillment. The betrayals and trials to synagogues and prisons, kings and governors are an expanded vision of the public character of the opposition to Christ and his kingdom. It is for his "name's sake" that they will suffer ... This is a conflict with principalities and powers, which should be no surprise to Jesus' followers.[3]

The proper stance of God's faithful people in the midst of tribulation is to *testify*, to bear witness to Jesus. This is not an activity we need to plan for. When the time of trial comes Jesus will give us words and wisdom. Cf. Luke 12:11-12 where the promise is that the Holy Spirit will give us the words to speak. These are incredible words of promise and presence for Christians seeking to find their way in a hostile culture. As our own culture grows increasingly hostile to the values of the kingdom we might find these promises of Christ to be of great comfort. The message is similar to that in 21:9. We are not to be terrified. God will stand with us in the time of trial: "... not a hair of your head will perish. By your endurance you will gain your souls" (21:18-19). This appears to be a promise of eternal life. Luther's great hymn puts it this way:

> Were they to take our house,
> Goods, honor, child, or spouse,
> Though life be wrenched away,
> They cannot win the day.
> The Kingdom's ours forever.

Homiletical Directions

Perhaps the most important reality in dealing with this week's text with its eschatological and apocalyptic overtones is to remember that the focus of this passage is much more on the *present* than on the *future*. Tribulations and trials will come but we need not be afraid. It is all part of God's plan. The world has not gone berserk. God's meaning and purpose are still in working order. In the darkest of hours we also will know what to say. We will know how to testify to Christ. The words will be given us. When death and hatred touch us we still need not fear. Not a hair of our head will perish. In losing even our very life we will find our new life, our true life.

There is not much in the way of narrative analogy in Luke's Gospel for this text. There is wonderful analogy with stories in the Book of Acts, however. We could tell, for example, the story in Acts 4:1-31. The Sadducees heard the disciples giving testimony to the good news of the resurrection and they locked them in jail. Peter, "filled with the Holy Spirit," gave their defense (Acts 4:8). God gave Peter the words to say in this time of trial. You can sort through the story yourself for its relationship to Luke 21. Note particularly the boldness of the testimony of Peter and John whom the Sadducees took to be uneducated, common men. The Lord truly touched their mouths! In the last verses of this story the disciples rejoice that though the Gentiles raged against them God had delivered them. God's plan (Acts 4:28) is in place! The closing prayer of this story (Acts 4:24-30) could be paraphrased for use within or after your sermon.

Acts 5:17-42 tells a similar story. Once again the Sadducees arrested the apostles and put them in prison. But God opened the prison doors for them and gave them words of *Life* to speak to the people. The apostles continue to testify. God protects them from all harm. Gamaliel comes on the scene. He speaks words that God must have given him. "And every day in the temple and at home they did not cease to teach and proclaim Jesus as the Messiah" (Acts 5:42). Their testimony went on. God was at work in time of trial!

These stories in Acts 4 and 5 appear to make the same point that this week's assigned text makes. Tell these stories as a sign that Jesus' words about our life in this world are true. Tell these stories to calm fear about trials and tribulations that may come upon us. Tell these stories to encourage people to continue to testify in the name of Jesus. These are wonderful stories for the telling.

215

Typically, Luke tells these stories with a happy ending! We know life's stories do not always end like that. There is no argument with Luke's conclusion, however. "By your endurance you will gain your souls."

---

1. Joseph A. Fitzmyer, *The Gospel According to Luke, X-XXIV* (New York: Doubleday, 1985), p. 1334.

2. David L. Tiede, *Luke: Augsburg Commentary on the New Testament* (Minneapolis: Augsburg, 1988), p. 355.

3. *Ibid.,* p. 361.

Chapter 44
Advent 1

Luke 21:25-36

Our first text from Luke is part of Jesus' final extended discourse in the temple. This final discourse begins in Luke 21:5. Luke 21:5-19, the first part of this final discourse, is treated in Chapter 43. An outline of the material in 21:5-36 is included there. This week's assigned text captures an Advent theme of the *coming* of the final judgment. It is very awkward, however, to begin our year of Luke in the middle of a discourse from one of the last chapters of this Gospel. We should not be surprised that our people have very little idea of the flow of Luke's story.

Material from the treasury of possibilities that is Luke 1 is not incorporated into the Lukan year until the Fourth Sunday in Advent. We encourage you to read the material for that Sunday in Chapter 1 as you prepare for the First Sunday in Advent. We would recommend that in some years it would be important to spend all four Sundays in Advent in Luke 1! That would get the year of Luke off to a proper start. It would also incorporate material that is vital to Luke's Gospel in our preaching sequence. It is very problematic that Luke 1 is so under represented in the lectionary. The chapter is filled with wonderfully unique Lukan stories and sets the tone for the entire Gospel.

It is further recommended that at the time of the reading of the Gospel at this beginning of the Lukan year you include a reading of Luke 1:1-4, the preface to Luke's Gospel. Some comments on the nature of Luke's Gospel would also be appropriate.

Commentators call the material from Luke 21:25-36 a dramatic Lukan restatement and reinterpretation of Mark 13. Jesus speaks in this material as a prophetic interpreter of history. He interprets for us the *plan of God.* As we spend a year in Luke we shall see that Luke interprets Jesus' ministry in light of God's plan. There is

217

nothing like Greek fate at work in these stories. Life and history have a proper destiny. Life has meaning and direction. There is a plan at work. "The Son of Man *must* undergo great suffering, and be rejected by the elders, chief priests, and scribes, and be killed and on the third day arise" (9:22). "... everything written about me in the law of Moses, the prophets, and the psalms *must be fulfilled* ... Thus it is written, that the Messiah is to suffer and to rise from the dead on the third day, and that repentance and forgiveness of sins is to be proclaimed in his name to all nations, beginning from *Jerusalem*" (24:44-47).

Jerusalem is crucial to the plan! Luke's story begins in Jerusalem (Luke 1). The entire Travel Narrative (9:51—19:27) tells of Jesus who set his face to go to Jerusalem. The Travel Narrative is the story of Jesus' journey to Jerusalem, to the temple. Luke's story ends in Jerusalem (24:44-53). The book of Acts begins in Jerusalem, Acts 1. Jesus promises the disciples that they will be filled with the Holy Spirit and be sent to bear witness to his name in Jerusalem, Judea, Samaria, and to the ends of the earth. The great event of church-birthing, Pentecost, takes place in Jerusalem, Acts 2.

The text appointed for this week is about Jerusalem — about the destruction of Jerusalem as part of God's plan. In three other passages in the Gospel of Luke Jesus speaks about the downfall of Jerusalem: 13:32-35; 19:41-44; 23:27-31. This is obviously an important motif, an important part of the plan, in Luke's Gospel.

Jerusalem will be trodden under by the Gentiles. That's the reality in verses 20-24. This happens according to the plan of God. It is to *fulfill all that is written* (v. 22). The time of Jerusalem and Israel will pass. But not forever. The end of Jerusalem becomes the beginning of the mission to the Gentiles. When the "times of the Gentiles are fulfilled" Jerusalem will get another chance to be grafted onto the vine. See Romans 9-11.

Luke 21:25-28 tells of the coming of the Son of Man. When these signs take place people can stand up and raise their heads because redemption is drawing near.

The past, present, and future are caught up in God's unfolding plan, and even the apocalyptic-images are fundamental assurances that God's reign will not fail. It is important to recognize that Luke's narrative does not yet know how God will finally fulfill the promises to Israel ... Shall the hopes of the prophetess Anna for "the redemption of Jerusalem" (1:38) or the hope of the travelers to Emmaus for Jesus "to redeem Israel" be unfulfilled? Perhaps this passage provides the needed assurance when Jesus declares the coming of the Son of Man to be the drawing near of your redemption *(v. 28). It may not be* clear how *God will accomplish this* redemption, *but it is inconceivable* that *God would not do so.*[1]

Tiede also points out that Luke is quite fond of the concept of the "drawing near" imagery. See 7:12; 10:9, 11; 18:35; 19:29, 37, 41; 21:8, 20. Much of this imagery has to do with the time of fulfillment.

The parable of the fig tree in verses 29-31 can probably be taken at face value. It is not difficult to see when the time of the kingdom drawn near is about to be realized. These seem to be words of comfort and assurance for those who might otherwise be anxious for their ability to recognize the signs of God's "drawing near."

Tiede is also helpful for us in noting that the focus of all of this eschatological and apocalyptic imagery finally falls on the present time of preparation:

Luke's account drives more to the point of instructing the disciples about what their proper concern should be (vv. 34-36) ... The question is, "When the Son of man comes, will he find faith on earth?" (18:8), and the command of Jesus departing on the cloud of heaven is, "You shall be my witnesses to the end of the earth!" (Acts 1:8-9). So also in Luke 21 Jesus redirects the attention of the faithful to attend to the present. In words that resound with apocalyptic tradition of 1 Thessalonians 5:1-11, Jesus counsels sobriety, watchfulness, and prayer, now. These are protections against temptation (see 8:13-15; 22:40,

46), lest the faithful fall away from their forthright witness
to Jesus' reign....[2]

Homiletical Directions

We have already proposed that in some years it would be wise to spend the four Sundays in Advent in Luke 1. Chapter 1 of this work provides commentary on the unity of Luke 1 as it sets the stage for the Gospel of Luke. We would particularly recommend the sermon possibilities suggested in Chapter 1 regarding a telling of the Zechariah and Mary stories and the matter of faith.

The material in this week's assigned text is didactic in character. Jesus is teaching about past, present, and future. This material is not very conducive to narrative analogy. The material is connected with the rest of the Gospel of Luke, however, in its center in Jerusalem and in its clear connection to God's plan. (The centrality of Jerusalem and the temple is dealt with in Chapter 3.) Jerusalem will be destroyed, after all, to fulfill what is written (21:22). In the preceding material we have mentioned some of the Jerusalem passages in Luke. Jerusalem is clearly a central location in the plan of God. That story begins in 2 Samuel 5:6-10 when David and his men captured the Jebusite city of "Zion" and made it the capital of a new kingdom which would encompass both northern and southern tribes. Solomon built the great temple in Jerusalem (1 Kings 5-9). Jerusalem has been the center of Israel's hope over the ages.

In Luke's Gospel Jerusalem is clearly the pivotal destination of Jesus. He comes to Jerusalem, goes to the temple, and gives an extended discourse. Part of that discourse is about the end of Jerusalem which Luke has referred to many times before. (See above.) The end of Jerusalem, however, will not be the end of God's plans! The disciples wait in Jerusalem. Pentecost occurs in Jerusalem. The church is born. From Jerusalem the disciples take the message of Jesus to the ends of the earth. The church grows. The message is finally passed on to us. We are members of the new Jerusalem, the new body of Christ on earth. God is present for us today neither in city or temple. God is present for us today in Jesus Christ. In Christ our redemption draws near. Advent is our time of preparation for the "drawing near" of our redemption. We are called upon to be sober, watchful people of prayer. The kingdom is very near.

If we choose to preach on the assigned Lukan text for this Sunday we can certainly introduce Luke's Gospel, deal with the role of Jerusalem in the overall plan of God, and call upon people to live advent lives of sober, watchful, and prayerful expectation. Advent lives will not be disappointed. God will fulfill God's plan. God's kingdom will prevail!

---

1. David L. Tiede, *Luke: Augsburg Commentary on the New Testament* (Minneapolis: Augsburg, 1988), pp. 365-366.

2. *Ibid.,* p. 370.

Luke 23:33-43

This week's appointed text from Luke is a fitting text for what is often called "Christ the King" Sunday. Jesus is taunted as king (v. 37), inscribed as king (v. 38), and acknowledged as king (v. 42). People today play these roles still.

Luke reports three words of Jesus from the cross. Jesus' first word from the cross is: "Father, forgive them; for they do not know what they are doing." (There is some textual dispute about the authenticity of this word in Luke.) The second word from the cross is also included in this text: "Truly I tell you, today you will be with me in Paradise." The third word from the cross is in Luke 23:46: "Father, into your hands I commend my spirit." Commentators have long noted that none of these words points to the real agony of Jesus' dying. What we appear to have in this version of the crucifixion story are the words of an "ideal martyr" bravely facing death. It is often noted that Stephen faces death with this same kind of tranquility (Acts 7). Stephen, too, could pray in the hour of his death: "Lord Jesus, receive my spirit," and "Lord, do not hold this sin against them" (Acts 7:59-60). Some suggest that Luke has an eye here on Christians who face persecution. Jesus and Stephen are models for those who face persecution for the faith.

Luke is ever mindful of the plan involved in Jesus' death. He notes that "they" cast lots to divide his garments. Psalm 22:18 would appear to be the Old Testament background for this activity. Jesus' death, that is, fulfills the Scripture!

> *The general statements in Luke 24 that the death of Jesus fulfills Scripture are supported by references to specific scriptural passages in other parts of Luke-Acts. In Acts the death of Jesus is interpreted by appeal to Psalm 118:22*

(Acts 4:11), Psalm 2:1-2 (Acts 4:25-26), and Isaiah 53:7-8 (Acts 8:32-33) ... To these texts we may add references in Luke to Psalm 118:22 (Luke 20:17), Isaiah 53:12 (Luke 22:37), Psalm 31:5 (Luke 23:46)....[1]

The rulers scoff at a dying Jesus: "He saved others; let him save himself *if* he is the Messiah of God, his chosen one!" (23:35). Here is the same kind of temptation that the devil put before Jesus in the wilderness (Luke 4:1-11). The voice from heaven had announced that Jesus was the "Son of God" (3:22) and a genealogical list confirmed this (3:23-38). The devil took up the challenge. *"If* you are the Son of God, command this stone to become a loaf of bread" (4:3). *"If* you are the Son of God throw yourself down from here ..." (4:9). See Chapter 7 above for a discussion of this "theology of glory" temptation that is put in Jesus' way. The devil and humans urged Jesus to forsake God's plan for his life and take matters into his own hands. Jesus refused. He went steadfastly to his death fulfilling his mission as Son of God.

Jesus is taunted three times in this week's text. The rulers scoffed, the soldiers mocked ("If you are the king of the Jews, *save* yourself!"), and one of the criminals derided him ("Are you not the Messiah? *Save* yourself and us!"). Each taunt includes the word for *salvation.* According to Fitzmyer this threesome of sayings

> *... highlights the salvific significance of Jesus' crucifixion in the Lucan Gospel: He is crucified precisely as "savior," a major theme in Lucan theology ... (The episode of the criminal on the cross) becomes the peak of the Lucan scene of crucifixion, for it not only presents the third taunt against Jesus, yet another (implicit) declaration of his innocence, but a manifestation of his salvific mercy to one of the dregs of humanity ... This episode, then, is Luke's way of presenting the salvific aspect of Jesus' death: the regal status that he will achieve, once he has entered "his glory" (24:26) and been exalted (Acts 2:32-36), will not be without saving effect on suffering human beings, even crucified criminals.*[2]

Commentators have long noted that Luke does not match Mark in his witness to the saving significance of Jesus' death.

> *Much has been writtten about the saving significance of Jesus' death in Mark's Gospel, and Luke's account has often been criticized for its lack of language of sacrifice. Luke does not describe Jesus' death as "saving" on the ground that his life was given "as a ransom for many" (cf. Mark 10:45). But Jesus' faith in God is unshaken throughout this passion story, and those who have faith in the faithful Jesus receive the saving benefits of his reign even as he dies (cf. the thief on the cross!) ... Jesus' death is a saving event in Luke becaue he dies as the "righteous one" whose trust in God's promises is saving faith. God is the one who will raise Jesus from the dead, and faith in the faithful Jesus is faith in God's righteousness, i.e. trust in God's promises ... Luke focuses upon Jesus' display of faithfulness and emphasizes the fulfillment of the law, prophets, and psalms (24:44).[3]*

The dying criminal whom Jesus invited into Paradise is an important figure in Luke's Gospel. In Chapter 37 we dealt with what Tannehill calls "Quest" stories in Luke's Gospel. Tannehill understands the repentant criminal to be one of those "Quest" stories. Tannehill also notes for us that the dying criminal is the only person who shows some awareness

> *that Jesus' death is part of a divine plan that will lead to Jesus' enthronement ... In this scene the repentant criminal is given the role of the reliable and perceptive interpreter of Jesus, whose insight contrasts with the blindness of all those who are rejecting Jesus ... The criminal is the last person who turns to Jesus for help during Jesus' ministry; he is also the one person who understands and accepts the path which Jesus must follow to fulfill God's purpose: through death to enthronement at God's right hand.[4]*

Homiletical Directions

We have discussed the "Quest" stories in Luke in Chapter 37. The story of the repentant thief could certainly be told along with a number of the stories mentioned there. The thrust of the "Quest" stories is that God seems to save quite unlikely people. We can tell some of these "Quest" stories in our sermon. Our concluding proclamation might be something like this: Jesus Christ speaks to us through these stories and says: "I offered forgiveness and healing to a helpless paralytic. I healed the slave of the Roman centurion. I showered my healing grace on a Samaritan leper. I opened the way to Paradise for a dying thief. I've dealt with some unlikely people in my day. Today, I offer salvation to you, as unlikely as that might seem. *Your* sins are forgiven. *Your* wounds are healed. *You* may enter Paradise with me."

A second sermon possibility with this week's text is to deal with the matter of temptation. "If you are the King of the Jews, save yourself!" We dealt with the temptation story in Chapter 7. See the Homiletical Directions there for sermon suggestions.

A third sermon possibility would be to take up the matter of *salvation*. The scoffing of the rulers, the mocking of the soldiers, and the derision of the dying thief all refer to Jesus' possibility to *save*. Tell the story of this week's text accenting this scoffing, mocking, and derision of the One who would save.

Salvation is a clear theme in Luke's Gospel. It is sung forth first in the prophecy of Zechariah in Luke 1:67-79. Our second story, therefore, might be the story of Zechariah. (See Chapter 1 for material on the parallel stories of Zechariah and Mary.) In his prophecy Zechariah sings of a "mighty savior" (v. 69) whom God will raise up to save us from our enemies (v. 71) and give knowledge of salvation to God's people through the forgiveness of their sins (v. 77).

The angels sing to the shepherds that there is good news of great joy for the people. "To you is born this day in the city of David a *Savior*, who is the Messiah, the Lord" (Luke 2:11). John the Baptist is the voice of one crying in the wilderness, preparing the way for "... all flesh [to] see the *salvation* of God" (Luke 3:6).

225

Several stories of salvation can then be told from Luke's Gospel. We can tell the story of the rich young ruler. When this fine commandment-keeping man turned sorrowfully away from Jesus the disciples wondered *who can be saved?* (Luke 18:26). In answer to their question Jesus states the incredible reality of God's salvation. "What is impossible for mortals is possible for God" (18:27).

Jesus' word to his disciples is confirmed in the Zacchaeus story. This impossible person is saved by God's possibility. "Today salvation has come to this house ..." Jesus says, "For the Son of Man came to seek out and to *save* the lost" (Luke 19:9-10).

The last story of this salvation theme is, of course, the story of the thief on the cross. If any person seems to be outside the possibility of salvation, it is he. But the dying thief repents. He cries out to Jesus: "Remember me." This is what has characterized faith throughout Luke's Gospel. People in their desperation turn to Jesus. That is the possibility of salvation. That is the possibility of our salvation. We can certainly shape a proclamation of good news to our people based on the impossible possibility that God has come to save us as well!

---

1. Robert C. Tannehill, *The Narrative Unity of Luke-Acts, Volume One* (Philadelphia: Fortress Press, 1986), p. 285.

2. Joseph A. Fitzmyer, *The Gospel According to Luke, X-XXIV* (New York: Doubleday, 1985), pp. 1501, 1508-1509.

3. David L. Tiede, *Luke: Augsburg Commentary on the New Testament* (Minneapolis: Augsburg, 1988), p. 421.

4. Tannehill, *op. cit.,* p. 127.

Chapter 46
Resurrection Of The Lord:
Vigil of Easter; Easter Day; Easter Evening

Luke 24:1-12; Luke 24:13-29

Luke 24:1-12 is the text assigned for both the Vigil of Easter and Easter Day. Luke 24:13-29 is assigned for Easter Evening. Luke 24 is one story of the resurrection of Jesus. We choose, therefore, to treat the whole of Luke 24 for preaching possibilities.

Luke 24 is a vital bridge in Luke's sweeping picture of Jesus and the early church. The whole of this chapter affirms the truth of Jesus' resurrection in a variety of ways. No other Gospel writer has taken so much time to speak of the meaning of the resurrection event. The climax of this chapter is one final review by Jesus of what his life's work has been all about. The law of Moses and the prophets and the psalms had to be fulfilled (v. 44). The Scriptures had to be understood (v. 45). It was necessary for the Messiah to die and be raised so that repentance and forgiveness could be proclaimed in his name to all nations beginning from Jerusalem (vv. 45-46). The disciples are to be the witnesses of these things once they have been clothed with power from on high (vv. 47-49). (Luke 24:44-53 is appointed for "The Ascension Of The Lord.") We recognize these verses as an introduction to the Book of Acts. Jesus' ministry is now complete. The Spirit will come and birth the Church. The Spirit-empowered Church will bring the message to generation upon generation to us.

Homiletical Directions

The end is the beginning! "God has brought down the powerful from their thrones and *lifted up the lowly* ..." (Luke 1:52). That's what Mary sang in the first chapter of Luke. That's what God does in the last chapter of Luke. That's what the resurrection of Jesus from the dead is all about! We have returned to this Lukan theme of *reversal* many times. Reversal took place in the life of a sinful woman (7:36-50). Reversal took place when we heard that in the great eschatological banquet the last will be first and the first last (13:22-30). Reversal took place when those invited came not to the banquet so that people from the highways and hedges of life had to be compelled to come in (14:11-24). Reversal took place when Lazarus ended up in Abraham's bosom while the rich man at whose gate he had groveled pleads to him to have mercy (16:19-31). Reversal took place when a Pharisee was sent home from the temple empty-handed while the tax collector was sent home justified (18:9-14). And now, in Luke's final chapter, we hear of the *reversal of all reversals.* The lowly one is lifted up. The dead one is raised. Life springs forth from death.

Our first sermon possibility, therefore, is a sermon which announces this reversal for all to hear. Start with Mary's song. Tell some of these reversal stories in Luke. After each story let God speak: "I observed the sinful woman who anointed Jesus' feet with ointment. I announced the forgiveness of her sins. I reversed her place in life from sinner to saint." A similarly structured proclamation can follow a brief retelling of some of these stories.

The climax of this telling, of course, is Luke 24. Tell this grand story of reversal. Spices for anointing. An empty tomb. An angelic announcement. In, with, and under this story God says to all of us: "I reversed the verdict on my Son. He was entombed and I opened the door. He was brought low and I lifted him up. He was dead and I gave him life. And so I promise to do for you. I will reverse the verdict when death strikes you down. I will open the door of your tomb. I will lift you up when you are laid low. I will give you life in place of death."

A second sermon possibility with the material in Luke 24 is to deal with the reality that Jesus' resurrection is a fulfillment of the *plan of God.* This dominant Lukan theme is called to mind in verse 6. The men said to the women: "Remember how he told you, while he was still in Galilee, that the *Son of Man must be handed over* to sinners, and be crucified, and on the third day rise again" (vv. 6-7). We have noted this "divine must" before. Jesus' word of prophecy on this matter is most clear in 9:22. The theme pulses through Luke's story: 2:49; 4:43; 9:51; 13:23; 17:25; 22:37.

Furthermore, this theme runs throughout Luke 24. In verses 26-27 Jesus explains to the disciples on the road to Emmaus that *it was necessary* that he suffer in order to fulfill that which Moses and the prophets spoke of him. In his last words (vv. 44-49, see above) to the disciples he speaks of his ministry as the fulfillment of the law, the prophets, and the psalms. It was written that the Christ should suffer.

In other words, *Jesus fulfilled the plan of God for his life.* His death and resurrection are the final events in what Jesus *must* do on earth. Robert Tannehill says this concerning Jesus' fulfillment of the plan:

> *A pattern of experience rooted in Scripture and applying to both Jesus and his witnesses helps to make sense of their stories. A sacred pattern assures those who accept it that events are not meaningless and chaotic, for they reflect the rhythm of God's work in the world. Events manifest a sacred pattern which hallows and reassures even when it cannot be rationally explained. A sacred pattern can be effective in sustaining faith and guiding life even when it does not lead to theological explanation. The narrator may have been content with this sacred pattern. It translates easily into narrative, while theological abstractions do not. Thus the narrative as a whole seems to suggest that the risen Christ illumines his blind disciples by conveying to them something like this pattern of* prophetic destiny *as a key to Scripture and his own story.*[1]

This quote from Tannehill provides some excellent ideas for a more didactic sermon. What we see coming to climax in the story of Jesus' resurrection is the whole plan of history. Life has a pattern, a meaning. We do not live in chaos. We do not live in a meaningless world. The world has meaning because Jesus carried out God's plan.

In our sermon on "God's plan for the world" we can tell some of the Lukan stories suggested above which show the necessity of Jesus' walk through life. Luke 24 touches upon this theme in verses

7, 26-27, and 44-49. The final verses give us the outcome of God's plan in perfect clarity. Because Jesus has fulfilled the plan the disciples can be commissioned to *preach repentance and forgiveness in his name* beginning in Jerusalem. This is precisely the message that they preached on the first Pentecost as told in Acts 2. "And Peter said to them, '*Repent*, and be baptized every one of you in the name of Jesus Christ so that your *sins may be forgiven* ...' " (Acts 2:38).

A Lukan Easter sermon, therefore, would very properly be a sermon which culminates in our stepping into the shoes of the disciples, calling for repentance and announcing the forgiveness of sins to repentant people. We have said before that Luke does not talk about Jesus dying as a ransom for our sins. For Luke, repentance and forgiveness are the heart of God's plan for the world. Through his suffering and death Jesus fulfilled God's plan and can therefore announce the message of repentance and forgiveness. We are not attuned to this way of telling the story. Luke's picture of the saving work of Jesus has not been much used in the history of Christian interpretation. *We* can use it! An Easter sermon in the Lukan mode would quite naturally culminate in our proclamation: "In the name of Jesus Christ I announce to all repentant sinners the entire forgiveness of all your sins. Easter means: your sins are forgiven. Go forth and live in the forgiven peace of mind of Easter."

A third possibility for preaching on this Easter text has to do with the gradual opening of the eyes and minds of the disciples so that they might grasp what has transpired. It was the women who first found the empty tomb. They were the first preachers of the resurrection! But the disciples did not believe them (24:11). The disciples on the road to Emmaus fare no better. Jesus himself came to join them and yet "their eyes were kept from recognizing him" (24:16). This Emmaus road encounter would seem to tell us that no one, not even the disciples, could have anticipated what God was up to in Jesus. It would take the Risen One himself to teach the faithful how to understand God's plan!

The conversation between the disciples and Jesus is filled with irony. The disciples tell Jesus the whole story of Easter! Here they were seeking to tell this story to the very One who lived the story!

230

This story "dramatizes human blindness by presenting an ironic situation. The disciples do not recognize that they are trying to inform Jesus about Jesus."[2] Part of the irony here is that divine and human purposes collide. "These experiences are sufficiently important in the plot to describe the God of Luke-Acts as the God who works by irony."[3]

When the disciples reach Emmaus they invite Jesus to eat with them. They still have not recognized their companion. Even a Bible study led by the Son of God has not opened their eyes. A meal will do what words would not! "Stay with us, because it is almost evening and the day is now nearly over," the disciples say to Jesus (v. 29). One is tempted to hear even this invitation as one full of irony. The disciples think the day is nearly over. They haven't figured out yet that the "day" is with them in the person of Jesus, and it has just begun!

The story then moves to the table, a very familiar setting in Luke's Gospel. Suddenly the guest becomes the host: "... he took bread, blessed and broke it, and gave it to them. *Then their eyes were opened and they recognized him* ..." (v. 31). Mealtime is revelation time! This is true throughout Luke's Gospel. Tannehill cites Richard Dillon who teaches that "the breaking of bread" is associated with instruction concerning Jesus' person and mission in Luke's Gospel.[4] There is more teaching by Jesus in the Lukan version of the Lord's Supper than there is in Matthew or Mark. A common theme of the instruction is that of Jesus' suffering (9:22; 22:15, 22; 24:25-26).

In Luke's story, revelation takes place in the context of the "breaking of bread." In Luke 9:12-22 we hear Luke's version of the feeding of the multitude. This passage is omitted from the lectionary. This means that during the Luke year we hear of no feeding miracles. We can tell it for Easter! In this story it is immediately after Jesus took "the five loaves and the two fish ... and blessed and broke them, and gave them to the disciples to set before the crowd," that Jesus asked the disciples who they thought that he was. Peter's answer was: "The Messiah of God." Jesus immediately began to teach the disciples that the Son of Man must undergo great sufferings. Mealtime is revelation time.

231

In Luke 22:7-23 we have the "breaking of the bread" which is the institution of the Lord's Supper. Here, too, Jesus teaches that he must suffer in a kind of Farewell Discourse (v. 15). In cup and bread Jesus presented himself to the disciples. Mealtime is revelation time.

On Easter Sunday when the Lord's Supper is celebrated among us these meals would make an excellent focus for preaching. Tell briefly the story of the supper and revelation in Luke 9, noting that mealtime is revelation time. Tell the story of supper and revelation in Luke 22 making the same point. Thirdly, tell the story of the Easter walk to Emmaus. It was at the table, in the breaking of the bread, that the disciples' eyes were opened to the reality of Jesus' presence. Mealtime is revelation time.

This is very good Easter news! We somehow think that it would have been much easier to believe the good news of Jesus if we would have been there ourselves. Not so! The disciples on the road to Emmaus were right there and they didn't "see" at all. Their eyes were opened only in the breaking of the bread. This means that the disciples have no advantage over us at all! We, too, are invited to the "breaking of the bread." Our eyes can be opened in this meal in just the same way that the disciples' eyes were opened. The disciples had their best access to the Risen Jesus in the breaking of the bread. So it is for us today. We have our best access to the Risen Jesus in the breaking of the bread as well. Mealtime is revelation time! Here we eat and drink the very life of the Risen One. From his life we have our life. Life here. Life forever.

A sermon that tells these three mealtime revelation stories ends in the proclamation of the supper itself. Our sermon might close by inviting people to the action itself. "Come now to this table," we might say. "The Risen Jesus will meet you here. The Risen Jesus will reveal himself to you here. The Risen Jesus reveals himself to you in simple words: 'This is my body. This is my blood.' Through these words Jesus announces his presence today to enter your life. Through these words Jesus announces his presence today to open your eyes. Through these words Jesus announces his presence to give you a foretaste of the Easter life that is to come."

1. Robert C. Tannehill, *The Narrative Unity of Luke-Acts, Volume One* (Minneapolis: Fortress Press, 1986), p. 288.

2. *Ibid.,* p. 282.

3. *Ibid.,* p. 284.

4. *Ibid.,* p. 290.